Palgrave Shakespeare Studies

Series Editors
Michael Dobson
The Shakespeare Institute
University of Birmingham
Stratford-upon-Avon, UK

Dympna Callaghan
Syracuse University
Syracuse, NY, USA

Palgrave Shakespeare Studies takes Shakespeare as its focus but strives to understand the significance of his oeuvre in relation to his contemporaries, to subsequent writers and to historical and political contexts. By extending the scope of Shakespeare and English Renaissance Studies, the series aims to open up the field to examinations of previously neglected aspects or sources in the period's art and thought. Titles in the *Palgrave Shakespeare Studies* series seek to understand anew both where the literary achievements of the English Renaissance came from and where they have brought us, and provide the reader with a combination of cutting-edge critical thought and archival scholarly rigour.

Sonya Freeman Loftis
Mardy Philippian • Justin P. Shaw
Editors

Inclusive Shakespeares

Identity, Pedagogy, Performance

Editors
Sonya Freeman Loftis
Department of English
Morehouse College
Atlanta, GA, USA

Mardy Philippian
English Studies
Lewis University
Romeoville, IL, USA

Justin P. Shaw
Department of English
Clark University
Worcester, MA, USA

ISSN 2731-3204   ISSN 2731-3212   (electronic)
Palgrave Shakespeare Studies
ISBN 978-3-031-26521-1   ISBN 978-3-031-26522-8   (eBook)
https://doi.org/10.1007/978-3-031-26522-8

Cover illustration: Anthony Harvie / Getty Images

This Palgrave Macmillan imprint is published by the registered company Springer Nature Switzerland AG.
The registered company address is: Gewerbestrasse 11, 6330 Cham, Switzerland

Paper in this product is recyclable.

Acknowledgments

First and foremost, thank you to our wonderful contributors: this collection would not have been possible without their hard work. Special thanks to Allison Kellar for her comments on the book's introduction and to David Houston Wood for his help in the book's early brainstorming phases. Sonya would like to thank the Shakespeare Association of America (SAA) for the opportunity to lead a seminar (with Sheila Cavanagh) on Inclusive Shakespeare at the annual SAA conference in 2021: about half of the chapters in this collection originated in that very fruitful meeting. Special thanks to Alexa Alice Joubin for her truly radical (and profoundly compassionate) listening. Finally, Mardy would like to thank Sonya and Justin for a productive collaboration and for modeling the habits of inclusive pedagogy in all of their many conversations and editorial exchanges.

CONTENTS

1   Introduction: Inclusion Is Hard, or Collaborating
    in Crip Time   1
    Sonya Freeman Loftis, Mardy Philippian, and Justin P. Shaw

Part I   Inclusive Shakespeares in Performance   23

2   Disability Embodiment and Inclusive Aesthetics   25
    Jill Marie Bradbury

3   Immersed in Miami/Bathed in the Caribbean: Tarell
    Alvin McCraney's *Antony and Cleopatra* Revisited   43
    Hayley R. Fernandez and James M. Sutton

4   "I am all the daughters of my father's house, and all the
    brothers too": Genderfluid Potentiality in *As You Like It*
    and *Twelfth Night*   63
    Eric Brinkman

5   "El español puede ser todo": Bilingual Grassroots
    Shakespeare in Merced, California   79
    William Wolfgang

6   Shakespearean Madness and Academic Civilization   97
    Avi Mendelson

7   Accessing Shakespeare in Performance: Northern
    Michigan University's Stratford Festival Endowment Fund 115
    David Houston Wood

Part II   Inclusive Shakespeares in Pedagogy   129

8   Blackfishing Complexions: Shakespeare, Passing, and the
    Politics of Beauty   131
    Kelly Duquette

9   Intersectionality, Inclusion, and the Shakespeare Survey
    Course   145
    Maya Mathur

10 Making First-Generation Experiences Visible in the
    Shakespeare Classroom   159
    Katherine Walker

11 Shakespeare Goes to Technical College   175
    John Gulledge and Kimberly Crews

12 "Let the Sky Rain Potatoes": Shakespeare Through
    Culinary and Popular Culture   191
    Sheila T. Cavanagh

13 "Let Gentleness My Strong Enforcement Be": Accessing
    San Quentin Prison with Inside-Out Shakespeare   207
    Perry Guevara

14 Radical Listening and the Global Politics
    of Inclusiveness: An Afterword   221
    Alexa Alice Joubin

Bibliography   235

Index   255

NOTES ON CONTRIBUTORS

Jill Marie Bradbury (she/her) is professor and chair of the Performing Arts Department at the National Technical Institute for the Deaf, Rochester Institute of Technology. Her areas of specialization include Deaf theater and Shakespeare in American Sign Language (ASL). In 2016, she received a grant from the National Endowment for the Arts for a DeafBlind Theater Initiative, which resulted in a documentary video, "ProTactile *Romeo and Juliet*." She also served as project director for the DC stop of *First Folio! The Book That Gave Us Shakespeare* national traveling exhibition sponsored by the Folger Shakespeare Library (2016), for which she co-curated a museum exhibit, *Shakespeare in American Deaf History*. Publications include the collaborative essay ProTactile Romeo and Juliet: Theater by/for the DeafBlind," *Shakespeare Studies* 47 (2019) and, with Miles Drawdy, "Shakespeare and Sign Language," *Stanford Encyclopedia of Shakespeare* (2021).

Eric Brinkman (they/them) is an instructional consultant for the Michael V. Drake Institute for Teaching and Learning at the Ohio State University. Their research focuses on the performance of race, gender, and sexuality in theater, film, and television. They have forthcoming articles on Iago in performance as a scapegoat for white anxiety, the centrality of the affect created by female actors to audience reception, and transgender potentiality in early modern drama.

Sheila T. Cavanagh (she/her) is Fulbright/Global Shakespeare Distinguished Chair in the United Kingdom and Professor of English at Emory University. She is founding director of the World Shakespeare

Project (www.worldshakespeareproject.org) and co-director of "First Folio! The Book That Gave Us Shakespeare" and Emory's Year of Shakespeare (2016–2017). She also held the Masse-Martin/NEH Distinguished Teaching Professorship. Author of *Wanton Eyes and Chaste Desires: Female Sexuality in the Faerie Queene* and *Cherished Torment: The Emotional Geography of Lady Mary Wroth's Urania*, she has her work published widely in the fields of pedagogy and of Renaissance literature. She is also active in the electronic realm, having directed the Emory Women Writers Resource Project (womenwriters.library.emory.edu) since 1994 and serving for many years as editor of the online *Spenser Review*.

Kimberly Crews (she/her) received her Bachelor of Arts from Agnes Scott College, where she majored in English Literature and Creative Writing, with a minor in Music. She received her Master of Fine Arts degree from California State University, Fresno (CSUF), while working as an instructor for the CSUF First-Year Writing Program. Her scholarship and research revolve around the intersection of Black women, policymaking, and organizational dissonance. She is working as the Department Chair of English and Social Sciences and is a full-time professor at Atlanta Technical College.

Kelly Duquette (she/her) is a PhD student in English specializing in Shakespeare and early modern literature. Her research focuses on representations of war and dissent, civil disobedience, and moral injury in the sixteenth and seventeenth centuries. Outside the classroom, her work focuses on Shakespeare service learning in the local community. She is co-founder of "The Puck Project," a Shakespeare summer program for homeless students in Atlanta. She holds an MA in Irish Literature from Boston College (2017) and a BA in English from the University of Florida (2010). She is a 2010 Teach for America alumna (Miami-Dade).

Hayley R. Fernandez (she/her) is a first-generation Cuban-American based in Miami, where she was born and raised. She received both her BA and MA in English Literature from Florida International University (FIU). Although she was initially intent on studies foregrounding Shakespeare, Renaissance drama, and dramaturgy, her focus shifted to the literature of the African diaspora and related fields, including history, anthropology, and gender studies. She is working on multiple projects covering the topics of AfroCuban literature, AfroCuban and African American relationships in the twentieth century, and the presence and influence of religion in diasporic communities. When she is not researching and writing, Hayley enjoys traveling, gardening, and spending time with friends and family in Miami's locally owned establishments.

Perry Guevara (he/him) joined the Dominican faculty in 2016 and is a visiting scholar at the University of California, Berkeley's Center for Science, Technology, Medicine & Society. Previously, he was a fellow at Emory's Scholars Program in Interdisciplinary Neuroscience Research. His essays have appeared or are forthcoming in *Configurations, Early Modern Culture, Shakespeare Studies*, and *Lesser Living Creatures of the Renaissance*. He is writing a book, *Inhuman Depressions: Cognitive Ecologies in English Renaissance Literature*.

John Gulledge (he/him) is an Assistant Professor of English at Wittenberg University, where he teaches courses on early modern litera-ture and disability studies. His current book project recovers the rhetorical and poetic method of energeia in early English drama and reveals the var-ied ways creative invention was patterned after encounters with disability. His most recent work can be found in the journal *Inscriptions* (2023) and the edited volume *Adaptations of Mental and Cognitive Disability in Popular Media* (2022). He is also the co-founder of "The Puck Project," a Shakespeare performance and ethics program for kids facing housing insecurity in Atlanta, GA.

Alexa Alice Joubin (she/her) is Professor of English, Women's, Gender and Sexuality Studies, Theatre, East Asian Languages and Literatures, and International Affairs at George Washington University, where she serves as founding co-director of the Digital Humanities Institute. She holds the John M. Kirk, Jr. Chair in Medieval and Renaissance Literature at Middlebury College Bread Loaf School of English. She is the inaugural recipient of the bell hooks Legacy Award and holder of the Martin Luther King, Jr. Award.

Sonya Freeman Loftis (she/her) is the M. Mitchell Chair of English at Morehouse College, where she specializes in Renaissance literature and disability studies. She is the author of *Shakespeare and Disability Studies* (2021), *Imagining Autism* (2015), and *Shakespeare's Surrogates* (Palgrave Macmillan, 2013), as well as the co-editor of Shakespeare's *Hamlet in an Era of Textual Exhaustion* (2017). Her work has appeared in *Shakespeare Survey, The Disability Studies Reader, Disability Studies Quarterly*, and *Shakespeare Bulletin*. She serves on the editorial boards of the *Journal of*

Literary and Cultural Disability Studies, Disability Studies Quarterly, Review of Disability Studies, and *Ought: The Journal of Autistic Culture.*

Maya Mathur (she/her) is Professor of English at the University of Mary Washington in Fredericksburg, Virginia. Her scholarship focuses on early modern comedy and popular protest, global Shakespeare, and the scholarship of teaching and learning. Her research on early modern drama has been published in *A Cultural History of Comedy,* the *Journal for Medieval and Early Modern Studies, Early Theater,* and the *Journal for Early Modern Cultural Studies,* among other venues. Her work on teaching Shakespeare has appeared in the MLA Approaches to Teaching series and is forthcoming in the volume *Teaching Race in the Renaissance.*

Avi Mendelson (he/him) recently received his PhD in English Literature from Brandeis University. Midway through graduate school, he expatriated himself to the United Kingdom, where he taught the English Literature GCSE and worked both in mental health advocacy—with organizations such as The Advocacy Project, Core Arts, and Mind UK—and in performed theater. In 2020, Avi was the in-house dramaturg for an adaptation of Middleton and Rowley's *The Changeling* at the Arcola Theatre in East London, and this year he co-directed *The Bacchae* at the Tower Theatre. Other essays appear in the edited collection *Performing Disability in Early Modern English Drama* (Palgrave Macmillan) and in the British Shakespeare Association's *Teaching Shakespeare* and San Francisco State University's *Interpretations.* His interest in early modern drama, histories of medicine and emotions, and disability studies is animated further by a drive to provide those with mental illnesses with equal access to education.

Mardy Philippian (he/him) is Associate Professor of English Studies and Director of the Literature and Language Concentration and former Associate Dean at Lewis University, where he teaches courses in Shakespeare, Milton, and early modern English literature. Since 2011, he has served as a member of the editorial board of *The Oswald Review: International Journal of Undergraduate Research and Criticism in the Discipline of English.* His reviews, articles, and book chapters have appeared in *Literature and Film Quarterly, Film Criticism, Prose Studies, Forum for World Literature Studies,* and *Early Modern Culture,* and in the edited collection *Recovering Disability in Early Modern England* (2013).

Justin P. Shaw (he/him) is Assistant Professor of English at Clark University, where he teaches and researches Shakespeare and early modern English literature. His work explores the intersections of race, emotions, disability, and medicine in sixteenth- and seventeenth-century texts. He is completing a book project that examines the work of melancholy and for-getting in the constructions of race in early modern drama. Committed to both public and traditional scholarship, his work appears in the peer-reviewed journal *Early Theatre* and in the anthology *White People in Shakespeare* (2022), and has been discussed publicly on NPR and *A Bit Lit*. He has helped to design exhibits for the Michael C. Carlos Museum at Emory University such as *Desire & Consumption: The New World in the Age of Shakespeare*, consulted on the exhibit *First Folio: The Book That Gave Us Shakespeare*, and has re-developed the extensive digital humanities project *Shakespeare and the Players* (Shakespeare.emory.edu).

James M. Sutton (he/him) is Associate Professor of English at Florida International University (FIU) in Miami; he acted as chair of his department from 2008 to 2016. He is the author of *Materializing Space at an Early Modern Prodigy House: The Cecils at Theobalds, 1564–1607* (2005) and several related articles. In February 2016, he served as project lead for FIU's exhibition of a Folger Shakespeare Library First Folio (as part of the nationwide tour of the Folio); this work initiated his interest in inclusive, community-based Shakespeare in the context of Miami and South Florida. His research foregrounds questions of "local Shakespeare" in both Miami and Slovenia, bridging Shakespeare to questions of exile, transplantation, immigration, and (in Miami) Latinx identities. Thus, his recent publications include the co-edited volume, with Asher Z. Milbauer, *Exile in Global Literature and Culture: Homes Found and Lost* (2020); an essay considering the importation of Shakespeare into Slovenia in light of recent immigration crises there (*Slovene Studies*, May 2020); and a chapter in *Shakespeare and Latindad* (2021) examining Latina appropriations of the author in Miami. With Stephanie Chamberlain and Vanessa Corredera, he co-directed a Shakespeare Association of America (SAA) seminar (Jacksonville 2022) investigating Shakespeare and exile.

Katherine Walker (she/her) received a PhD in English and Comparative Literature from the University of North Carolina at Chapel Hill. Her book project *Instinct, Knowledge, and Science on the Early Modern Stage* situates instinctive, intuitive, or embodied ways of knowing in sixteenth- and seventeenth-century culture. Dr. Walker's work is particularly interested in how marginalized figures adopt or advance methods of reading the environment on the stage. Dr. Walker's work appears in the journals *Prose Studies, Comitatus, Early Modern Literary Studies, Studies in Philology, Preternature: Critical and Historical Studies on the Preternatural*, and *English Literary History*, and is forthcoming in *English Literary Renaissance* and the *Journal of Marlowe Studies*. Her *Shakespeare and Science: A Dictionary* is forthcoming.

William Wolfgang (he/him) is a theatre practitioner and an independent scholar. He has produced 23 Shakespeare plays during a decade with the OrangeMite Shakespeare Company in York, Pennsylvania, as the founding executive director. Wolfgang has also directed and managed productions with Merced Shakespearefest and Shakespeare in Yosemite while serving as a lecturer in the Department of Literatures and Languages at the University of California, Merced. He recently completed the first major study of community-based Shakespeare performance in the United States. These findings will be published, in part, in an upcoming article in *Shakespeare Bulletin* entitled "Grassroots Shakespeare." Wolfgang's research has been used to increase membership in the Shakespeare Theatre Association after locating hundreds of decentralized Shakespeare-performing organizations across the nation. His research interests include rural- and community-based arts in addition to Shakespeare in bilingual performance.

David Houston Wood (he/him) serves as Distinguished Professor of English at Northern Michigan University. He teaches Renaissance, medieval, and classical literature. Having his work published widely in top journals ranging from *Shakespeare Yearbook* to *Renaissance Drama*, from *Prose Studies* to *Interfaces*, from *Disability Studies Quarterly* to the *Blackwell Literature-Compass Online*, he is also the author of a monograph titled *Time, Narrative, and Emotion in Early Modern England* (2009) and the co-editor of two essay collections, both completed with Allison P. Hobgood (Willamette University): the first, a special issue of the journal *Disability Studies Quarterly*, titled "Disabled Shakespeares" (29.4 Fall 2009); and the second, *Recovering Disability in Early Modern England* (2013).

CHAPTER 1

Introduction: Inclusion Is Hard, or Collaborating in Crip Time

Sonya Freeman Loftis, Mardy Philippian, and Justin P. Shaw

We have to work actively against any ineffectual default to political correctness. When implemented unilaterally as a one-size-fits-all imposition, some gestures of inclusion risk becoming empty rituals.—Alexa Alice Joubin and Lisa S. Starks, "Teaching Shakespeare in a Time of Hate" (Joubin and Starks 2021)

S. F. Loftis (✉)
Morehouse College, Atlanta, GA, USA

M. Philippian
Lewis University, Romeoville, IL, USA
e-mail: philipmd@lewisu.edu

J. P. Shaw
Clark University, Worcester, MA, USA
e-mail: jshaw@clarku.edu

© The Author(s), under exclusive license to Springer Nature
Switzerland AG 2023
S. Freeman Loftis et al. (eds.), *Inclusive Shakespeares*, Palgrave
Shakespeare Studies,
https://doi.org/10.1007/978-3-031-26522-8_1

PART 1: "WHO'S THERE?"

Sonya Freeman Loftis

The old cliché about *Hamlet* is that it starts with the question of identity ("Who's there?" [1.1.1]). Of course, the titular character spends most of the play running around in a state of (teenaged?) angst about his identity.[1] His identity in flux includes paradoxes: he manages to be both punningly wise ("I know a hawk from a handsaw") and potentially mad ("to put an antic disposition on"), both hesitant ("to be or not to be") and viciously active ("not shriving time allowed"), he is in the clouds and also "too much in the sun" (2.2.379; 1.5.172; 3.1.55; 5.2.47; 1.2.67).[2] If the world of the play represents a functioning social system (debatable), Hamlet's identity breaks the system. In my experience, having a disability is a little like that. In fact, individual identity is often the thing that breaks the systems (even the ones that were already secretly broken when we found them). For example, almost everything in the world is designed for an imagined able-bodied/neurotypical human. This inevitably means that most things in the world were not designed with me (an autistic woman) in mind. Actually, any identity outside of what is falsely assumed as the "normative" or "majority" default tends to break various social systems. This book is about inclusion, so it is also about identity, about the unique places we come from and the life experiences that help make us into the people we are.

I would argue that academia is currently having a very Hamlet kind of moment. As we try to acknowledge and grapple with the past (also known as history, also known as ongoing institutionalized discrimination against various people and communities, also known as the uncomfortable truths that many people try to ignore), we may find ourselves focused on identity, especially on the broken systems surrounding identity and particularly on the identities that were (through ignorance or violence or hate) excluded from the systems.[3] In our scholarship, we want to know "who's there." In our scholarship, we want to know who speaks. Identity matters. Knowing who speaks matters. This is certainly true in disability communities. The motto of the disability rights movement is "nothing about us without us." How will we know that people with disabilities are included unless we know who speaks? It is hard to practice "nothing about us without us" unless we first identify the "us."[4] But even once we identify the "us" (and we have successfully navigated all the complexity of professional identity disclosure), inclusion is still hard to define and even harder to practice.

Inclusion has become a powerful concept in contemporary scholarship, a term that combines the search for social justice with academic and scholarly pursuits.[5] While the desire for inclusion drives pedagogical and theatrical innovation, however, it remains a multifaceted term that is difficult to define, a lived practice that is challenging to enact, and a hoped-for result that is almost impossible to achieve. The desire to include, so often the heartfelt attempt to create a more just world, is too often met with the paradox of its own forgone failure—no attempt to be inclusive will ever succeed in including everyone. In my mind, inclusion usually means that everyone both participates equally and participates together: however, I can also think of many situations in which both participating equally and participating together is logistically impossible—or situations in which radical changes would be needed to create equal access that would allow all people with different kinds of disabilities to participate equally and together with able-bodied/neurotypical people.[6] In some situations, full and true inclusion may be idealistic and impossible. In fact, this book may be doomed to inevitable failure based on this very premise—no one book can hope to include and/or examine every possible identity. Thus, real inclusion is hard (maybe sometimes impossible) to achieve.

I would argue that inclusion's forgone failure doesn't mean that we should stop trying to achieve it—in fact, it might mean that we need to try even harder; we have to keep trying to exercise imagination and empathy, to be open to and with each other, and to remember that if individual identity is the thing that breaks the system then creating more systems won't create real inclusion. Indeed, my lived experience as a person with a disability has taught me that inclusion isn't created by systems—it is created by people. Sometimes when we try to make inclusion a part of the system, we run the risk of what Alexa Alice Joubin and Lisa S. Starks describe as "empty rituals" in the epigraph to this chapter. For many years now, I have attended disability panels at various conferences that have tried to signal acceptance of neurodiversity and to create more autistic safe spaces. They often do this by announcing to the audience at the beginning of the panel that "you can stim in here."[7] As desperately as we need more autistic safe spaces (the vast majority of spaces in the world are decidedly autistic unsafe), those words never make me feel welcome as one of the only autistic people in the room (more often the only autistic person in the room). Ironically, it doesn't even make me feel free to engage in stimming during the panel. (Can I really stim in here? Probably not. Some forms of stimming are large, loud, and extremely distracting. Even assuming the speaker can handle it, it doesn't mean other people in the room won't react adversely.) There is something in "you can stim in here" that signals the performance of political correctness to me rather than real acceptance. It is a gesture of inclusion that actually makes me feel more excluded—the very opposite of what the speaker intends. In studying inclusion, I've often been amazed by how quickly (and unintentionally) attempts at inclusion can turn into their opposite. There's certainly plenty of theoretical work out there to warn of this ever-present danger. Disability theorist Ellen Samuels writes about the dangers of comparing or conflating one identity group's experience with another's, examining how such comparisons might aid in empathy and understanding but also showing how they devalue the unique experiences of the communities thus compared (Samuels 2013). How do we include different identities while avoiding comparison or conflation? Ayanna Thompson examines how "neo-colonial agendas" can spring from attempts at inclusion (Thompson 2011). What happens when the attempt to include covertly becomes the attempt to colonize? These are the things that inclusion is not. But if saying "you can stim in here" isn't real inclusion for autistic people, then what is?

In my personal experience, real inclusion is more like collaborating in crip time. Because I was a part of this book project, everyone who was involved with this book had to accelerate to crip time. On the most basic level, "crip time" is the term disability theorists use to describe the way disability interfaces with time.[8] While the most common situation is that people with disabilities might need more time (someone with a mobility impairment might walk more slowly or a student with a learning disability might need more time to take an exam), disability theorists also agree that the experience of crip time is variable and complicated.[9] In my case, my mental disability means that I am often working very rapidly—and while that pace accommodates my short attention span and unusually fast changes in thought and emotion, it creates challenges for neurotypical collaborators, co-authors, editors, colleagues, and students.[10] Collaborating in crip time looks like me emailing Mardy: "Hey Mardy, can you please do X?" And then an hour later, "I already did X. Can you do Y?" And then an hour later, "Actually, I did X and Y. But could you do Z?" Real inclusion means that neurotypical people have to speed up their timeline so that I can participate. Real inclusion means that I have to slow down my timeline so that neurotypical people can participate. But crip time isn't always fast: sometimes other people have to slow down for me. Professional conferences are full of overwhelming crowds, loud noises, bright lights—the kind of sensory input that often renders me painfully disoriented. Real inclusion is Justin taking the time to stop for a colleague in distress, helping me from the crowded hallway and guiding me where I was trying to go. My experience of mental disability has taught me that the work of inclusion is inherently relational—you have to know, understand, and communicate with people in order to include them.[11] Inclusion usually involves collaboration—because one person probably won't be a part of all possible communities. Inclusion is group work in which people from different communities have leadership roles, in which people from different backgrounds listen carefully to each other. It has to be group work that is incredibly flexible and that is not afraid to break the system—whether that system is prioritizing the voice of a single author or adhering to a supposedly normative time frame. Inclusion is not polite or superficial; in fact, inclusion is radical and disruptive. (Since academia imagines itself as the realm of the able mind, the very presence of mental disability in academia is inherently subversive, a disruption at the assumed core of the system [Price 2011].) Including neurodiverse colleagues in academic spaces requires more than saying "you can stim in here"—it requires us to collectively reimagine and redefine the terms of social and intellectual engagement. In short, inclusion is hard to do because it almost always means breaking the existing systems and rewriting the so-called rules (and sometimes those rules are so deeply ingrained that we don't even recognize them as the rules until someone starts breaking them). Inclusion is hard to define because it is relational and highly individual—because it is a way to bring individuals together. A way to bring individuals together has to be individual by definition—and because it is individual, whatever it looks like, it won't be a part of the system. Inevitably, individual identity breaks the systems.

The primary problem with Hamlet, as a character, is that he doesn't fit into the play's systems. The other characters think Hamlet is mad because he is rebelling (or contemplating rebelling) against the established organizing principles of the world as they understand it: linguistic ("these are but wild and whirling words"), gendered ("Tis unmanly grief …"), temporal ("do not forever … seek for thy noble father …"), theological ("or that the Everlasting had not fixed his canon 'gainst self-slaughter"), social ("with his doublet all unbraced … his stockings fouled …"), emotional ("what's Hecuba to him or he to Hecuba …") (1.5.133; 1.2.94; 1.2.70–1; 1.2.131–2; 2.1.75–6; 2.2.559–60). The command of the past (his father's ghost) has already set up a deeply flawed set of systemic expectations ("revenge his foul and most unnatural murther") about masculinity ("What is a man …") and violence ("from this time forth / My thoughts be bloody or be nothing worth") (1.5.25; 4.4.33; 4.4.65–6). The secret of Hamlet's madness, his apparent disunity with the world around him, is that all of these systems were already broken when he found them.[12]

PART 2: "AM NOT I CHRISTOPHER SLY?"

Mardy Philippian

Just as crip time is a temporal state of being that varies from disabled individual to individual, a state of being that is defined from within by the unique experiences of a single person and from without by an outside world emotionally averse to temporal variance, socio-economic identity is similarly defined by such an inter-antagonism of pressures. The emotional and psychological challenges faced by first-generation college students in most instances stem from quantitative and qualitative differences that social scientists in recent years have studied in a larger effort to provide classroom teachers with a detailed understanding of the specific hurdles to acceptance, belonging, and inclusion that these students confront, a process of confrontation that generates psychological discomfort and emotional pain.[13]

Unknowingly becoming a version of Christopher Sly, first-generation college students enter with one identity and find their new cultural world hard at work to transform them into another.[14] While the ideological work of the college or university is not as mean spirited as the brutal jest perpetrated against the beggar Sly, the effects of "waking" to find oneself ignorant of so many social scripts, pressed for pocket change, and loaded down with expectations—from how to read a course syllabus, to backward planning for the completion of assignments, to how to properly address a professor in a face-to-face encounter and through email—leaves so many of these students palpably aware of their status as outsiders. To look directly at *The Taming of the Shrew's* first induction, we see class distinction in high relief. Setting aside the intention to engage in mockery as a form of entertainment, we might note that a radical alteration of an individual's environment combined with only a rudimentary knowledge of the expectations created by that new environment results in a destabilizing of identity. Even when the outward signifiers, the accoutrement, of rightfully belonging to a particular place and purpose are made available, self-understanding and identity remain beneath the surface. As the huntsmen and the Lord discuss plans to transform Sly from beggar to his "honor," the hypothesis they forward is quite similar to the now widespread and staid conviction in college and university Shakespeare classrooms that learning "the moves" of academic writing and of the careful historicizing of a play, or the sophisticated application of our most cherished interpretive strategies, will remake the uninitiated into more convincing versions of "proper students" of Shakespeare:

> Lord: What think you if he were conveyed to bed,
> Wrapped in sweet clothes, rings put upon his fingers,
> A most delicious banquet by his bed,
> And brave attendants near him when he wakes--
> Would not the beggar then forget himself?
>
> First Hunstman: Believe me, lord, I think he cannot choose.
> (Induction 1.33–38)

The First Hunstman moves well beyond the suggestion of the Lord to confirm ("Believe me") that identity is outward, external, and performative. But without the means to construct such an identity as that of an honorable Lord, a figure like Christopher Sly is left a beggar, his identity in contrast defined by stereotyping conceived of as rags and drunkenness. Agreeing with the huntsman, the Lord admonishes his servants,

> Persuade him that he hath been lunatic
> And, when he says he is, say that he dreams,
> For he is nothing but a mighty lord.
> This do, and do it kindly, gentle sire:
> It will be pastime passing excellent
> If it be husbanded with modesty.
> (Induction 1.59–64)

Persuasion, kindness, and modesty are marshaled in support of a remaking of identity. In the midst of this very strange and cruel prank, we unexpectedly find the kind of advice that still goes a long way toward reassuring first-generation students that belonging in some new and unexpected sense is possible. For some first-generation college students, inclusion may begin as performance, self-conscious or otherwise, but it may solidify into identity in the same way that practicing various interpretive reading strategies eventually solidifies into dynamic expertise.

In yet another old cliché from so much scholarship, namely that Shakespeare wrote for a wide audience of broadening social class, eclectic interests, and varying degrees of cultural awareness, the student bodies in college and university classrooms since the end of the second world war have grown increasingly complex in, as administrators are often fond of saying, profile. The GI Bill and related tuition benefits led to a massive influx of students all over the United States into the college and university sphere and, further, their children went on to populate faculty ranks on most if not all campuses in the country. And while this was primarily true for white males initially, the development of inroads into the historically exclusive world of higher education has since led to wider inroads for women, BIPOC, disabled, LGBTQ, and undocumented college students. Such a dramatic shift in the profile of faculty should, it seems to me, have made us more aware of the vital importance of seeing such a widening of the eye of the needle as a critical moment of inclusivity and accessibility. Our audience or classroom-goers, to deploy an awkwardly constructed though nonetheless pointed Shakespearean term, is not a group we have researched or tried to understand in an effort to make our subject matter outward facing, relevant, or even interesting to individuals whose collective personal histories do not include a conversational awareness of race, class, gender, and disability related issues. As Doug Eskew has recently related from his own experiences of teaching at a university whose student body is largely first-generation college students, "A lot of the time (perhaps even 'usually'), a student's honest answer to [the] question of what Shakespeare means to people today is that Shakespeare doesn't mean much at all. Shakespeare is a requirement in school—that's it" (2019). Perhaps for the better part of the last forty years we've focused so much on the portion of the textual iceberg below the surface of the water, so to speak, that we may have imperiled the initial meaningful connection to and value of Shakespeare Studies to incoming students and so contributed to the shrinking percentage of freshman declaring English as a major. Relatedly, in another sector of Shakespeare Studies, Patrick Grey has raised the question of high theory's value toward making the study of Shakespeare consequential in our own time, noting that the new materialism in particular, with its intense focus on the minutiae of the sixteenth-century's physical world and not on issues of more present cultural relevance such as those related to ethics, has devalued embracing uncertainty and complexity as a cognitive tool. And Scott Newstok forcefully argues for a return to many of the pedagogical practices of the early modern period, particularly the emphasis on using imitation of literary forms as a program for orienting students' focus beyond mere skills acquisition to thinking. Newstok notes that education must be about thinking and not simply accumulating data about a text (2020). Here the data points of recent trends in Shakespeare Studies must be seen as just that and not as the end in themselves. But to enable our students to use such points of historical information to shape their larger understanding of the past may be more germane to graduate education in the discipline than to making the undergraduate reading experience of the plays meaningful. Emma Smith has also offered a lengthy and cogent defense of inviting students into a different kind of interpretive space in which they confront and value the "gappiness" of Shakespeare's plays by asking useful but seemingly odd, obvious, historically naïve, or even side-glancing questions rather than overly focusing on historicizing as the primary means of gaining understanding. And here we might also cite Denise Albanese who recalls a Shakespeare student's blunt statement that efforts to make Shakespeare's texts historically alien to our own contemporary moment through so much historicizing trained him "how to hate the English Renaissance."[15] All of this is not to say that scholarship should become a kind of market-driven pandering or twee pastime. Rather, I am advocating that we ask ourselves, in what ways do teaching and scholarship in Shakespeare Studies demonstrate an understanding of the complex backgrounds from which so many students come? And how might this understanding be made to influence how we teach and write about our subject?[16]

As a first-generation college student who is descended from Armenian genocide survivors, Kentucky coal miners, a number of grandparents and other family members who did not graduate from high school, several more who struggle to read as a result of undiagnosed dyslexia, and an aspirationally lower-middle-class family of origin, I understand the unpredictable effects of students' underpreparedness and their attendant anxieties in the face of leaving home to begin a bachelor's degree program, perhaps especially when that program is in the discipline of English (see Osborne 2019). Entering college in the early 1990s at a time when high theory was causing consternation between an older generation of faculty in our department committed to New Critical close-reading practices and a newer generation practiced in the maneuvers of deconstructive reading, for example, I was lost as to what to think, say, or even feel about a literary text. The only solace was my Shakespeare course, the first in which I had ever enrolled. Taught by a beat-generation holdout who wore a leather sport coat, tie, and ghost-white lambchops, and who always sought to confirm our collective understanding with the expression, "dig?" I came to realize that eclecticism was allowed and even in some sense appreciated. But when it came to reading the plays, Dr. Canney, unlike his colleagues of the same generation, slowly walked us through various theoretical approaches and never assumed we would catch on like born-experts. He included us in the ongoing debate within the discipline and in this new way of approaching the reading of a literary text. His persuasion, kindness, and modesty opened up Shakespeare's plays for me and set me on a path to aspiring toward a life and profession that I did not, like many first-generation college students, believe was available to me. Dr. Canney was patient, available, and relational, and that made the study of Shakespeare and the wider world of college accessible to me.

Part 3: "Infinite Variety"

Justin P. Shaw

At the start of my second year on the faculty of my university, I was invited to attend a lunch with incoming first-year first-generation multicultural students. It was exciting for me in many ways because, due to the COVID-19 pandemic, I had not had a chance to meet many students on campus. Midway through my mouthful of butternut squash soup, one student who shared my physical complexion (she later identified as Ghanaian), asked me with the widest of eyes what it meant to me to study Shakespeare. There were several important components to her brilliant question, each with its own nuance and specificity: what does it mean, in the meta sense, to study Shakespeare at the collegiate level? What does it mean for me, as a Black person, to study Shakespeare—or in other words, to be a "Shakespeare scholar"? What does it mean for me to study Shakespeare at a predominately white institution? I got a similar question from a white student in a class a few weeks later, this time in the context of hoping to manage chronic illness with academic productivity. Taken together, these two students allowed me to ponder what it meant to study Shakespeare as a Black person in the academy with chronic illness. What are the benefits and difficulties of doing Shakespeare as such? Does "Shakespeare"—the man and the myth, the job and the hobby—even include someone like me or my Black, disabled, international, and first-generation students? To imagine the dream of an inclusive Shakespeare, we must also bear witness to the realities of an exclusive one.

The hard truth of the second question I raise is that, as much as I enjoy Shakespeare, discourses of Shakespeare have historically and systematically excluded people like me. As Kim F. Hall has shown us, the early modern archive itself is more than exclusive; it is harmful (Hall 2020). From the criminalization of Blackness and disability in his texts to the marginalization and/or tokenism of Blackness and disability in the academy and theater—spaces where "Shakespeare" is traditionally done—the idea of an inclusive Shakespeare remains just that, an idea. Without inclusivity, or when it comes in the form of something like "diversity," Shakespeare continues to fall flat as his work fails to meet the cultural moment. To differentiate diversity from inclusion, we might see the first as a kind of aggregation of difference that may or may not be directed toward a singular purpose. The latter, then, might be defined as seeing oneself incorporated into, supported by, cared for, and engaged in the purposeful work of some larger entity. Inclusion, then, seems to require relationship, responsibility, and redistribution on the part of the entity in power—that into which one is included. Thinking about an inclusive Shakespeare will require us to reframe our debt to Shakespeare as, instead, Shakespeare's debt or responsibility to us as readers, storytellers, and interpreters. It will challenge us to imagine a Shakespeare that is made and remade in our images—our "infinite variety," à la Cleopatra—as we acknowledge both the cultural limits and the currencies of his (*Antony and Cleopatra* 2.2.277).

The drive and desire for an inclusive Shakespeare is by no means a new phenomenon. Scholars and practitioners have long employed strategies to either make Shakespeare more inclusive or reveal his work's inherent inclusivity. But whom or what does inclusivity serve? What is at stake when we believe something to be inherently inclusive? Recall, for example, *The Sea Voyage*, John Fletcher and Philip Massinger's 1622 adaptation of *The Tempest*, or William D'Avenant and John Dryden's version, *The Enchanted Island*, that premiered in 1667. Both plays expand the role of women from Shakespeare's original—the latter would've even featured women actors—for sure, but to what end? Colley Cibber's enormously popular eighteenth-century revision of *Richard III* makes the language and plot more "inclusive"—in this sense, meaning palatable—for his audiences while further degrading as evil the disability of its title figure. These early adaptations however remain inaccessible to this day and in fact increased the exclusivity in their Shakespearean sources and the culture surrounding them.[17] More modern attempts to make Shakespeare more inclusive, diverse, or accessible have innovated in casting, language, setting, and in some cases revising the plots to focus on marginalized voices. In my undergraduate Shakespeare seminars, I demonstrate some of this work by centering texts like Toni Morrison and Rokia Traore's *Desdemona* (2012), Caroline Randall Williams' *Lucy Negro Redux* (2015), and *The Death of a Chief*, Yvette Nolan's 2008 feminist and Indigenous adaptation of *Julius Caesar*. These texts capture something about the work of inclusivity that requires that we start at the margins of society.

One of the most malleable modes we have for imagining an inclusive Shakespeare over the last two centuries is that of film. Shakespeare has been integral to filmmaking since the genesis of the industry, but its relative accessibility and mass appeal does not guarantee inclusivity. In fact, as one might see in Herbert Beerbohm Tree's 1899 silent film *King John*, upstart filmmakers—as do celebrated ones today—looked to Shakespeare precisely because of the cultural perception of his exclusivity and prestige. Aside from simply reproducing Shakespeare's texts for the silver screen, some filmmakers have also tried to craft a more inclusive Shakespeare by making Shakespeare disappear behind the characters, setting, and/or revised language such as in the films *Deliver Us from Eva* (2003), *O* (2001), and the fan-favorite, Disney's *The Lion King* (1994). I wonder if I see myself in any of these. Perhaps the play that garners the most immediate name recognition as "inclusive" is *Romeo and Juliet* which, in a film like *Ram-Leela* (2013), fluidly highlights the complexities of class transgression, inheritance, and marriage already present in caste-based social systems. The film *Mississippi Masala* (1991), as Joyce Green MacDonald discusses in her recent monograph, shows how *Romeo and Juliet* can take on power structures rooted in race, ethnic, and class identities muddled together under the veil of romance in the American South (MacDonald 2020). Perhaps the film only shows what's already present in the original play thus allowing itself to be made available to more inclusive renderings. Does adaptability entail inclusivity? If yes, then Shakespeare is perhaps the most inclusive literary figure in history. But I would argue, and perhaps you would too, that inclusive Shakespeare requires something more than an ability to be Disney-fied by animated lions.

What stands out to me as I search for inclusivity in these modern examples is that they tend to have one implicit goal in common—decentering or even deconstructing whiteness. In doing so, they highlight what we today might note as the white supremacy, or anti-black racism, native to the original text and contexts. Innovative productions such as Jude Kelly's 1997 *Othello*, which featured Patrick Stewart in the title role opposite an all-Black cast, or Iqbal Khan's 2015 *Othello* for the Royal Shakespeare Company, which featured Black and South Asian actors—Hugh Quarshie, Lucian Msamati, and Ayesha Dharker—in the roles of Othello, Iago, and Emilia, seemed to gesture toward arguments about racial inclusivity, or the lack thereof, in Othello's world. However, in these productions, anti-black racism remained a guiding force in the play's discourse.[18] In cases such as these, the focus on Blackness, without the accompanying spectacle, ought to give audiences a chance to make legible white racial power—too often ignored as neutral or absent—and those it deputizes in both Shakespeare's original and on the stage before them. Playwright James Ijames arguably succeeds in this regard when he turns *Hamlet* inside out in his 2021 adaptation *Fat Ham*. This play features an all-Black cast but moving beyond simply casting BIPOC bodies in Shakespeare's white shoes, this revision invites audiences to embrace and participate in the joy, queerness, madness, and complexity of Blackness.[19] As Hamlet becomes Juicy, the play explores the character's inability to function in normative social systems while allowing other characters the flexibility to question and/or reject those systems as well. *Fat Ham*'s invitation to embrace the complexity of Blackness also challenges audiences and readers to confront the unbearable, tragic, and dazzling whiteness of Shakespeare's most famous tragedy and the irreparable harm this exclusive White gaze has done to us as inclusive readers over time (Dadabhoy 2020).

I say "dazzling whiteness" intentionally and provocatively to call attention to how conversations about inclusion often ignore and efface the complex politics of identity, such as where race and disability intersect. "Dazzling" connotes how seductive and disorienting Shakespeare can be both on the stage and in the academy when made exclusive by systems of whiteness and compulsory able-bodiedness. Under this guise, the hard work of inclusion is diluted and ultimately ends up bolstering the exclusivity of Shakespeare and Shakespeare studies. In other words, with whiteness and/or ability at the center, inclusion will fail in its objective, reduce its impact, and risk causing harm. Thus, the work of inclusive Shakespeare in the theater, classroom, academy, and beyond must be an intersectional endeavor. It should start and end with the work and lives of individual people rather than with theoretical propositions. As such, it is necessary to survey the ever-evolving goals and scope of inclusion. What does it include and to what does it aim? An inclusive Shakespeare production or pedagogy that purportedly de-centers whiteness but retains its ableism and misogyny, for example, is not fully inclusive. Doing Shakespeare that purports to be inclusive but considers the intersections of race, gender, class, sexuality, religion, and/or disability to be marginal phenomena not only refuses inclusivity, but also undermines decades of scholarship that persuasively argues for and documents the centrality of these in the literary culture of Shakespeare's time and our own. When I speak of the "dazzling whiteness" of Shakespeare, I mean to point to the nefarious ways that white supremacy shapes and interrupts gender, race, disability, sexuality, and so forth, often obscuring and undermining the constant need for and benefits of intersectional discourse. Inclusive Shakespeare, then, must witness and then escape these tendencies. It must resist the ways that systems of power seek to disrupt or dilute the work of inclusion, creating new barriers for people doing—or hoping to do—inclusive Shakespeare in the world.

What, then, does inclusive Shakespeare mean to me? What does it mean to do Shakespeare inclusively in the world—this world—today? Inclusive Shakespeare will take what Christina Sharpe calls "wake work" (Sharpe 2016). It will require a rupture at the center, wading with the ripples, discomforting those committed to Shakespearean exclusivity. As we stand or sit in the wakes of Black Lives Matter protests, of continued assaults on reproductive freedom and disability rights, of global refugee crises, of climate change and human-led environmental destruction, of pandemic losses, doing Shakespeare inclusively means amplifying and centering voices that Shakespeare subdued, ridiculed, and never meant to include. Doing Shakespeare inclusively means engaging meaningfully with "infinite variety," embracing the contributions and bodies of scholars and practitioners who have historically been marginalized and rejected by the traditional institutions and archives of Shakespeare curation like the theater and the university. Doing Shakespeare inclusively means following the lead of activists, creators, and leaders working in spaces beyond those traditional institutions to curate new ways of imagining Shakespeare that do what Shakespeare's work always does—center people.

PART 4: CREATING INCLUSIVE THEATERS AND CLASSROOMS

The first section of this volume focuses on inclusive Shakespeares in performance. In the book's first chapter, Jill Bradbury offers an analysis informed by disability studies, embodiment theory, and performance theory, examining both American Sign Language and ProTactile (designed for DeafBlind audience members) productions of *Romeo and Juliet*. Her analysis raises key questions about access and inclusion as theoretical concepts. Specifically, Bradbury's chapter interrogates how the presence of disabled actors on stage deconstructs traditional conceptions of theatrical aesthetics. The chapter argues that "inclusion" and "access" should be redefined and points out ways in which hearing audiences may misappropriate or misuse these terms in relation to Deaf performance. Continuing the volume's attempts to evaluate inclusion as a critical concept in Shakespearean performance, Hayley R. Fernandez and James M. Sutton argue that Tarell Alvin McCraney's *Antony and Cleopatra* represents "exemplary" inclusion. Although originally conceived at the Royal Shakespeare Company, McCraney designed the performance with an audience of Miami youth in mind. Fernandez and Sutton argue that this under-appreciated performance forms an important benchmark in McCraney's oeuvre, noting that "the inclusivity of his Shakespeare work, bent towards young people (particularly South Floridian youth), however misunderstood and poorly grasped, served as the artistic springboard that propelled him to his much-acclaimed film and television work, well-noted for its intersectional inclusivity and appeal to youth." Fernandez and Sutton conclude that this "'forgotten' or 'overlooked' Shakespearean production is in fact central to the artist's entire body of work, key to understanding the plays that came before, and the screen dramas that follow."

In Chap. 3, Eric Brinkman examines Shakespeare performances with genderqueer potentiality. Theorizing how early modern play texts and contemporary stage performances may both contain and use genderqueer potentiality, Brinkman offers a particular focus on Simon Godwin's 2017 National Theatre production of *Twelfth Night*, a performance that depicted Malvolia as having a coming out scene that elicited varied reactions from different audiences. Continuing Bradbury's investigation of what it means to be "inclusive," Brinkman examines "productive and nonproductive" uses of inclusion in a variety of contemporary performances. Ultimately, the chapter concludes that inclusion is not a matter of success or failure but rather one of more (and less) productive possibilities and ways of learning from each other. In the next chapter, William Wolfgang examines a *Richard II* coming from and created for the Latinx community. In collaboration with co-directors, Ángel Núñez and Maria Nguyen-Cruz, Wolfgang participated in the construction of a bilingual *Richard II* that premiered on Youtube during the 2020 pandemic. Informed by autoethnographic approaches, the chapter provides a discussion of how Merced Shakespearefest's "mission of inclusivity" meant that "participants in this project took ownership of the text of *Richard II* with the creation of a collaborative and equally divided Spanish/English script." Specifically, Wolfgang's analysis focuses on the role of code-switching in the play text, as well as the ways in which the tensions and difficulties of the pandemic informed the dynamic of the production's construction and final product.

Continuing the discussion of inclusive performance, Avi Mendelson's chapter focuses on stage performances by and for neurodiverse people. The chapter combines discussion of Mendelson's own work as a dramaturg with the Arcola Theatre in East London with examination of various Shakespeare performances engaging neurodiverse audiences and actors. Mendelson's discussion moves from performance to pedagogy: the chapter concludes with a discussion of neurodiversity's tenuous role in the academy. Finally, David Houston Wood concludes the book's section on performance by giving a first-hand account of the ways in which his university has made live Shakespeare performances more accessible for first-generation students and students from different backgrounds and majors. Outlining the details of Northern Michigan University's annual trip to the Stratford Festival in Ontario, Wood's chapter offers practical suggestions for teachers interested in implementing similar programs.

Kelly Duquette opens the volume's section on inclusive pedagogy by discussing her use of cultural artifacts from the 1960s "Black is Beautiful" movement in the Shakespeare classroom. Duquette argues that bringing varied discourses about the historical and cultural construction of beauty into dialogue with each other may "offer students of Shakespeare a new understanding of racism in the discourse of cosmetics" found in Shakespeare's sonnets. In the next chapter, Maya Mathur focuses on teaching "intersectional Shakespeare," specifically by using four primary critical approaches (gender, sexuality, race, and disability) in her teaching of Shakespeare's plays. Arguing that "students will be more likely to study Shakespeare if instructors engage in conversations about the racism, sexism, and ableism in his plays," Mathur gives practical tips for employing an intersectional lens in classroom readings of Shakespeare as well as analyzing the varied ways in which her students have responded to this approach. In Chap. 9, Katherine Walker focuses on encouraging first-generation students to "talk back to Shakespeare." Her work in the classroom toward "dethroning Shakespeare … shape[s] … pedagogy around the idea that if we allow for alternative narratives … then we can provide pathways for a new, more diverse generation of scholars. With this framework, students … are active participants in a thorough and eclectic, but ultimately productive, iconoclasm." By drawing overt comparisons between moments of political rebellion in the plays and moments of "rebellion" in the classroom, Walker creates a forum that centers the needs and experiences of students rather than the mythos of Shakespeare. In the next chapter, Gulledge and Crews examine Shakespeare's potential place in the curriculum of technical colleges. Focusing on their College's mission of "transformation," they reflect not on how Shakespeare transforms technical college students but rather on how technical college students transform our understanding of Shakespeare's text and Shakespearean pedagogy.

Although at many universities the students most likely to encounter Shakespeare are English and theater majors, Sheila Cavanagh's chapter explores innovative ways to include students from a variety of majors in the study of Shakespeare. Specifically, this chapter offers an analysis of two classes ("Cooking with Shakespeare" and "The Many Faces of Shakespeare") to offer suggestions for making Shakespeare classes more hands-on (cooking in the Shakespeare classroom) as well as more accessible (combining Shakespeare with the study of popular culture). In the final chapter, Perry Guevara discusses the pedagogical approaches used in engaging undergraduate students in Shakespeare prison programs. Guevara's course combines "inside-out" pedagogy with the Marin Shakespeare Company's arts-in-corrections program, Shakespeare for Social Justice. The chapter approaches "access" as a two-sided theoretical concern: contemplating the challenges that arise both in creating access to Shakespeare for incarcerated people and in finding access to "a highly disciplinary, heavily policed, and culturally stigmatized space, only then to transform that space through theater." The chapter concludes by providing "a review of the curriculum, the theory shaping the curriculum, and the logistics of accessing the prison … as a guide to other educators seeking to pair the study of Shakespeare with social justice pedagogy."

Finally, Alexa Alice Joubin's Afterword draws the book to a close by focusing on the concept of radical listening and on engaging global perspectives in the classroom. This discussion both returns to the theoretical tensions of inclusion and exclusion explored in the book's early chapters and continues the pedagogical analysis begun in its second section. Joubin calls for classrooms that invite students to listen to the motivations of people and characters in ways that undermine testimonial oppression, build empathy, and teach the potential powers of inclusion.

NOTES

1. Although the gravedigger states that Hamlet is 30 years old (5.1.142–48; 5.1.161–62), it hasn't stopped generations of critics from conjecturing endlessly about his age.
2. Far be it from me to claim that the neurodiverse can't also be the wise. I'm just noting that cultural stereotypes usually (falsely) depict them as opposites.
3. In using Hamlet's struggle with identity as a metaphor for the individual's clash with social systems, I do not mean to imply that Hamlet's story is somehow "universal." I am merely pointing out that Hamlet's struggle with identity mirrors some of my own experiences as a person with a disability.
4. On the issues surrounding disability disclosure in disability studies, see Corbett O'Toole, "Disclosing Our Relationships to Disabilities: An Invitation for Disability Studies Scholars," *Disability Studies Quarterly* 33.2 (2013): http://dsq-sds.org/article/view/3708.
5. The phrase "inclusive education," often abbreviated to the watchword "inclusivity," first appeared in peer-reviewed literature in the late 1980s as a more ethically informed response to the experiences of people with disabilities, with the phrase "inclusive education" slowly replacing the older descriptive "special education." Inclusive education is at once a philosophical understanding of the forces that lead to the individual's experience of exclusion and, in application, a pedagogical response to the historical challenge of addressing forms of disenfranchisement. The most comprehensive survey and discussion of research to date that relates to the subject of inclusive education in colleges and universities is Christine Hockings, "Inclusive Learning and Teaching in Higher Education: A Synthesis of Research" (York: Higher Education Academy, 2010). Hockings defines inclusive learning in higher education as "the ways in which pedagogy, curricula and assessment are designed and delivered to engage students in learning that is meaningful, relevant and accessible to all. It embraces a view of the individual and individual difference as the source of diversity that can enrich the lives and learning of others" (Hockings, 2010, p. 1).

6. I've explored these questions about disability and inclusion more fully else-where. For a more detailed discussion, see *Shakespeare and Disability Studies* (Oxford: Oxford University Press, 2021).

7. Autistic stimming includes a variety of body movements like pacing, rocking, and hand flapping. Although stimming is a natural form of movement and self-expression for autistic people, it often makes one the object of negative judgement in neurotypical spaces.

8. For more on crip time, see Ellen Samuels, "Six Ways of Looking at Crip Time," *Disability Studies Quarterly* 37.3 (2017).

9. For more on how crip time interfaces with mental disability, see Michael Bérubé, *The Secret Life of Stories* (New York: New York University Press, 2018).

10. Autism is a spectrum, which means that it includes a wide variety of diverse impairments. Thus, autistic people may experience crip time in many different kinds of ways.

11. For more on inclusion as a relationship, see Kelsie Acton et al., "Being in Relationship: Reflections on Dis-Performing, Hospitality, and Accessibility," *Canadian Theatre Review* 177 (Winter 2019).

12. I'm inspired by Price's description of madness: "for what is madness but a radical disunity of perception from that held by those who share one's social context?" (Price, Mad at School, n.p.).

13. The term "first-generation college" student has been used by higher-education researchers since the early 1980s. The term refers to college and university students whose parents have no college, university, or postsecondary experiences. For foundational discussions of the term and its many cultural implications, see Janet Mancini Billson and Margaret Brooks Terry, "In Search of the Silken Purse: Factors in Attrition among First-Generation Students," *College and University* 58 (1982): 57–75; Patrick T. Terenzini, Leonard Springer, Patricia M. Yaeger, Ernest T. Pascarella and Amaury Nora, "First-Generation College Students: Characteristics, Experiences, and Cognitive Development," *Research in Higher Education* 37.1 (1996): 1–22; Anne-Marie Nunez and Stephanie Cuccaro-Alamin, *First-Generation Students: Undergraduates Whose Parents Never Enrolled in Postsecondary Education*, Washington, D.C.: U.S. Department of Education, National Center for Educational Statistics (NCES) (1998); Laura Horn and Anne-Marie Nunez, "Mapping the Road to College: First-Generation Students' Math Track, Planning Strategies, and Context of Support," *Education Statistics Quarterly* 2.1 (Spring 2000): 81–86; Susan P. Choy, *Students Whose Parents Did Not Go to College: Postsecondary Access, Persistence, and Attainment*, Washington, D.C.: U.S. Department of Education, National Center for Educational Statistics (NCES) (2001); Edward C. Warburton, Rosio Bugarin, and Anne-

Marie Nunez, *Bridging the Gap: Academic Preparation and Postsecondary Success of First-Generation Students*, Washington, D.C.: U.S. Department of Education, National Center for Educational Statistics (NCES) (2001); Ernest T. Pascarella, Christopher T. Pierson, Gregory C. Wolniak and Patrick T. Terenzini, "First-Generation College Students: Additional Evidence on College Experiences and Outcomes," *The Journal of Higher Education* 75.3 (May/June, 2004): 249–284.

14. For the fullest and most authoritative discussion to date of how the subject of classism has been ignored in professional literary studies, see Sharon O'Dair, *Class, Critics, and Shakespeare: Bottom Lines on the Culture Wars* (University of Michigan Press, 2000).

15. See Patrick Grey, "Shakespeare After the New Materialism," presented as part of the panel entitled, "Shakespeare and Intellectual History," at the Shakespeare Association of America (SAA), 30 March–4 April 2021; Newstok; *How to Think Like Shakespeare*; Emma Smith, *This is Shakespeare* (Pantheon, 2019); Denise Albanese, "Identification, Alienation, and 'Hating the Renaissance,'" *Shakespeare and the 99%: Literary Studies, the Profession, and the Production of Inequity*, ed. Sharon O'Dair and Timothy Francisco (Palgrave, 2019), 27.

16. In recent years, social class has come much more to the fore as a topic of research and pedagogical concern in the Shakespeare classroom. As the community of Shakespeareans in the Anglo-American world especially has separated into classes defined by differences in workload, resources, and guarantees of permanency, two distinct formations of Shakespeare Studies have formed. One formation is defined by advanced archival preparation in graduate school and rich and available resources that result from proximity to important collections and hubs of conference activity. The other formation is defined in contrast by, in a word, scarcity of such resources and opportunities.

17. For more on Shakespeare's elevated status in the eighteenth century, see Michael Caines, *Shakespeare and the Eighteenth Century* (Oxford: Oxford University Press, 2013).

18. For some of Quarshie's earlier thoughts on this subject, see Hugh Quarshie, *Second Thoughts about Othello* (Chipping Camden: International Shakespeare Association, 1999).

19. I am thinking here about the expansiveness of Blackness, such as in its capacity with madness to "exceed and shift the boundaries and definitions of human," as conveyed by Therí Alyce Pickens, *Black Madness:: Mad Blackness* (Durham: Duke University Press, 2019), 16.

References

Ambereen Dadabhoy, "The Unbearable Whiteness of Being (in) Shakespeare," *Postmedieval: A Journal of Medieval Cultural Studies* 11.2–3 (2020): 228–235.

Doug Eskew, "Shakespeare, Alienation, and the Working-Class Student," *Shakespeare and the 99%: Literary Studies, the Profession, and the Production of Inequity*, ed. Sharon O'Dair and Timothy Francisco (Palgrave, 2019), 40.

Kim F. Hall, "I Can't Love This the Way You Want Me To: Archival Blackness," *Postmedieval: A Journal of Medieval Cultural Studies* 11.2–3 (2020): 171–179.

Alexa Alice Joubin and Lisa S. Starks. "Teaching Shakespeare in a Time of Hate," *Shakespeare Survey* 74 (2021): 28.

Joyce MacDonald, *Shakespearean Adaptation, Race and Memory in the New World* (New York and Basingstoke: Palgrave Macmillan, 2020), 47–76.

Scott Newstok, *How to Think Like Shakespeare: Lesson from a Renaissance Education* (Princeton University Press, 2020).

Jeffrey Osborne, "Rural Shakespeare and the Tragedy of Education," *Teaching Social Justice Through Shakespeare: Why Renaissance Literature Matters Now*, eds. Hillary Eklund and Wendy Beth Hyman (Edinburgh University Press, 2019), 106–114.

Margaret Price, *Mad at School: Rhetorics of Mental Disability and Academic Life* (Ann Arbor: University of Michigan Press, 2011), Kindle edition.

Ellen Samuels, "'My Body, My Closet': Invisible Disability and the Limits of Coming Out'," *The Disability Studies Reader*, ed. Lennard J. Davis, 4th edition. (New York: Routledge, 2013), Kindle edition, 308–24.

Christina Sharpe, *In the Wake: On Blackness and Being* (Durham: Duke University Press, 2016), 18.

Ayanna Thompson, *Passing Strange: Shakespeare, Race, and Contemporary America* (Oxford: Oxford University Press, 2011).

PART I

Inclusive Shakespeares in Performance

Disability Embodiment and Inclusive Aesthetics

Jill Marie Bradbury

Aesthetics is born as a discourse of the body.—Terry Eagleton (1988, p. 327)

Performative bodies, Pascale Aebischer remarks, are "a barometer on which cultural changes of attitude can be registered as each generation makes them mean differently" (Aebischer 2009, pp. 5–6). Gauging by a number of recent productions, the cultural meanings of disabled bodies are in flux. Once almost invariably played by able-bodied actors and used to enact narrative prosthesis or to manifest inner defects, disability embodiment is now more frequently undertaken by disabled actors and used dramaturgically in ways that respect the lived experiences of people with atypical bodyminds.[1] In a few productions, disability embodiment is being explored as the basis for new kinds of theatrical practices and standards of artistic achievement. As my opening quote from Terry Eagleton alludes, assumptions of normative embodiment underpin the conventions of

---

J. M. Bradbury (✉)
Rochester Institute of Technology, Rochester, NY, USA

S. Freeman Loftis et al. (eds.), *Inclusive Shakespeares*, Palgrave
Shakespeare Studies,
https://doi.org/10.1007/978-3-031-26522-8_2

Western theater. Vision and hearing are primary senses to which performance is directed, and physical control of the body is the predominant
measure of artistic achievement. Theater grounded in disability embodiment challenges these normative paradigms, leading to new practices, new
modes of experiencing performance, and new aesthetic principles. This
chapter explores these emergent modalities via analysis of Shakespeare
productions centered in senses of taste, smell, and touch, and in deaf and
DeafBlind perceptual experiences.[2]

PARTY ON

*The audience mingles outside the auditorium until they are offered a plain
black mask. After donning the mask, they are guided inside one by one. Their
first stop is a table, where their usher draws their hands down to feel an assort-
ment of masks festooned with pipe cleaners, beading, pom pom balls, and other
tactile decorations. They are gently encouraged to pick one and place it over
their plain masks. Then, the usher takes their hand and leads them carefully
up steps onto the stage.*

PROTACTILE *ROMEO AND JULIET*

*The audience has arrived and friends chat animatedly in tactile sign language
while waiting for the play to begin. Soon a townsman, dressed in coarse linen
clothes in a style reminiscent of the sixteenth century, approaches the first patron.
He takes her hand and greets her, sharing his character's sign name. He guides
her hand from his head to his chest and down his arms, allowing her to feel his
costume. Then, he brings her to the cast, waiting in a line. Each actor introduces
their character's sign name and family affiliation, then brings the patron's hand
across their hair, face, and costume. When the patron has finished meeting all the
characters, the townsman guides her through curtains into the Capulet party,
where she is invited to eat, drink, and socialize until Romeo approaches her.*

Critical disability studies explores "questions of embodiment, identity
and agency as they affect all living beings" (Shildrik 2013, p. 30).
Influenced by phenomenology, critical disability studies treats bodily existence as more than just a social or cultural construct. Instead, such physical experience fundamentally structures the mind's perception of itself. As
Rosemarie Garland Thomson puts it, "The self materializes in response to an
embodied engagement with its environment, both social and concrete"

(Thomson 2008, p. 33). Disabled bodies generate unique perceptual experiences of the world and understanding of the self in relation to these experiences. These experiences, Tobin Siebers writes, form "a body of knowledge—a collection of skills, qualities, properties, and characteristics, among other things—both driven by the built environment and transformed by the variety and features of bodies" (Siebers 2016, p. 443). Disability knowledge is both situated, adhering in social locations, and phenomenological, adhering in physical experience of the material world (Siebers 2008, pp. 22–23).

For Siebers, as for other scholars of aesthetics such as Eagleton, embodiment is fundamental to theories of art and artistic evaluation. Concepts of ability and disability are aesthetic values in that they are part of "a system of knowledge that provides material for and increases critical consciousness about the ways that some bodies make other bodies feel" (Siebers 2008, p. 20). Kirsty Johnston applies Siebers' concept of disability aesthetics to theater, noting that certain types of embodiment are privileged in professional training, casting, and representations of bodily experience onstage (Johnston 2016, p. 2). As Philip Zarrilli points out, the actor on stage also literally embodies a theory of acting, one informed by cultural narratives about bodies (Zarrilli 2002, p. 4). Most acting traditions, whether realistic or codified, emphasize physical control over movement, vocalization, and facial expressiveness as preeminent artistic values. These technical prescriptions, theater historian Joseph Roach argues, construct ideological meanings from material bodies, foregrounding favored representations and erasing undesirable ones. For Roach, acting methodology is the primary technique through which cultural narratives about ideal bodies and behaviors are inscribed in theatrical practice (Roach 1989, p. 159, 161). Normative embodiment is thus the neutral material of performance, allowing actors to transcend their own embodied selves to become a character. Ironically, the physical artistry of able-bodied actors is often seen as best displayed when they are simulating disability embodiment.[3] Disabled theater makers such as Christine Bruno have frequently remarked that disability simulation is not only "*accepted* as a technical skill tucked away in an actor's bag of tricks, it is always applauded and more often than not, rewarded" (Bruno 2014).

John Heilpern's review of Peter Dinklage's 2004 performance in *Richard III* exemplifies this aesthetics of normative embodiment. Heilpern begins by recounting the virtuosity of past actors in the title role—Anthony Sher's "astonishing" performance ("all anyone could talk about was the crutches") and Ian McKellen's "amazing feats" with one hand. Such is the physicality of the "theatrical tricks of great actors." Comparing Dinklage to Sher and McKellen, Heilpern remarks that "it shouldn't be relevant that Mr. Dinklage is a dwarf, only how well he plays the role." But Heilpern's emphasis on physical artistry implies that because Dinklage is a dwarf, he can't physically embody the role as well as an able-bodied actor. In contrast to Sher and McKellen, Dinklage is "sluggish" and "clumsy" (Heilpern 2004).[4] The aesthetic of normative embodiment can lead not only to negative judgments about the artistic skill of disabled actors but also questions about the nature of their art itself. Able-bodied actors may receive critical praise for performing disability, but disabled actors performing disability are often met with critical suspicion (Sandahl 2018). Are they really acting or are they just being themselves? Such questions result from the essentialization of normative embodiment in theatrical traditions. As Siebers writes, "Because the theater is a theater of nondisabled bodies, they are supposedly the most visible on the stage, but because they are the norm, they are in effect invisible" (Siebers 2016, p. 441).

Disability performance scholars challenge the normative assumptions of conventional theatrical practices and aesthetics. Petra Kuppers' work, particularly in *Disability and Contemporary Performance*, explores how individuals with a variety of disabilities create performance art that is structured by their embodied experiences of the world, as well as the aesthetics suggested by such art (Kuppers 2003). Several essays in Carrie Sandahl and Philip Auslander's edited collection *Bodies in Commotion* examine how disability performance advances principles that challenge the aesthetics of corporeal homogeneity and strict demarcations between performers and audiences (Sandahl and Auslander 2005), in particular Brueggerman and Smith. Kanta Kochhar-Lindgren's *Hearing Difference* advances an aesthetics of integrated deaf/hard of hearing/hearing theater that is founded in diverse sensorial embodiments (Kochhar-Lindgren 2006). While not yet applied to performance, recent work by autistic scholars has proposed an aesthetics of neurodiversity; unique artistic practices of seeing, interpreting, and expressing that are grounded in non-normative embodiments (Rodas 2018). This chapter offers another contribution to the field of disability aesthetics, examining how productions grounded in deaf and DeafBlind perceptual experiences develop new theatrical practices and principles.

PARTY ON

The usher lets go of the audience members' hands and gently urges them forward. Hands outstretched, they walk slowly through a tunnel filled with thin strips of fabric that softly brush their faces and shoulders. Without the sense of sight, the tunnel seems to go on for a long time, though it is no more than ten feet long. As they exit, an usher takes their hand again and leads them to a series of tables. Each one contains food in little cups, with distinctive scents wafting from diffusers. The foods are grouped by taste—sweet, bitter, spicy, and sour. Audience members explore the food given to them by touch, smell, and then taste.

PROTACTILE *ROMEO AND JULIET*

The actor playing Romeo seizes the patron's hand and asks urgently about a woman he has just met, who smells of sweet lavender. He leads the patron in search of this mysterious woman, finding her in the crowd. With the patron in the middle, the two actors perform the famous "pilgrim's hands" scene. Suddenly the Nurse appears and sends Juliet away to her mother. The Nurse informs Romeo that Juliet is a Capulet. Heartbroken at this news, Romeo exits. The Nurse then guides the patron outside the party room to a balcony patio where they meet Juliet, who learns from the Nurse that Romeo is a Montague.

Kaite O'Reilly has proposed the aesthetics of access as a mechanism for "escaping the tyranny of normalization" in theater (O'Reilly 2017). But in my experience, access merely allows diversely embodied people to partake in theatrical practices based on normative embodiment. Access decisions also do not always serve the needs of the community at which they are aimed. For example, captioning boxes may be positioned in such a way that it is impossible to have a view of both the captioning and the production simultaneously. Nor does the presence of disabled bodies onstage necessarily entail consideration of those in the audience. In her analysis of two productions by the National Theatre of the Deaf, Shannon Bradford identifies several instances where aesthetic decisions made by the hearing director excluded deaf audience members by making it impossible to understand the signing on stage (Bradford 2005, pp. 91–93; see also Kochhar-Lindgren 2006 pp. 107–108). If artistic vision and access needs conflict, an aesthetics of access can reinforce the marginalization of disabled audiences. Inclusion, on the other hand, enables participation in performance modes that are based on the particular embodiments of the intended audience. An aesthetics of inclusion focuses on how individuals remake theatrical practices and spaces in ways that best suit their unique perceptual experiences. It discovers the principles guiding these practices and evaluates them on their own terms.

Shakespeare in ASL offers a possible model for an aesthetics of inclusion. In productions by deaf directors, characters inhabit a world in which being deaf and communicating through sign language is the norm. Deafness as disability disappears, both as a social-cultural construct and as a dramaturgical frame. As an extension of deaf people's sensorial experience of the world, visual language is used artistically in performance. For example, the linguistic principle of spatial indexing can be mapped onto the theatrical space by associating major characters with stage right or left. Those actors enter/exit from their assigned locations and other actors point to these directions when referring to these characters in their absence. Translations of Shakespeare's play-texts also create visual equivalences for spoken language poetic techniques. Rhyme, allusion, and extended metaphors can be created through repetition of similar hand shapes, while rhythm can be expressed through pacing, repetition, and transformational signs (where the same handshape is kept across different signs). Depiction, the sign language equivalent of "show, don't tell," uses linguistic features such as classifiers, tokens, role shifting, and sign space to create visual narratives. Classifiers are handshapes representing specific nouns that can be manipulated to show action.[5] A bird is sitting on a tree, for example, can be shown using two different classifiers—1 (index finger) and bent V. The index finger represents the branch and the bent V represents the bird sitting on the branch. Tokens are sign-entities established in the sign space and used to show action and dialogue. Continuing the example, the bent V classifier is the bird token. It can be manipulated to show the bird's action, such as hopping from branch to branch. Role shifting is a narrative technique where the signer adopts different perspectives. These are shown by shifting the body or eye gaze. For example, suppose the signer wants to describe a cat seeing the bird in the tree. By gazing up, the signer shifts to the cat's perspective, as if looking at the bird in the tree.

ASL translations of Shakespeare use classifiers, tokens, role shifting, and sign space to create visual equivalences for his richly poetic language. However, the linguistic and structural differences between spoken and signed languages require different principles for evaluating the artistry of the translation. Consider, for example, Manny Hernandez's performance as the Ghost in Gallaudet University's 2012 production of *Hamlet*. During the Ghost's scene, a filmed video of Hernandez was projected onto the backdrop of a darkened stage. Hernandez's face was not visible, eliminating grammatical elements such as facial expressions and mouth movements. He thus created a richly detailed picture of the Ghost's murder and Gertrude's seduction by Claudius using only a limited number of handshapes and classifiers. The translation of "sleeping in my orchard,/a serpent stung me" (1.5.35–36) (Shakespeare 1603), for example, uses the bent V and open hand classifiers to set the scene of the King's murder. At first, the open hand represents the ground and the bent V shows the King laying on the ground sleeping. Then the open hand transforms into a second bent V classifier, becoming a snake that crawls around to bite the first bent V (the King). The first bent V shakes and then stills, depicting the King's death. The second bent V then straightens into an index finger, which moves in a half circle, shaking. This can be interpreted as the sign for "where" and as a person walking (or chasing/seeking). Hernandez then signs TRICK TRICK TRICK (a sign that incorporates the index finger) in a half circle, then repeats the depiction of the snake bite and death. "The serpent that did sting thy father's life / now wears his crown" (1.5.38–39) (Shakespeare 1603) is translated by the snake bent V moving to the right and the bent V representing the King moving atop the snake, becoming a crown.

This translation incorporates several ASL poetic techniques. A small number of handshapes are used, with frequent repetition of several classifiers. Depiction predominates, with classifiers showing the narrative actions. Multiple transformational signs are used, suggesting thematic as well as narrative connections. For example, the use of transformations signs to depict Claudius's assumption of power (when the King bent V becomes the crown atop the serpent bent V) parallels Shakespeare's transmutation of the literal serpent reported to have killed the King into the figurative serpent responsible for his murder. Signs are also repeated for emphasis, with the repetitions moving in a half circle. This arc delineates not only the gestural space of the actor, but also the cosmological space in which the Ghost is confined, "Doom'd for a certain term to walk the night,/And for the day confin'd to fast in fires" (1.5.10–11) (Shakespeare 1603). To sum up, this translation cannot be evaluated with principles drawn from spoken language. Instead, a visual poetics must be created. This shows, on a granular level, how Shakespeare in ASL can model theatrical practices and aesthetics founded on disability embodiment.

Some Shakespeare productions have also incorporated ASL in ways that center deaf embodiment. To draw from Jessica Berson's discussion of deaf performance continuums, these productions reject reductive and stereotypical uses of deafness in favor of dramaturgy and characterizations grounded in the experience, language, and visual aesthetics of the deaf world (Berson 2005, p. 49). Lindsey Snyder's 2014 *Richard III*, featuring deaf actor Ethan Sinnott, is one such production. Productions of *Richard III* typically reduce Richard's complex psychology to the trauma of his embodied experience, as shown through adaptive appendages and physical contortions.[6] These disability simulations are often explained with compensatory narratives that focus on physical limitations, rather than social attitudes and access barriers. Playing Richard in Sam Mendes' 2011–2012 production, for example, Kevin Spacey described his character as triumphing over the stigma of his twisted body, turning weaknesses into strength (Whelehan 2014). In Snyder's production, disability (in the form of deafness alone, as Sinnott was not outfitted with the usual prosthetic trappings) is also a significant contributor to Richard's psychology and behavior. However, the presence of other deaf characters and moments when they communicate directly with Richard through ASL (without voice interpreting, thus excluding the non-signing audience from the conversation) suggest that the handicapping element of Richard's disability comes from social barriers, rather than from internal flaws that are manifested as an aberrant body.[7] Snyder's production also included deaf humor, as when Lord Hastings spoke slowly and loudly to Richard, who has all along been lip-reading with skill. The set design also artistically leveraged ASL. During some of Richard's soliloquys, for example, an actor appeared behind a shadowed mirror to provide voicing. Because shadows, mirrors, and external/internal perceptions are all recurrent motifs in the play-text, access for hearing audience members was provided in ways that intensified the thematic content.

R+J: The Vineyard, a 2015 production by Red Theatre Chicago, also centered the experience of deafness. Director Aaron Sawyer and dramaturg Claire Alston (both hearing) transported the audience to nineteenth-century Martha's Vineyard, a place where hereditary deafness and a stationary population led to a unique society in which "everyone spoke sign language." In this community, deaf people were included in everyday life and not set apart by their hearing status (Groce 1985). *R+J: The Vineyard* also referenced deaf history by framing the strife between the Capulets and the Montague families as a clash of communication modalities. The Capulets stressed speaking and lipreading, while the Montagues used ASL. Audiences were thus introduced to the divisive struggle between oral and manual philosophies of deaf education.[8] Furthermore, relationships between characters dramatized the ways language use shapes the experience of deafness. The only deaf person in the Capulet family, Juliet (played by hearing actress McKenna Lieseman) prefers signing over speaking. She depends on her nurse (played by hearing actress Beth Harris), to communicate for her when she interacts with others. Harris interprets for Juliet behind Lady Capulet's back, popping her hands down quickly when her mistress turns around. This defiance of the Capulet communication philosophy made Juliet's isolation from her family visible. It added another dimension to the relationship between Juliet and her nurse, and it subtly prepared us for their collaboration in Juliet's elopement.

The dramaturgical use of deaf history in *R+J: The Vineyard* amplifies the conflict between Juliet and her parents and deepens our understanding of the relationship between the two lovers. Romeo and Juliet connect not just because of physical attraction but also because of their shared experience of disability embodiment. When deaf actor Brendan Connelly first catches sight of Juliet, he literally beholds her. *Who is this person?* he asks, reaching out as he signs "person" so that she is framed by his hands. In Sawyer's staging, Juliet stands off from the crowd at the Capulet feast. She holds an old-fashioned ear trumpet, underscoring the social isolation caused by her inability to communicate with hearing people. Then a curtain is pulled across the stage, leaving Romeo and Juliet alone at opposite ends. *I see you*, they sign to each other, beginning an interlude of ASL word play that is not in Shakespeare's script but that allows us to see how the joy of direct communication drives their courtship.

These examples of Shakespeare in ASL and deaf performance demonstrate how disability embodiment can engender new theatrical practices and principles for evaluating these artistic practices. Yet there are pitfalls in taking deaf performance as a model for an aesthetics of inclusion. Deaf ASL users largely reject the label of disability, emphasizing their close-knit community, cultural identity and language minority status. ASL Shakespeare is also predominantly white and deaf theater in general has yet to rethink its aesthetics and poetics from intersectional frameworks. Additionally, deafness also has a unique type of social and cultural capital that other types of disability embodiment do not. The typical response to Shakespeare in sign language, for example, is to comment on its aesthetic appeal and emotional expressiveness. Reviewing Snyder's *Richard III*, Conrad Geller praises Sinnott's "forceful, poetic, even balletic use of sign" which "showed its power and its beauty" (Geller 2014). Would the same be said about autistic communication, the hands and bodies that stim, flick and flap? As Michele Friedner and Pamela Block observe, "there is a difference between 'beautiful' signing that is a 'feast for the eyes' and 'loud hands' in that 'loud hands' challenge us to consider and recognize non-linguistic intelligibility in addition to both our language and semiotic ideologies" (Friedner and Block 2017).

In looking for models of inclusive performance, we must acknowledge cultural attitudes toward various kinds of disability embodiment. Consider, as another example, Ian Merrill Peakes' portrayal of Timon in the Folger Shakespeare Theatre's 2017 *Timon of Athens*. Peakes incorporated behaviors such as obsessive hand-washing/sanitizing, responding to touch with anxiety, and compulsively skipping the third step when ascending/descending from a staircase on stage left. After Timon's world collapses, these compulsions disappear. Critical reviews of his performance were positive. *Washington Post* critic Peter Marks, for example, called Peakes' use of these behaviors "an intriguing indicator of human frailty" (Marks 2017). Was the tenor of the response due to the subtlety of Peakes' performance or the director's notes identifying modernity, materialism, and social media as far more important contributors to Timon's downfall (Richmond 2017, p. 4)? Or was it because this form of disability embodiment is aesthetically and experientially privileged over others? Would reviewers have praised a Timon with schizophrenia or Tourette's? What if Peakes had been a person of color, rather than a white actor? Living as we do in a society where black and disabled men are killed by police, we must not forget how race intersects disability aesthetics (Thompson 2021; Shaw 2019).[9] New models for thinking about performance embodiment should acknowledge the intersections of lived experiences—an intersectionality that is generative, rather than additive, exploring how systems of oppression differ, interrelate, and reinforce each other (Thomson 2008; Strand 2017).

Party On

Ushers take audience members' hands and begin dancing. Music which may or may not have been audible before, depending on the audience members' sensory abilities, becomes louder. The bass grows stronger. Audience members and ushers change partners; it's soon unclear who is who. Eventually, everyone ends up holding hands with two people. The bass grows even stronger and audience members find themselves being pulled from both sides. A tug of war ensues and continues almost to the point of being physically uncomfortable.

ProTactile *Romeo and Juliet*

Alone on the balcony with the patron, Juliet pours her heart out. As she feels her way along the railing, she bumps into a strange pair of hands. It is Romeo! They plot their clandestine marriage and then kiss. Romeo leaves, taking the patron with him. As they attempt to sneak out of the Capulet house, they bump into Mercutio. A fight ensues. Romeo stabs Mercutio, who falls down unmoving. Romeo and the patron then flee to a door, where Romeo leaves the patron with townsman.

Throughout this chapter, I have described two performances of *Romeo and Juliet* that use senses other than sound and sight for dramatic storytelling. *Party On*, produced by the now-defunct theater company dog & pony dc, was the culmination of an initiative exploring movement, smell, and taste inspired by DeafBlind writer John Lee Clark's article "My Dream Play" (Clark 2015). In one workshop, participants were invited to express passages from Shakespeare's plays using food. The picture below shows my gustatory translation of Puck's closing lines from *A Midsummer Night's Dream*.[10]

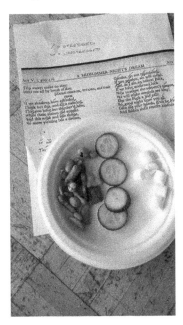

The crunchy party mix stands for the dream, suggesting the discomfort and bewilderment experienced by the mortals as a result of the fairies' tricks. The cucumbers cleanse the palate and represent Puck's "mending," with the sweetness of the marshmallows signifying that it was all just a dream. Fairly conventional taste symbolism, but I added a pinch of dirt to the party mix. This gave it an extra grittiness that stayed in the mouth, suggesting how the residue of the dream lingers on even after awakening.

dog & pony dc first applied this sensory exploration in a performance of the seven ages of man passage in *As You Like It*. Audience members wore blindfolds and earplugs (if needed) and were led through a series of scenes that depicted the cycle of life through touch, taste, smell, and movement. Throughout the play, no language-based interaction took place between actors and patrons. In a second production, called *Party On*, dog & pony dc again used touch, taste, smell, and movement to explore the themes of conflict in *Romeo and Juliet*. Participants, wearing blindfolds and earplugs as needed, faced choices and contrasts from masks, to dance partners, to food and drink. A subwoofer mimicked a beating heart and vapor machines created distinct scent zones in the performance space. Audience members interacted with both actors and each other, without knowing who was who. *Party On* was not designed solely for deaf or DeafBlind audiences, but its experimentation with non-dominant senses created an inclusive experience for attendees with auditory and visual disabilities who are excluded by conventional theatrical practices.

The second adaptation of *Romeo and Juliet* I have described throughout this chapter took place during a DeafBlind theater institute that I organized in 2018. The project, funded by the National Endowment for the Arts, explored how immersive theater techniques could be leveraged to create theatrical practices grounded in the emerging language of Protactile (PT) and the perceptual experiences of DeafBlind people.[11] Rather than a deficit model in which DeafBlind individuals depend on sighted helpers, the Protactile Theater Institute centered DeafBlind autonomy and ways of being in the world. After an intense week of playing with Shakespeare, PT, and sensory props, participants performed scenes from *Romeo and Juliet* for a small audience of mixed hearing/vision abilities. The adaptation was similar in approach to immersive theater productions such as Punchdrunk's *Sleep No More*, in which audiences move through a series of rooms and view tableaus portraying *Macbeth*. Unlike *Sleep No More*, however, interaction between actors and audience members was central to the experience. PT requires contact—hands touching hands—in two-way or three-way communication. Each patron, as we called the audience members, could engage with one or two actors at a time.[12] Patrons also needed to maintain physical contact with an actor as they travelled through the performance space. The fourth wall was thrown out, and the set was transformed to fit how DeafBlind people interact and move through space. Institute participants refined techniques for navigating the performance space and establishing tactile cues for the actors' entrances and exits. They also experimented with costuming, props, and using scent and taste for character development. The end product was a performance that was designed for DeafBlind actors and patrons alike, demonstrating how disability embodiment can create inclusive new theatrical practices (Bradbury et al. 2019).

PARTY ON

The patron must finally choose to go with one person. They stand together, hands touching, as the underlying bass of the music becomes strong and stronger, until all that is left is the feeling of a beating heart. After a time, the rhythmic thumping gradually begins to slow. As it fades away, patrons are led back down the stairs and into the lobby where they began.

PROTACTILE *ROMEO AND JULIET*

The townsman tells the patron that Mercutio has died and Romeo is banished from Verona. War has broken out between the Capulet and Montague families, leaving Juliet heartbroken. The last is signed with two hands forming the shape of a heart over the breast. The heart breaks open and falls down, down, down. The townsman pauses for a long moment, head bowed, then slowly leads the patron back to the waiting area.

This chapter has drawn on concepts of embodied aesthetics in critical disability studies to discuss how theater can move beyond simply providing access to conventional performance modes. I have shown how theater makers can embrace an aesthetics of inclusion that invites people with diverse embodiments to remake theatrical practices and spaces in ways that best suit their unique ways of being in the world. Such new artistic practices call for new principles of assessment. How do we evaluate a performance that is primarily tactile? What concepts can we use to discuss the choreography of smells? We might look to fields such as culinary aesthetics or aromachology, the study of scents and their emotional resonances. The aesthetics of everyday experience is also a rich field to explore. Yuriko Saito describes everyday aesthetics as an evaluative practice that focuses on distinctive characteristics of an object, phenomenon, or activity—an approach that nurtures "an attitude of open-mindedness by encouraging us to appreciate each kind of object for what it is, rather than imposing a certain predetermined standard of beauty" (Saito 2007, p. 129). Applying such an aesthetics to theater, this would mean understanding the type of embodiment that structures a theatrical practice, the formal possibilities inherent in this embodiment, and the artistic expression of those formal possibilities in performance.

It is impossible, of course, for any one theater production to be inclusive of all. People with disabilities have various needs and preferences that may sometimes be in conflict. Some deaf people prefer captioning over ASL interpreting of performances or vice versa. Through the experiences, conventions, and sensory associations it draws on, PT theater unavoidably creates new lines of exclusion. It may be inaccessible to audience members with sensory processing disorders such as hyper-sensitivity to touch. Race, class, gender, and sexuality also shape the experience of disability in performance. In its very nature, theater is a selective re-presentation of the phenomenal world around us and our embodiment in it. Theater inevitably creates spheres of inclusion and exclusion—thus, the importance of diversifying performative bodies and practices so that theater embodies the full spectrum of human experience.

NOTES

1. On narrative prosthesis, see David T. Mitchell and Sharon L. Snyder, *Narrative Prosthesis: Disability and the Dependencies of Discourse*, University of Michigan Press, Ann Arbor, 2000.
2. I use deaf to refer a continuum of positions along the audiological/language use/cultural spectrums that may not align with clearly identified communities, cultures, or language practices, rather than the reductive, but more common Deaf/deaf to distinguish between those who identify as part of the deaf world and those who identify with the hearing world. DeafBlind is the term used by those who identify with this community.
3. Samuel Yates proposes 'disability simulation' to describe normatively embodied actors performing disability embodiment over the more common 'cripping up' to foreground disability in the language use to examine disability in performance (Yates 2019, pg. 68).
4. In contrast, Ben Brantley's review suggests that Dinklage's casting allows us to better understand Richard's psychology: "Once you see him, in the

show's second half, climbing so uncomfortably into his newly won throne, you realize that such concentrated effort is what has always defined him. And because he has had to work harder than his peers to belong to a morally diseased society, he plays that society's rotten games better than anyone" (Brantley 2004).

5. Videos and pictures of classifiers can be found at this link: https://www.startasl.com/american-sign-language-classes-asl2-5/

6. As Marcela Kostihova points out, Shakespeare's play is surprisingly opaque about Richard's actual physical appearance. With the discovery of Richard's physical remains in 2012, we now know that he had only scoliosis, rather than the withered hand and limp (Kostihova 2013, pg. 136, 140–41).

7. New York City's Nicu's Spoon Theater production of *Richard III* in 2015 also invited audiences to consider how disability is socially constructed, by casting actors with visible disabilities in every role except Richard.

8. In the nineteenth century, the mostly hearing proponents of oralist methods believed deaf people should learn to speak and read lips. Led by Alexander Graham Bell, they viewed sign language as a crutch that prevented deaf people from integrating into hearing society. In contrast, manualists believed ASL gave deaf people the best possibility of developing their full intellectual and civic potential. At the 1880 Milan Conference on deaf education, a contingent of oralists succeeded in passing a resolution declaring their method superior. For almost a century afterward, ASL was suppressed in schools for the deaf, often by corporal punishments such as hitting children's hands with rulers if they signed. However, teachers could not stop the hands from flying when their backs were turned. ASL was the language of choice in the residential school dorms which were often supervised by deaf adults, unlike the classrooms managed by hearing teachers (Bayton 1998). The conflict between oralists and manualists still resonates today, as a visit to cochlear implant discussion boards and Facebook groups quickly reveals.

9. Peakes' performance also raises interesting questions about disability visibility and disclosure. We do not know where Peakes himself falls on the neurodiversity spectrum. How might disability disclosure change our understanding of his performance?

10. If we shadows have offended,
Think but this and all is mended:
That you have but slumbered here
While these visions did appear.
And this weak and idle theme,
No more yielding but a dream,
Gentles, do not reprehend.
If you pardon, we will mend. (5.1.440–47) (Shakespeare 1600).

11. While ASL is a visual-spatial language, Protactile is haptic-spatial. It incorporates movement and touch to communicate visual and auditory information. DeafBlind PT users have developed unique linguistic features to convey environmental information, nonverbal cues, and noises/facial expressions (Edwards 2016). The PT philosophy also emphasizes autonomy and direct interaction between DeafBlind individuals, rather than mediated via sighted interpreters or support providers (granda and Nuccio 2018).
12. We needed a different name because the sign for 'audience' assumes normative vision. Bodily experience is deeply embedded in language.

References

Aebischer, Pascale. 2009. *Shakespeare's Violated Bodies: Stage and Screen Performance*. New York: Cambridge University Press.

Bayton, Douglas C. 1998. *Forbidden Signs: American Culture and the Campaign against Sign Language*. Chicago: University of Chicago Press.

Berson, Jessica. 2005. Performing Deaf Identity. Towards a Continuum of Deaf Performance. *Bodies in Commotion: Disability and Performance*, edited by Carrie Sandahl and Philip Auslander, 42–55. Ann Arbor: University of Michigan Press.

Bradbury, Jill Marie, John Lee Clark, Rachel Grossman, Jason Herbers, Victoria Magliocchino, Jasper Norman, Yashaira Romilus, Robert T. Sirvage, and Lisa van der Mark. 2019. ProTactile Shakespeare: Inclusive Theater by/for the DeafBlind. *Shakespeare Studies* 47: 81–115.

Bradford, Shannon. 2005. The National Theatre of the Deaf Identity: Artistic Freedom and Cultural Responsibility in the Use of American Sign Language. *Bodies in Commotion: Disability and Performance*, edited by Carrie Sandahl and Philip Auslander, 86–94. Ann Arbor: University of Michigan Press.

Brantley, Ben. 2004. A Big Throne to Fill, and the Man to Fill It. *The New York Times*. October 12.

Bruno, Christine. 2014. Disability in American Theater: Where is the Tipping Point? Howl Round Theatre Commons. https://howlround.com/disability-american-theater. Accessed 14 March 2022.

Clark, John Lee. 2015. My Dream Play: A DeafBlind Man Imagines a Pro-Tactile Theatre. *Scene4 Magazine*. https://www.scene4.com/archivesqv6/2015/apr-2015/0415/johnleeclark0415.html. Accessed 14 March 2022.

Eagleton, Terry. 1988. "The Ideology of the Aesthetic." *Poetics Today*, 9 no. 2, 327–338.

Edwards, Terra. 2016. Sign-Creation in the Seattle Deafblind Community: A Triumphant Story about the Regeneration of Obviousness. *Gesture* 16, no. 2, 307–332.

Friedner, Michelle and Pamela Block. 2017. Deaf Studies Meets Autistic Studies. *The Senses and Society* 12.3: 282–300. https://doi.org/10.1080/1745892 7.2017.1369716.

Geller, Conrad. 2014. Theatre Review: *Richard III* by NextStop Theatre Company at Industrial Strength Theatre. MD Theatre Guide. https://mdtheatreguide. com/2014/02/theatre-review-richard-iii-by-nextstop-theatre-company-at-industrial-strength-theatre/. Accessed 14 March 2022.

granda, aj, and Jelica Nuccio. 2018. Protactile Principles. Seattle: Tactile Communications LLC. https://www.tactilecommunications.org/ ProTactilePrinciples. Accessed 14 March 2022.

Groce, Nora. 1985. *Everyone Here Spoke Sign Language: Hereditary Deafness on Martha's Vineyard*. Cambridge, MA: Harvard University Press.

Heilpern, John. 2004. A Sluggish *Richard III*: Where Is Our Royal Psycho? *The Observer*, October 25.

Johnston, Kirsty. 2016. *Disability Theatre and Modern Drama: Recasting Modernism*. New York: Bloomsbury Press.

Kochhar-Lindgren, Kanta. 2006. *Hearing Difference: The Third Ear in Experimental, Deaf, and Multicultural Theater*. DC: Gallaudet University Press.

Kostihova, Marcela. 2013. Richard Recast: Renaissance Disability in a Postcommunist Culture. *Recovering Disability in Early Modern England*, edited by Allison P. Hobgood and David Houston Wood, 136–149. Columbus: Ohio State University Press.

Kuppers, Petra. 2003. *Disability and Contemporary Performance: Bodies on Edge*. New York: Routledge.

Marks, Peter. 2017. Shakespeare's *Timon* Takes a Rare Washington Bow. *The Washington Post*, May 17.

O'Reilly, Kaite. 2017. The Necessity of Diverse Voices in Theatre Regarding Disability and Difference. Howl Round Theatre Commons. https://howl-round.com/necessity-diverse-voices-theatre-regarding-disability-and-difference. Accessed 14 March 2022.

Richmond, Robert. 2017. "From the Director." *Timon of Athens* Program. Folger Theater.

Roach, Joseph. 1989. Theatre History and the Ideology of the Aesthetic. *Theatre Journal*, 41, no. 2, 155–168.

Rodas, Julie Miele. 2018. *Autistic Disturbances: Theorizing Autism Poetics from the DSM to* Robinson Crusoe. Ann Arbor: University of Michigan Press.

Saito, Yuriko. 2007. *Everyday Aesthetics*. New York: Oxford University Press.

Sandahl, Carrie. 2018. Using Our Words: Exploring Representational Conundrums in Disability Drama and Performance. *Journal of Literary and Cultural Disability Studies*, 12, no. 2, 129–144. https://doi.org/10.3828/jlcds. 2018.11.

Sandahl, Carrie, and Philip Auslander, eds. 2005. *Bodies in Commotion: Disability and Performance*. Ann Arbor: University of Michigan Press.

Shakespeare, William.1600. *A Midsummer Night's Dream*, edited by Sukanta Chaudhuri. New York: Bloomsbury Press.

Shakespeare, William. 1603. *Hamlet*, edited by Ann Thompson and Neil Taylor. New York: Bloomsbury Press.

Shaw, Justin. 2019. "Rub Him About the Temples": *Othello*, Disability, and the Failures of Care. *Early Theatre* 22, no. 2, 171–184. https://doi.org/10.12745/et.22.2.3997.

Shildrik, Margrit. 2013. Critical Disability Studies: Rethinking the Conventions for the Age of Postmodernism. In *Routledge Handbook of Disability Studies*, edited by Nick Watson, Alan Roulstone, and Carol Thomas, 30–41. New York: Routledge.

Siebers, Tobin. 2008. *Disability Theory*. Ann Arbor: University of Michigan Press.

Siebers, Tobin. 2016. Shakespeare Differently Disabled. *The Oxford Handbook of Shakespeare and Embodiment: Gender, Sexuality, and Race*, edited by Valerie Traub, 435–454. New York: Oxford University Press.

Strand, Lauren Rose. 2017. Charting Relations between Intersectionality Theory and the Neurodiversity Paradigm. *Disability Studies Quarterly* 37, no. 2. 10.18061/dsq.v37i2.5374.

Thompson, Vilissa. 2021. *Understanding the Policing of Black, Disabled Bodies*. Center for American Progress. https://www.americanprogress.org/article/understanding-policing-black-disabled-bodies/. Accessed 14 March 2022.

Thomson, Rosemarie Garland. 2008. Integrating Disability, Transforming Feminist Theory. In *Feminist Disability Studies*, edited by Kim C. Hall, 13–47. Bloomington: Indiana University Press.

Whelehan, Jeremey. 2014. *NOW: In the Wings on a World Stage*. Treetop Productions. Film.

Yates, Samuel. 2019. Choreographing Conjoinment: *Side Show*'s Fleshly Fixations and Disability Simulation. *Studies in Musical Theatre* 13, no. 1, 67–78. https://doi.org/10.1386/smt.13.1.67_1.

Zarrilli, Peter B. 2002. *Acting (Re)Considered: A Theoretical and Practical Guide*. 2nd ed. New York: Routledge.

CHAPTER 3

Immersed in Miami/Bathed in the Caribbean: Tarell Alvin McCraney's *Antony and Cleopatra* Revisited

Hayley R. Fernandez and James M. Sutton

This chapter advances Tarell Alvin McCraney's *Antony and Cleopatra* (2013–2014) as an exemplary but overlooked inclusive Shakespearean performance. The show afforded McCraney the opportunity to bring big-budget, high-end production values home to Miami; in doing so, he chose to "shift the scene" of the tragedy from its original West-East binary of ancient Rome's encounter with Egypt to a late eighteenth-century framework featuring the fracturing relationship between Napoleonic Paris and pre-Revolutionary Haiti. He reduced and rearranged Shakespeare's text in a "radical edit," and employed casting, costuming, scenography, dramaturgy, and music that bathed the production in Caribbean waters. Thus,

H. R. Fernandez (✉)
Doral Academy Preparatory School, Miami, FL, USA
e-mail: hfern055@fiu.edu

J. M. Sutton
Florida International University, Miami, FL, USA
e-mail: suttonj@fiu.edu

S. Freeman Loftis et al. (eds.), *Inclusive Shakespeares*, Palgrave Shakespeare Studies,
https://doi.org/10.1007/978-3-031-26522-8_3

he reimagined the play in light of a familiar creolized Miami, in conversation with a Haitian imaginary. The production was designed, rehearsed, and staged in autumn 2013 at the RSC, playing at Stratford's Swan Theater that November. The show then transferred to Miami in late December, and ran at the Colony Theater on Miami Beach, in January–February 2014. Finally, it appeared at New York's Public Theater from late February–late March 2014. Despite its daring inclusivity and Caribbean setting, this performance was poorly received by critics, especially in the UK and New York, and has been mostly neglected in academic scholarship; it thus stands out in McCraney's oeuvre as un(der)appreciated and largely forgotten. This chapter aims to address this anomaly, opening up dialogue around this remarkable production.

McCraney is renowned as a visionary African-American playwright and screen-writer, and as demonstrated by *Tarell Alvin McCraney: Theater, Performance and Collaboration*, his work often receives attention in academic scholarship (Luckett et al. 2020). Born in Miami in October 1980, McCraney grew up in the vibrant, historic African-American neighborhood of Liberty City, adjacent to Little Haiti (Cote 2014) (Francis 25, Dunn 164–168, 280–290). McCraney's lifework celebrates his home city and its Black neighborhoods, through an inclusive, collaborative dramatic art. This theme of Black life is pronounced in all of his work, most notably his Miami-based screenplay *Moonlight*, and his adaptation of *Antony and Cleopatra* placed in colonial Haiti that is the focus of this chapter. Setting much of his work either in Miami or in close proximity (geographically or culturally) to Miami propels this prioritization of the city and its people. His creative work embodies homecoming: McCraney discovered his talent for theater as a teenager in Miami, first in the nurturing environment of Teo Castellanos' Village Improv, and then as a student at the New World School of the Arts (NWSA), a nationally acclaimed arts magnet high school in downtown Miami. Graduating from NWSA in 1999, he received the "Exemplary Artist Award" and the "Dean's Award in Theater" ("Tarell Alvin McCraney: A Career Chronology" 2020).

His undergraduate and graduate education and early professional career seem to show McCraney "breaking away" from Miami, establishing his name in theater centers such as Chicago, New York and the east coast, and England: nevertheless, we assert that Miami always remained close to his heart (his *Antony and Cleopatra* underscores this fact). McCraney attended DePaul University, earning his BFA (Acting) in 2003 and winning its Sarah Siddons Award, and Yale's School of Drama (YSD), where in 2007 he received his MFA in playwriting. While at Yale, he worked with August Wilson on Radio Golf, and penned his own trilogy, *The Brother/Sister Plays*. These three plays, *In the Red and Brown Water*, *The Brothers Size*, and *Marcus; Or the Secret of Sweet*, were first staged at Yale, then performed, between 2007–2009, at venues such as the Public Theater, the Young Vic, the Alliance Theater (Atlanta), The Vineyard (New York), and the McCarter Theater Center (Princeton). Contemporaneously, he co-wrote *The Breach* (premiering at the Southern Rep Theater, New Orleans) and composed *Wig Out!* (debuting at The Vineyard). Acclaim for these earliest plays came rapidly. In 2007 he won the Cole Porter Playwriting Award from YSD, a Whiting Award, and *The Brothers Size* (Young Vic) was nominated for a Laurence Olivier Award. In 2008 he won the Paula Vogel Playwriting Award from the Vineyard, was named "Most Promising Playwright" by the Evening Standard, and recognized by the National Endowment for the Arts for the Outstanding New American Play (for his *Brother/Sister* trilogy) ("Tarell Alvin McCraney: A Career Chronology" 2020).

In such contexts, his nomination as the RSC/Warwick International Playwright in Residence (2008–2010) appears bold and visionary. This residency in England fostered new works such as *American Trade* (co-produced by the RSC and Hampstead Theater, 2011) and *Choir Boy* (opening in 2012 at the Royal Court). McCraney also reworked and directed two Shakespearean tragedies due to this residency, 2010's *Young People's Hamlet* and the 2013–2014 *Antony and Cleopatra* under discussion here ("Tarell Alvin McCraney: A Career Chronology" 2020). In the past seven years, McCraney's creative and academic success has continued unabated. *Head of Passes*, which premiered in 2013 at Chicago's Steppenwolf Theater, and the 2016 Barry Jenkins film *Moonlight*, adapted from McCraney's unpublished script, "In Moonlight Black Boys Look Blue," predominate artistically; his 2015 appointment to the University of Miami's Theater department, and his selection as Chair of Playwriting at the Yale School of Drama, 2017–present, underscore his scholarly stature. He was named a MacArthur Fellow in 2013 ("Tarell Alvin McCraney: A Career Chronology" 2020). His most recent work, the television series *David Makes Man*, features Miami as its setting and focuses on the adolescence of Black youth in the city and its surrounding communities. Coupled with *Moonlight*, it sets the tone for McCraney's recent work, rooted in telling stories about his home, the vibrant Black neighborhoods of South Florida.

Despite rocketing to fame on global stages, screens, and streaming services in the past 15 years, three aspects of his practice have kept McCraney grounded, humble, and inclusive. First, he prizes collaboration, generosity, and dialogue, especially as a director and writer in the rehearsal space. Theater partners repeatedly mention such traits. Alana Arenas considers him "a gracious collaborator, which is a testament to his character because he is a meticulous craftsman. When you see an actor come into rehearsals suggesting [her line readings], it's endearing to watch Tarell effortlessly relent … because … nothing Tarell writes is happenstance" (Luckett et al. 2020). Tina Landau claims "he's an open book. A shy one, sometimes, but open nonetheless. He is startlingly candid about his own life and experiences" (189). Michael Boyd, reflecting on McCraney's RSC residency, recollects "a deeply principled artist who would always listen with grace and care, and then take what was useful from what he heard" (189). Tina Landau, who directed many of his premieres, reminisces that when "he is in the room [, w]e are a team. It's not about my executing some vision or directive he has. It's about us discovering together what is there on the page and us experimenting together on what can be there on the stage" (191). In a recent interview with T. Cole Rachel, McCraney claims: "collaboration also breeds community, and as a person who is deeply interested in making sure that communities thrive—and that art helps the community thrive—I'm trying to find ways to inoculate those communities from the pressures that performance can sometimes create" ("On Redefining What it Means to be Successful" 2021).

Although the particular "collaborative community" that McCraney denotes in this interview with Rachel is the Yale School of Drama, his words evoke another precious community to which he perpetually returns: Miami. This hometown connection exemplifies the second of his inclusive practices. Indeed, in interviews and accounts of others about him, his commitment to telling stories about his birthplace, and thereby fostering a better understanding of Miami's creolized diversity, emerge repeatedly. Thus, in speaking with Rachel, musing about the possibilities of "community theater," he remarks,

> I grew up in Homestead, Florida and if you go to Homestead you'll see all of these migrant workers who are from various parts of Central America and South America… and they tell stories. There's literal storytelling, there's joke telling, there're songs, there's music. You go to Little Haiti and their cultural center, there's a band coming down the street making music, doing

plays, and doing dances. Theater, live performance, and storytelling are alive and well in marginalized communities. ("On Redefining What it Means to be Successful" 2021)

Following upon McCraney's claim that "all of my plays are about Miami; the bayous are the Everglades" (Mandell 2014), scholar Donette Francis proposes that all his work crystallizes what she terms a "black Southern hemispheric epic" perspective. This includes his "Louisiana" plays (the *Brother/Sister* trilogy, *The Breach*, and *Head of Passes*), which should be approached by way of McCraney's roots in hemispheric Black Miami (19–21). She writes, "in the post-1970s Miami of McCraney's plays, the presence of Haitians, Afro-Latinos, Bahamians and other immigrants from the Anglophone Caribbean demonstrate the plurality with which African American identity is lived" (22).

A strong indicator of this creolized Miami/Caribbean sphere in McCraney's work surfaces in his consistent use of water imagery. Whether referred to solely in the titles of his works—*In the Red and Brown Water*—or existing as a major stage component or dramaturgical element within his productions, water constantly seems to flow through the stage scenes he creates. Sometimes contained as navigable channels, water just as often presents itself in overflowing torrents that reshape human activity and relationships. Deep (and troubled) waters abound in the "Louisiana" plays. Water is complex and dual in nature; sometimes it baptizes, sometimes it drowns. The former prevails in *Moonlight*, where Chiron finds himself in healthy relationships with the men in his life when he is bathed in or located near the water, and both are source and symbol of positive masculinity. Juan teaches him how to swim in the Atlantic Ocean as a young boy, and later he has two watery experiences with Kevin, first a beach-front sexual initiation in their youth, and secondly, reconnecting as adults, they spend the night together in Kevin's apartment by the beach. Alternatively, in the first season of *David Makes Man* (2019), water threatens David and his community at the height of hurricane season (a yearly rite of passage for Miamians). His place of residence lies in an evacuation zone, a hazardous area determined primarily by the threat of destructive surge waters, not by potentially damaging high winds. Moreover, these zones are spaces of urgency and conflictual time: when the call comes to evacuate one's home due to impending storm and tempest, concerns for one's own safety and that of family and friends prevail. Leave-taking done under the threat of high winds and flooding waters is hurried and anxious, not leisurely.

A son of Miami, McCraney (like many of his characters) comprehends such hurried departures, and understands how geography, socioeconomic status, race, and class might condition and attend to the very ground that patterns such forms of awareness (Wardi 2011). Furthermore, economic and other determinants always dictate that many in the "evacuation zone" will not leave: against all odds, folks risk staying at home. Such are the "winds" and the "rains" and the prevailing human conditions that McCraney well knows, and they blow through, water, and season all his plays. Bathed in comparable fluidity, and structured by serial comings and goings, toing and froing, Shakespeare's "Egyptian" play offered safe harbor for McCraney's scenic imagination to anchor. Through set design and dramaturgy, McCraney's *Antony and Cleopatra* prioritized the abundant, overflowing water imagery of Shakespeare's original.

Thus, in all his work, water draws individuals together or splits them apart, adding natural conflict to the narrative, creating fluidity, especially for his intended creolized Miami audiences. To be from Miami often means either to be an immigrant, or to be a descendant of one, from the diaspora; Miami's exiled, diasporic communities are, prima facie, seafarers, water-borne, ship-wrecked. As water-facing people, Miamians understand travel across water in its various forms. Thus, McCraney, Miami born and raised, in turning to *Antony and Cleopatra*, could not evade its fluid, oceanic textures: water is his, and his production's, and Cleopatra's natural element. Water creolizes, mixes, levels; it seeps, it permeates. Contemporary Miami dissolves into (pre)revolutionary Haiti.

This melding of Miami to the Caribbean is echoed in Donette Francis' formulation of the "black Southern hemispheric" as McCraney's realm: a space of creolization, contradictory omens, and a troubled "poetics of relation" (Boyd 2013; Glissant 1997). The emphasis on Miami, his affiliation with his home community, is clear (while the Caribbean sphere remains more shadowed, folded into the edges of his creative work, lurking and awaiting discovery). His commitment to Miami is also evidenced both through his tenure at the University of Miami ("Tarell Alvin McCraney: A Career Chronology" 2020), and annual visits to his alma mater, the New World School of the Arts (NWSA), where he engages current students in conversation and "talk backs" (Ogle 2017; Smalls 2019). McCraney's strong affinity for the youth of Miami was especially obvious during his January 2017 visit to NWSA to perform readings of "In the Red and Brown Water" and "The Brother's Size" from his trilogy *The Brother/Sister Plays*. Proceeds from ticket sales enhanced the Tarell Alvin

McCraney Audition Fund, which he established in 2010 to aid NWSA students with travel costs, fees, and other charges associated with applying to BFA programs. At the height of Moonlight's popularity—the film was nominated for the Best Picture Academy Award on January 24, 2017 and won this honor that same February 26—McCraney's visit to Miami showcased his care for his community and its youth. Students and theater enthusiasts alike witnessed readings from his signature plays, never staged or produced in Miami, and saw McCraney partake in the readings; author Hayley Fernandez, then a college sophomore, was present at this event. NWSA students, alumni and faculty, and other Miami-based actors participated in these readings. In addition, Jeremy Pope, an openly gay Black actor from Orlando, was featured; Pope's breakthrough role came when McCraney cast him in the 2013–2014 Off-Broadway production of Choir Boy, as Pharus Jonathan Young, the show's titular character. Thus, McCraney's visit, which included a Q&A session with attending students, exemplifies how he continuously considers and prioritizes Miami, its young actors, and its too often ignored and neglected communities: Black Miami, Afro-Caribbean Miami, gay and trans Miami, and the intersections thereof, from which he himself emerged.

Here surfaces his third inclusive practice: he is committed to arts education and ensuring that school children encounter his work and ideas. The interview with Rachel illuminates his generosity in training youth. Asked what advice he might offer to a beginning playwright, McCraney replies,

> it depends on the student and it depends on the person. I always try to look at their work and help them assess their situation based on the type of work they want to do... My fear... is that there's a brilliant artist who doesn't see themselves or the type of work that they're looking at doing reflected in [our current models]. Or maybe I don't even fully understand what they are trying to do... I try to guide them to follow their instincts as much as possible. ("On Redefining What it Means to be Successful" 2021)

This predisposition toward youth and his strong commitment to Miami coalesced in his *Young Person's Hamlet*, 2010–2013. The first incarnation of this "reduced Shakespeare," clocking in at 70 minutes and featuring memorable use of umbrellas (again, an emphasis on water), was crafted for the RSC. Starring Dharmesh Patel in the title role, this 2010 production opened in Stratford's Courtyard Theater, then transferred to London for ten schools performances. Peter Kirwan, reviewing the Stratford staging, wrote glowingly,

> Reimagining Shakespeare's longest tragedy for a school-age audience can't have been easy, but the RSC pulled it off with style and wit in a production that seemed to appeal to all members of the families that packed out the Courtyard. Fascinatingly, despite being only 70 minutes long, the play felt in no ways compromised; rather than giving a cut version, this was simply a different *Hamlet*, complete and coherent in itself. (Kirwan 2010)

In an interview with *The Guardian*'s Nosheen Iqbal, McCraney underscored the inclusive practices undergirding the show. Iqbal notes that this "cast mirror[s] the ethnic variety of the audiences they're playing to. This production sees 29-year-old Patel become the RSC's first British-Asian Hamlet; opposite him is Simone Saunders, the company's first black, female Horatio" (Iqbal 2010). Amid rehearsal, Iqbal queried McCraney about these choices. He explained, "It was hugely important for me to cast a Hamlet of colour … We're in London, for God's sake, where around 40% of people are non-white" (Iqbal 2010). As for bringing Shakespeare to young children, McCraney expounds, "something happens when your first theater experience is at a young age… but if you're from a minority and in the first show you see, everyone is white, followed by another that's the same and so on, you think: 'Oh, this is for them.' A pattern builds. And it's difficult to overcome" (Iqbal 2010).

The Miami connection? Three years later, in early 2013, McCraney transported a 90-minute cousin of this 2010 show to GableStage, re-cast with local Latinx, Black, and "Anglo" actors, but with a comparable frenetic energy aimed at youth.[1] "What can I say about the insertion of certain anachronistic musical interludes, such as Arielle Hoffman singing City and Colour's 'O' Sister' on a ukulele?" asks *Miami New Times* reviewer, John Thomason: "Like much of McCraney's *Hamlet*, it's radical, and it works" ("Hamlet at GableStage: Shakespeare for the Twitter Generation" 2013). As in London, this Miami production transformed into a schools' show, moving to high schools in Cutler Bay and Liberty City—both communities of color—where it was performed for 15,000 high-school students ("Hamlet at GableStage: Shakespeare for the Twitter Generation" 2013).

These three hallmarks of McCraney's inclusive theater-making practice—collaborative, generous theater-making open to diverse creolized perspectives; a commitment to Miami; and a willingness bordering on a mission to engage with schoolchildren (especially in South Florida)—powerfully shaped his 2013–2014 *Antony and Cleopatra*. Unlike his other plays, adaptations, films, and TV shows, however, this production was poorly received by critics and has been largely neglected in scholarship on McCraney. The poor reception of *Antony and Cleopatra* forces us to ask why the play was so poorly received and to posit that the inability of many "elite" audience members and critics ("privileged playgoers," reimagined) to agreeably experience and comprehend Shakespeare's play transported to a Caribbean setting severely damaged its reception. Did this production over-reach in some manner, going astray in its radical re-scripting of this Mediterranean tragedy into a transatlantic and colonial affair foregrounding the postcolonial in its emphasis on racial, cultural, and religious difference? Was the production a misstep? Or did the play, with its intense focus on Cleopatra's Black body, celebration of Haitian negritude, and importation of cultural and religious practices from the Black Atlantic and Caribbean, encounter a white Shakespearean elite unable, or unwilling, to incorporate and accept its perspectives, thus ironically reproducing or rescripting Rome's failure to accommodate Egypt as figured in the play? Was McCraney's *Antony and Cleopatra* an inclusive Shakespeare staged six or seven years before its time? We believe so.

The casting of the production signaled its inclusivity. The American actor Joaquina Kalukango was the first Black woman to ever portray Cleopatra on stage in Stratford. The British Black actor Sarah Niles doubled as Charmian and Menas. Cuban-American Charise Castro Smith, born in Miami and educated at Brown and YSD (and most recently, co-director of the Disney animated film, Encanto), doubled as Iras and Octavia, a blending indicative of the crossings in geography and race this production explored. Similarly, mixed-race actor Ash Hunter took on both sides of the story, playing Roman Scarus, Pompey, and Egyptian Alexas (Verzuh n.d.). African American actor Chivas Michael portrayed Eros, Mardian and the Soothsayer. Nigerian-born, British educated actor Chukwudi Iwuji depicted Enobarbus. White British actors Jonathan Cake and Samuel Colling performed Antony and Octavius Caesar, respectively, while white American actors Henry Stram and Ian Lassiter played Lepidus/Proculeius and Agrippa/Thyreus (Program for William Shakespeare 2013).

The rehearsal space McCraney fostered for this production was collaborative and generous. Shakespearean scholar James Shapiro, who observed the company in rehearsal, recalled in personal correspondence that "Tarell was a superb presence in the room—open-minded, clear about what he wanted, humble (in a way that few directors are), always open to input from anyone" (Shapiro 2020). These grace-notes on McCraney's practice reverberate from a director's rehearsal note dated October 21, 2013, three weeks prior to the Stratford premier. Recollecting an underwater sculpture off the coast of Grenada, depicting enchained Africans, submerged and holding hands, joined in a circle, McCraney told his company,

> I asked you all to recreate a circle and before I even gave instruction to do anything, together as a group you all decided to move, sing, hum, breathe together. For some reason the light and the movement reminded me of this... sculpture at the bottom of the sea in Grenada of African slaves who were thrown or sometimes who jumped overboard ships darting the Caribbean... This particular sculpture is a group chained together, who went in together. (McCraney 2013)

What surfaces here? For one, his commitment to forging inclusive attachments and shared purpose in the company. But also visible, and aligned with Brathwaite's assertion that "unity is submarine" (64), is McCraney's strong predisposition toward uncovering the Black hemispheric Atlantic, the creolized Caribbean, in this production—he and this show bend toward pre-revolutionary Haiti, gesture toward the diasporic community of Little Haiti, and lean into Black Miami (Francis 2020). Casting and costuming clearly demarcated the struggle of Black Haitians to achieve independence from their white, European, Napoleonic colonizers; so too dramaturgy, choreography, and music. A large rectangular pool of water upstage, accompanied by soft, clear lighting and a white billowing canopy adorning the backstage created the atmosphere of a Caribbean late afternoon, approaching sunset. Michael Thurber's musical score, performed by Akintayo Akinbode and two other musicians, bathed the production in Caribbean sound and rhythm. Haitian cultural and religious practice were most pronounced in the production's fourth act, showcasing a Haitian chant, originally penned and performed by Toto Bissainthe in 1977, sung here by Charmian, Iras and Scarus, "Dèy O / n ap rele dèy o / Ayiti Woy" (Mourning o / We're screaming, mourning o / Haiti Woy) (Bissainthe 1977). Antony and Cleopatra appeared together, center stage, during the song, but did not participate; they faded to black as the song progressed. Channeling voudou ritual, the Soothsayer emerged during the lament, carrying an "Antony" doll, with which he danced, then exited. Singing solo at the end, Charmian proclaimed Haiti's resilience—"Yes Haiti will rise / Haiti will stand / Haiti will strive ... for working together"—while Enobarbus silently watched, and then made his grand, final departure from Antony's Haitian sphere (Bissainthe 1977). Sung in Creole by Black actors, this powerful performance of Bissainthe's chant memorably stamped this production as a Haitian-focused *Antony and Cleopatra*, a re-formed perspective trumpeted by the bold decision to open the show with Enobarbus' famous celebration of Cleopatra's erotic beauty, "the barge she sat in, like a burnis'd throne / Burn'd on the water" (II. ii. 224–225) instead of concern over Antony's seeming-emasculation, "this dotage of our general's / Overflows the measure" (I. i. 1–2). Decisions regarding setting, props, and movement contribute to McCraney's inclusive vision, enfolding familiar symbols and cultural modes for South Florida audiences, proximate to and ever-cognizant of Haiti and the Caribbean. By repositioning an otherwise inaccessible Shakespearean play in a place and history intimately known by his desired audience, McCraney practiced inclusivity.

From Haiti to Little Haiti, the connection between Port au Prince and Miami has always been strong and vital, especially in times of trauma, such as following the devastating January 2010 earthquake. In this regard, McCraney's production was a Black Atlantic show, encompassing and especially oriented to McCraney's creolized Miami (not Stratford, and not New York, either.) The central run of this show, in Miami in January 2014 (four years after the earthquake), was always meant to represent its heart. Michael Boyd, the Artistic Director responsible for McCraney's RSC residency, noted in the production program, "I asked Tarell if he would lead an intimate ensemble ... in producing a repertoire of Shakespeare and a new work of his own. As a brilliant young theater-maker who wanted to... establish a repertoire company that could speak to the whole of the community in his native Miami, Tarell said yes ... [this] *Antony and Cleopatra* is the beginning of that journey" (Boyd 2013). Shapiro, in personal correspondence, concurs that the Miami run took precedence for McCraney:

> I sensed that for Tarell, the Miami audiences mattered most. It's tough enough staging a production that works in both New York and Stratford. The younger demographic, and the far more racially mixed audiences in Miami, meant that whatever Tarell did with the play would register quite differently there—[Thurber]'s music too. It speaks to the ambition of the production and to Tarell's not much caring if it didn't please the old (and

soon pro-Brexit) crowds in Warwickshire. He knew what he wanted to achieve and worked to that end. (Shapiro 2020)

The focus on Miami audiences can also be perceived in the educational outreach of the production: only in South Florida was a schools' program pronounced. In Stratford, the show ran at the Swan from November 7–30, 26 performances total. There was a single day of outreach to schools: the RSC's Education Department arranged programming for school groups on the morning of Wednesday November 27, and these students attended the matinee show that afternoon, the 21st performance there. Julia Wade, the Company Stage Manager, reported that this was "a very well received show and marvelous audience response at the curtain call. The school groups that had been involved in the education workshops this morning also thoroughly enjoyed themselves" (Wade n.d.). In this single school's show in Stratford's Swan, at most 450 students attended. In New York, where the show was performed at the Anspacher Theater 40 times, from February 18–April 23, no record of educational outreach exists. In Miami, by contrast, more than half of the 31 performances were schools' shows. Opening Thursday January 9 and closing on February 9, each week of this month-long run included four 10 a.m. shows, every Tuesday, Wednesday, Thursday, and Friday morning, 16 school shows in all. The Colony seats some 430, so just under 7000 high-school students in Miami potentially experienced this production (Wade n.d.).

The inclusivity of McCraney's *Antony and Cleopatra* did not translate into success or honors, however. In transparently focusing on Haiti and the Caribbean in the adaptation, the production ironically became inaccessible to those who perhaps routinely see themselves reflected in Shakespeare's plays. The reviews suggest that critics did not recognize McCraney's choices. Particularly in the UK, press reviews were highly critical. Kate Bassett skewered the show in *The Times*, admitting that "perhaps I needed more background info to grasp why McCraney's take… might be a snug fit, socially or historically. It struck me as muddle-headed, unlike the company's post-colonial-Africa … *Julius Caesar*, directed in 2012 by Gregory Doran, which fitted like a glove" (Bassett 2013). Charles Spencer, writing in the *Daily Telegraph*, also attacked the show, labeling it a "travesty of a masterpiece," wherein "for reasons best known to himself, McCraney has relocated the action to Haiti … there is a scene depicting slavery undreamt of by Shakespeare … there is also a good deal of calypso music and spirituals, and moments of voodoo. The arrogance of all this is matched only by its incompetence. Far from making the play seem fresh and accessible, McCraney's crass interventions actually make it harder to follow, especially as the verse speaking is often abysmal." Singling out Iwuji's as a "moving Enobarbus," and praising Michael's counter-tenor vocals, Spencer concluded, "in every other respect the show is an utter dud" (Spencer 2013). Both Bassett and Spencer, with their lack of knowledge of Haiti and the elements McCraney drew from its history and culture, choose to demean the production without remorse. They admit as much, both mentioning that they do not have knowledge of their own regarding Haiti. There exists a stark difference between these two critiques and one that can, at the very least, identify a reason for a colonial, Haitian setting of this adaptation. Claiming this middle ground, Andrew Dickson of *The Guardian* found the Haitian setting "astutely recast... draw[ing] out the racial tensions that underlie the play," but nevertheless an "idea [that] vastly overpromises." Arguing that "McCraney's broader point feels more rickety," he castigated the lighting, the frolicking in the pool, the wriggling of hips, and concluded that the transformation of Enobarbus into "a voodoo-style spirit of the dead is overkill at its most literal" (Dickson 2013). Similarly, Ian Shuttleworth writing in *The Financial Times* equivocated, "McCraney's restless imagination has repeatedly explored various present, past and simultaneously superimposed dimensions of black American identity; if this is not one of his greatest successes, it is by no means a failure either" (Shuttleworth 2013). Alone among UK reviewers, Ian Hughes of *The Observer* lauded the racialized production, remarking that "the creole-tongued delivery of some of the canon's finest poetry is actually very pleasing on the ear," and concluded "this is a bold and vibrant production well worth catching" (Hughes 2013).

The show fared only slightly better in New York. Called out as "Shakespeare on the Beach" in Ben Brantley's *NYT* review, he speared it as "squishy" and "misbegotten," where everything "is dampened by its soggy high reconception." Highlighting the "lack of chemistry" between Cake and Kalukango noted by many critics, Brantley repudiated their relationship as less "an immortal marriage of soul mates than a summer fling" (Brantley 2014). The show received more positive reviews in *Time Out*, where David Cote noted that it "takes liberties but... remains strikingly faithful"; and in *New York Theater*, where Jonathan Mandell extolled its "entertaining" "Haitian frame" (Cote 2014; Mandell 2014). Even Mandell's seemingly positive language veers into danger zones, however, belittling not only the production but also the serious image of Haiti and Caribbean Blackness the show is at pains to extol. In reducing the "frame" and its elements to merely "entertaining," Mandell challenges the validity of Haiti as a space where Shakespearean works can exist in their own right. Although his and the other New York reviews are less negative than those from the UK, their language subtly reproduces the stereotyping of Haiti as the poorest and most corrupt Western nation, a site for "entertainment" and "summer flings" but not a space for serious cultural production. We assert then that in New York as in London, McCraney's adaptation failed to win credibility.

South Florida reviewers, such as Christine Dolen (*The Miami Herald*), Bill Hirschman (*Florida Theater on Stage*) and John Thomason (*Miami New Times*), were more appreciative than their UK or New York counterparts. Thomason's even-handed approach encapsulates the view from Miami: "McCraney's decision to have it both ways—to suggest Haiti while otherwise remaining faithful to Shakespeare's historical period—is one of his few experiments that isn't fully realized. But otherwise, his decision to suture his personality into Shakespeare's is more than welcome" (Thomason 2014). Even his use of the word "suture" signals that Thomason implicitly seems to have understood the cultural poetics of this Caribbean-oriented production far better than did his English or New York contemporaries (Hall 1994). Several Florida-based critics also commented upon the delicious imbalance of big-budget, world-class theater venues (the RSC and the Public) collaborating with a high-quality but low-budget, small company such as GableStage; while this mismatch created many headaches for company director Joe Adler and his creative team, it also brought to Miami a level of Shakespearean performance rarely experienced in South Florida.

Nevertheless, the language and tone marshaled by several of the London and New York-based critics exceeds the limits of polite critique and generous understanding, instead flirting with the ugly assertion that spaces outside of these two theatrical foci (the UK and New York), such as might be found in Miami and the Caribbean, cannot be considered serious in their contributions to theater art. Mocking disrespect bordering on racist gaslighting characterizes several of these diatribes: they respond to McCraney's inclusive practices and watery scenography with the exclusivity of the landed. For example, by constricting the production to its beach imagery, Brantley's review subtly reinforces stereotypes of the Caribbean as a tourist destination intended solely for holiday and entertainment rather than a serious sphere of cultural, historical and theatrical production in its own right. When thinking of the Caribbean, McCraney, channeling creolized Miami, does not subscribe to Disneyesque images of calypso-singing crabs or the hyperfeminine image of Carmen Miranda with fruit on her head and a smile; yet these are the very fantasies that seem to underwrite the reviews of the New York and English critics. These images do not reflect the lived realities of the diaspora, nor are they conducive to who Cleopatra was as a royal adjacent to Antony and the rest of Rome. But as long as she can be thus categorized and characterized, as a sashaying Caribbean goddess, hips wriggling provocatively, then too McCraney's production does not have to be afforded respect or seen as worthy of polite reception. Instead, the production can be trashed, even though it ostensibly bore the RSC and New York Public stamps of approval, their imprimatur. Although this *Antony and Cleopatra* validated Haiti as a place worthy of serious-minded cultural and geo-political consideration, the show was laughed out of town: in this reception history, England and New York eerily emulate Rome; the elite critics of these cities channel Caesar.

As previously noted, the RSC, where this production was initially designed and produced, now seems neglectful of McCraney's effort, more fervently showcasing other performances of *Antony and Cleopatra*, such as the 2006 Gregory Doran production, starring Patrick Stewart and Harriet Walter; the 2010 Michael Boyd show, performed in the Swan, with Darrell D'Silva and Katy Stephens in the titles roles; and the 2017 Iqbal Khan main-house performance, starring Antony Byrne and Josette Simon. McCraney's 2013–2014 show founders in this mix, squeezed out perhaps by the Company's change in artistic direction in 2012, from Boyd to Doran, and overlooked due to the splashy success of Khan's vehicle: witness Simon, not Kalukango, wrongly hailed as the first Black Cleopatra to perform in Stratford (Jays 2017).

In the end, however, neither negative reviews nor general neglect can lessen the true impact of McCraney's bold and inventive reworking of this Roman tragedy in the waters of the Caribbean. The true measure of this show, as an agent of change, will be discovered neither in London nor New York reviews, nor in the records of the RSC or Public Theater. If we take seriously its inclusive aims, the real story of McCraney's Haitian-inspired *Antony and Cleopatra* will be uncovered only in the schools and theaters of urban, Black Miami, in the stories that the next generation of youth from Liberty City and Homestead choose to tell, in the manner these stories might further pry open access to the creolized Caribbean as a subject worth dramatizing.

Thus, McCraney's inclusive *Antony and Cleopatra* permits Black Miamians the right to speak, authentically and creatively, as themselves. The production combats an external, negative view of Miami and the Caribbean by making these spheres visible, giving them instant credibility. It breaks through the white-washing of Shakespeare and theater to which Black youth are too often and too quickly exposed. This white-washing goes against what McCraney believes theater, including Shakespeare's work, ought to be: drama in service to its locale, that is, "community theater." In his recent interview with T. Cole Rachel, he claims:

> And yes, it's community theater. I mean, Shakespeare told us with *A Midsummer Night's Dream* that sometimes the plumber is going to want to be in a play, and he might even steal the show. Everybody doesn't have to be royal. You don't have to invite the President to every show you do. I think the moment we let go of that and realize just how wide and varied and beautiful the tapestry of theater is in America, we will then not have to engage in these really weird conversations where we're like, "Oh, well, no one cares about that." That makes no sense. ("On Redefining What it Means to be Successful" 2021)

Having given voice to a creolized, Black Miami with his *Antony and Cleopatra*, McCraney expanded such work with *Moonlight*, which affords value to queer, Black youth troubled by violence and addiction. *David Makes Man* continues in this vein, again shining a spotlight on Black youth in Miami. David, like *Moonlight*'s Chiron, acts from perspectives and worldviews that McCraney intimately knows.

The Black student who watched *Antony and Cleopatra* in Miami in January 2014, with a homelife similar to David or Chiron—this youth is McCraney's intended audience, not the New York or London critic, nor, for that matter, the Miami-based academics writing this piece. This imagined student, seeing themselves reflected on the Colony stage, unlocks the hidden potential of McCraney's inclusive production. This transaction—Shakespearean tragedy enfolded within the sphere of the creolized Caribbean—did not end with the final curtain call at The Colony; it remains vital in Miami, now and tomorrow. We eagerly await the stories and plays of the next generation of Black Miami youth, who, following

Tarell McCraney, and perhaps channeling his example, are inspired too by a newly accessible and inclusive Shakespeare, a Shakespeare in which they can see and recognize themselves.

NOTE

1. The term "Anglo" is commonly used in Miami.

REFERENCES

Bassett, Kate. "Antony and Cleopatra at the Swan, Stratford." *The Times*, Nov. 15, 2013, https://www.thetimes.co.uk/article/antony-and-cleopatra-at-the-swan-stratford-673qnvhb6db. Accessed Feb. 15, 2021.

Bissainthe, Toto. "Dèy." 1977. Text and translation appear in Julia Wade, RSC/SM/1/2013/ANT1. and associated SM script, also held at the Shakespeare Birthplace Trust, Library and Archives, Stratford-upon-Avon.

Boyd, Michael. "A New and Trusted Voice." Program for William Shakespeare's *Antony and Cleopatra* at the Swan Theatre, Stratford-upon-Avon. Playbill, 2013.

Brantley, Ben. "Shakespeare Hits the Beach." *New York Times*, March 5, 2014, https://www.nytimes.com/2014/03/06/theater/an-antony-and-cleopatra-set-in-the-caribbean.html. Accessed Feb. 15, 2021.

Cote, David. "*Antony and Cleopatra*—Theater Review." *Time Out*, March 5, 2014, https://www.timeout.com/newyork/theater/antony-and-cleopatra-1. Accessed Feb. 15, 2021.

Dickson, Andrew. "*Antony and Cleopatra*—Review." *The Guardian*, Nov. 15, 2013, https://www.theguardian.com/stage/2013/nov/15/antony-and-cleopatra-tarell-alvin-mccraney-rsc-review. Accessed February 15, 2013.

Dunn, Marvin. *Black Miami in the Twentieth Century*. University Press of Florida, 1997.

Francis, Donette. "Juxtaposing Creoles: Miami in the Plays of Tarell Alvin McCraney." *Tarell Alvin McCraney: Theater, Performance, and Collaboration*, edited by Sharrell D. Luckett, David Roman, and Isaiah Matthew Wooden. Northwestern University Press, 2020, pp. 19–36.

Glissant, Édouard. *Poetics of Relation*. University of Michigan Press, 1997.

Hall, Stuart. "Cultural Identity and Diaspora." *Colonial Discourse and Post-colonial Theory: A Reader*, edited by Patrick Williams and Laura Chrisman. Columbia UP, 1994, pp. 392–403.

Hughes, Ian. "Electric New Production in Charged Up and Vibrant." *The Observer*, Nov. 15, 2013.

Iqbal, Nosheen. "How Tarell Alvin McCraney Took Hamlet Back to School." *The Guardian*, Feb. 5, 2010, https://www.theguardian.com/stage/2010/feb/05/shakespeare-school-theatre-hamlet. Accessed Feb. 12, 2021.

Jays, David. "Josette Simon: 'Powerful Women Are Reduced to Being Dishonourable'." *The Guardian*, March 21, 2017, https://www.theguardian.com/stage/2017/mar/21/josette-simon-cleopatra-rsc-shakespeare. Accessed Feb. 15, 2021.

Kirwan, Peter. "*Hamlet* (RSC Young People's Shakespeare) @ the Courtyard Theatre." University of Nottingham Blogs, The Bardathon, Aug. 27, 2010, https://blogs.nottingham.ac.uk/bardathon/2010/08/27/hamlet-rsc-young-peoples-shakespeare-the-courtyard-theatre. Accessed Feb. 12, 2021.

Luckett, Sharrell D. "Backstage Pass: An Artist Roundtable on the Work of Tarell Alvin McCraney." *Tarell Alvin McCraney: Theater, Performance, and Collaboration*, edited by Sharrell D. Luckett, David Roman, and Isaiah Matthew Wooden. Northwestern University Press, 2020, pp. 183–206.

"Tarell Alvin McCraney: A Career Chronology." *Tarell Alvin McCraney: Theater, Performance, and Collaboration*, edited by Sharrell D. Luckett, David Roman, and Isaiah Matthew Wooden. Northwestern University Press, 2020, pp. xi–xvii.

Luckett, Sharrell D., David Roman, and Isaiah Matthew Wooden, editors. *Tarell Alvin McCraney: Theater, Performance, and Collaboration*. Northwestern University Press, 2020.

Mandell, Jonathan. "*Antony and Cleopatra* Review: Shakespeare's Tragedy in Haiti and Miami." *New York Theater*, March 5, 2014, https://newyorktheater.me/2014/03/05/antony-and-cleopatra-review-shakespeares-tragedy-in-haiti-and-miami. Accessed Feb. 15, 2021.

McCraney, Tarell Alvin. "Director's Notes." Stage Manager's Script and Prompt Book, *Antony and Cleopatra*, RSC 2013, Shakespeare Birthplace Trust Library and Archives, Stratford-upon-Avon.

"On Redefining What it Means to be Successful." *The Creative Independent*, Feb. 1, 2021, https://thecreativeindependent.com/people/playwright-tarell-alvin-mccraney-on-redefining-notions-of-being-an-artist. Accessed Feb. 12, 2021.

Ogle, Connie. "The Miami Writer behind 'Moonlight' is Coming Home for a Reading." *The Miami Herald*, Jan. 9, 2017, https://www.miamiherald.com/miami-com/things-to-do/article225704015.html. Accessed Feb. 15, 2021.

Program for William Shakespeare's *Antony and Cleopatra* at the Swan Theatre, Stratford-upon-Avon. Playbill, 2013.

Shapiro, James. Personal Correspondence conducted via e-mail. July 8, 2020.

Shuttleworth, Ian. "*Antony and Cleopatra*, Swan Theatre, Stratford-upon-Avon—Review." *Financial Times*, Nov. 15, 2013, https://app.ft.com/content/1b11740e-4d24-11e3-9f4000144feabdc0. Accessed Feb. 15, 2021.

Smalls, C. Isaiah, II. "This 'Moonlight' Oscar Winner Returned to His Alma Mater—And He had a Message for the Kids." *The Miami Herald*, Dec. 16, 2019, https://www.miamiherald.com/article238421728.html. Accessed Feb. 15, 2021.

Spencer, Charles. "*Antony and Cleopatra*, RSC, Review." *The Daily Telegraph*, Nov. 14, 2013, https://www.telegraph.co.uk/culture/theatre/theatre-reviews/10449633/Antony-and-Cleopatra-RSC-review.html. Accessed Feb. 15, 2021.

Thomason, John. "*Antony and Cleopatra* is McCraney's Masterpiece." *Miami New Times*, Jan. 16, 2014, https://www.miaminewtimes.com/arts/antony-and-cleopatra-is-mccraneys-masterpiece-6394553. Accessed Feb. 15, 2021.

"Hamlet at GableStage: Shakespeare for the Twitter Generation." *Miami New Times*, Jan. 15, 2013, https://www.miaminewtimes.com/arts/hamlet-at-gablestage-shakespeare-for-the-twitter-generation-6511977. Accessed Feb. 16, 2021.

Verzuh, Jennifer. "Ash Hunnter—Harlots." An Interview. *Starrymag*, n.d. https://starrymag.com/ash-hunter-harlots/. Accessed Dec. 27, 2021.

Wade, Julia. RSC/SM/1/2013/ANT1 and associated SM script, also held at the Shakespeare Birthplace Trust Library and Archives, Stratford-upon-Avon, n.d.

Wardi, Anissa Janine. *Water and African American Memory: An Ecocritical Perspective*. University Press of Florida, 2011.

CHAPTER 4

"I am all the daughters of my father's house, and all the brothers too": Genderfluid Potentiality in *As You Like It* and *Twelfth Night*

Eric Brinkman

I've auditioned and appeared at callbacks or in talks with something, hearing, 'We don't know if we want to make that statement with this show.' And I get that on a certain level it does make a statement, because as ridiculous as it is, hiring trans people is not done enough. But the only way to get beyond it being a statement is to make it so common that it's not a statement anymore.—Parker Guidry[1]

While female actors frequently play male parts and several actors of color have now played lead roles at well-funded Shakespeare theaters, no female

E. Brinkman (✉) (They/them)
Michael V. Drake Institute for Teaching and Learning,
The Ohio State University, Columbus, OH, USA
e-mail: ericbrin@iu.edu

© The Author(s), under exclusive license to Springer Nature Switzerland AG 2023
S. Freeman Loftis et al. (eds.), *Inclusive Shakespeares*, Palgrave Shakespeare Studies,
https://doi.org/10.1007/978-3-031-26522-8_4

or male transgender actor has had any similar level of visibility: none of the Shakespeare productions of the National Theatre, Shakespeare's Globe, Stratford Festival, or Oregon Shakespeare Festival have cast a self-identifying transgender actor in a lead role.[2] The Globe, when still under the direction of Emma Rice, cast several performers who are notable for performing in drag, but drag and transgender are not equivalent.[3] Across dozens of recent productions, no transgender performer has ever performed on any of these highly visible stages.[4] Historically, however, there is evidence that people we might now consider nonbinary or transgender did appear on early modern stages in highly visible ways. Actor Richard Robinson is textually reported by Ben Jonson to have worn feminine clothing outside of the theater, and the historical figure of Middleton and Dekker's *The Roaring Girl*, Mary Frith, was known to have sat on stage in male clothing while wearing a sword.[5] Most of the scholarship to date, however, has focused on early modern roles played by boy actors "crossdressing."[6] The evidence around Robinson and Frith suggests that there were people in London in the early modern era choosing their gender presentations irrespective of their assigned gender at birth. What happens when we stop thinking of early modern "crossdressing" through the assumption of cisgendered actors? This chapter starts from the historical precedent for nonbinary and transgender actors and attempts to imagine the possibility of Shakespeare for and by nonbinary and transgender actors and spectators, exploring which kinds of access are and are not present in Shakespearean texts and how they can be approached and adapted to be more inclusive of the needs and interests of nonbinary and transgender actors and audiences.

According to José Esteban Muñoz, potentiality is the present possibility embodied in the contemporary reading and performance of theatre and art. In his seminal 2009 *Cruising Utopia*, he theorizes potentiality as an already ontologically present queer reality: potentiality does not occur in an always deferred futurity—it is instead already present in the queer here and now, even if it only exists at the edges of our vision. In this chapter, I apply this concept to a discussion of how the reading and performance of certain early modern plays, like Shakespeare's *Twelfth Night* or *As You Like It*, enacts an already present nonbinary, genderfluid, and transgender space. Early modern "crossdressing" as it is performed in contemporary productions of *As You Like It* or *Twelfth Night* can allow us to visualize an already existing ontological space available for genderfluid and transgender becoming, a radical performative outside of cisgender cultural norms that is alive during select genderfluid transitional moments that occur during the performance of early modern plays such as *As You Like It*, *Twelfth Night*, *Gallathea*, and *The Roaring Girl*.[7]

Nevertheless, the danger of theorizing about the potentiality of Shakespearean drama is ignoring the lived experiences of those it purports to uplift by using the rhetoric of queer and transgender theory to defend current Shakespearean production practices. Sawyer Kemp's "Shakespeare in Transition: Pedagogies of Transgender Justice and Performance" makes an important scholarly intervention into the current critical discourse on genderfluid Shakespeare production by arguing that the focus on "disguise" and clothing potentially erases the lived experience of transgender people. Unlike characters in a Shakespeare play, simply changing their clothing does not automatically allow transgender people to easily "pass" and avoid systemic transphobic oppressions. Critical approaches that offer seemingly "liberal" or progressive readings of genderfluid productions that cast cisgender actors in "crossdressing" roles, therefore, ignore and potentially erase the actual needs and concerns of transgender and nonbinary actors and audiences. In their conclusion, Kemp suggests:

> Shifting away from the interior/exterior rhetoric of truth and disguise, and toward a model developed with a perspective of experience and the self-in-context (which is to say, often either in community or in danger) can help us put Shakespeare to work for justice by training us to see and witness the broad range of experiences of trans people. If we as scholars are going to engage in a practice that believes trans people are integral to Shakespeare, it is important at every phase to make scholarship that is rooted in experience, not abstraction.[8]

Thus, to fully actualize the potentiality present in a performance of Shakespeare, productions should implement casting practices that support a desire to represent nonbinary and transgender experience, not just appropriating them rhetorically to justify the (re)production of Shakespeare.

PRODUCTIVE AND NONPRODUCTIVE FAILURE

To clarify the differences between Shakespeare in the service of social justice versus social justice rhetoric in the service of Shakespeare, I will distinguish between the terms productive and nonproductive failure. In his 2019 ATHE keynote address, Bill Rauch, formerly of the Oregon

Shakespeare Festival and Cornerstone Theatre Company, claimed that theatre is always successful. As a theater practitioner, while empathetic on an emotional level, I want to take the opposite approach: theatre always fails. All the focus placed on awards, sold-out theatrical runs, or even Rauch's idealization of a theatre that builds community and creates change agents who make a difference, belies the fact that at the heart of the theatrical experiment lies perpetual failure: theatre will never fully achieve the goals it sets for itself because, by definition, theatre cannot become the thing it represents itself to be. More simply—no amount of theatre, by itself, will succeed in instituting social justice and creating a just world free of discrimination for nonbinary and transgender folx. That is also no excuse not to do better, and in fact, Nicolas Ridout has argued that failure, in many ways, is constitutive of theater.[9] Yet, that theatrical "failure" is inherently productive is also not true; therefore, I define *nonproductive failure* as theater that (re)produces existing systemic injustices that marginalize, while *productive failure*—"failure" in that it cannot possibly achieve all the goals of social justice—allows the practice of recognizing potentiality, one in which we can see a genderfluid future present in the here and now.

In order to circumscribe the limits as well as the possibilities of representing genderfluid potentiality as productive failure on stage, I offer a close reading of two large scale productions of "crossdressing" plays as case studies: the Shakespeare's Globe 2018 production of *As You Like It* (Federay Holmes) and Simon Godwin's 2017 National Theatre production of *Twelfth Night*. Both of these productions purport to explore "crossdressing" in a socially conscious way yet notably fail to reflect in their productions key aspects of nonbinary or transgender experience.

Federay Holmes' 2018 *As You Like It*

In 2018, Federay Holmes directed two plays in the inaugural season of Michelle Terry's artistic directorship at the Globe: *Hamlet* and *As You Like It*. Performed by an ensemble with a 50:50 gender parity cast, both productions featured genderfluid casting but with differing effects. In *Hamlet*, Ophelia was played by male actor Shubham Saraf. In an interview, Saraf claimed that his Ophelia was "beyond gender."[10] Reading this in performance was difficult, however, because rather than portraying someone existing outside of gender, his choice simply seemed vague and unspecific. He put on a dress, but kept his short, "boy" haircut, abstained from wearing a wig or sculpting his hair in any visibly feminine way, and did not try to pitch his voice higher. One way to interpret his performance would be to suggest that he was performing Ophelia in a way that was genderfluid: he was playing Ophelia as feminine, and as such wears a dress, but adds stereotypically masculine behaviors as well. These elements could encourage a reading that engages in genderfluid potentiality, but, in watching his performance, this was difficult because when Saraf delivered her/his/their lines in a masculine tone of voice,[11] the audience's response was to laugh.[12] If Saraf was trying to present a genderfluid Ophelia, then what were the results of provoking or seeming to encourage the audience to laugh? Perhaps this is a failure of my imagination, but to me, encouraging the audience to laugh does not imply being "beyond" gender. Rather, claims of being "genderblind" ignore histories of female and transgender oppression rather than somehow mystically transcending them. Though interpreting audience laughter is largely understudied and can convey multiple meanings, my experience of this moment was to perceive it as a significant nonproductive representational failure: not only is Saraf not genderfluid or transgender, or reflective of those experiences, but provoking laughter at someone depicted as genderfluid fails to challenge normative stereotypes or increase any awareness of the social justice issues around nonbinary or transgender performers. Although Saraf's intentions in performing the role this way might have been to somehow transcend gender, from a social justice perspective the response his interpretation provoked is more significant politically than whatever his intention might or might not have been.

As with Saraf's Ophelia, the 2018 Globe production of *As You Like It* also cast a male actor, Jack Laskey, to play a woman, in this instance Rosalind. At the time, I heard several complaints from scholars and practitioners at events around the production over the course of that summer complaining that the largest "female" part in Shakespeare was "being taken away from them." I'm not exactly sure what that means, since the role was not regendered: that is, Laskey was playing a woman. The argument that an important "female" role was lost by casting Laskey rests on the assumption that gender is based on biological sex characteristics. Although—as far as I know—Laskey has not come out as nonbinary or transgender, I find the assumption that he cannot be female troubling.[13] In fact, this production was cast as a 50:50 ensemble and so several significant roles traditionally performed by men were played by female actors

and none of the parts were regendered.[14] Therefore, although this production was also a nonproductive failure in that it failed to cast any self-
identifying nonbinary or transgender actors in its "crossdressing" roles, its
insistence that gender is not biologically determined enacts a genderfluid
potentiality that allows the spectator to participate in an experience of
gender as free from biological determinism. For example, both of the
Duke characters that appear in the play were played by a female actor
(Helen Schlesinger) and seemed comfortable wielding direct political
power. The genderfluid potentiality embodied by this performance choice
suggests a less heteronormative world in which nonbinary people are
accepted in roles that require the careful handling of political power. This
was mirrored by another intersectional genderfluid moment in which the
male mythological god Hymen was portrayed by Tanika Yearwood. In the
final sequence of this production, Rosalind appears from under Hymen's
skirts and then Hymen is lifted up via wires into the heavens through a
trap door above. Although unfortunately Hymen had only a few lines,
visually representing the god of marriage as embodied by a woman of
color, who literally rises above all of the action on stage, is significant in
terms of its representational politics because it also allows an audience to
visualize a genderfluid woman of color with masculine and feminine characteristics who wields power and influence.

Laskey last performed at the Globe in Thea Sharrock's 2009 production of *As You Like It* as Orlando; thus, his appearance as Rosalind in
Holmes' production reverberates as both masculine and feminine on that
stage and in that play, an intertextual friction that is suggestive of a continued exploration of gender as fluid. In contrast to Saraf's Ophelia, Laskey's
Rosalind spoke in a higher pitch and wore flowers in her/his/their hair.
While a high-pitched voice and wearing flowers could be interpreted as
reinforcing stereotypes—not all women have high-pitched voices nor do
they all love flowers—Laskey's Rosalind deconstructs these traits as overt
markers of being female since these choices were carried over to her/his/
their presentation of a woman "disguised" as the male character Ganymede:
as this character, she/he/they continued to pitch her/his/their voice
higher, wore a small flower in her/his/their hair, and also wore a shirt
with a prominent embroidered flower stitched on it, creating a blend of
stereotypically masculine and feminine characteristics in the character of
Ganymede. As Rosalind, Laskey appeared more butch, but as Ganymede,
Laskey also maintained an air of femininity, never fully conforming to the
vocal and visual tropes of either gender. Watching Laskey's performance

also raises interesting historical questions: how did boy actors, playing female characters in the early modern period, signal to the audience that they were still playing women when they were "disguised" as boys? Does the boy actor playing a female character just return back to wearing male clothes, or, as Laskey chose, did they somehow signal to the audience that they were boys playing woman presenting themselves again as boys? Laskey's choices are suggestive without being definitive, given that our historical record of these early modern performance choices is limited, but Laskey's Rosalind invites a continued exploration of genderfluid potentiality, one that a nonbinary or transgender actor with lived experience of dressing to pass in different contexts could continue to develop.[15]

Another important genderfluid casting choice in this production of *As You Like It* included the fact that in casting the role of Rosalind with a male actor, the ensemble in response cast Orlando with a female actor, played by Bettrys Jones. Casting Jones to play a masculine character provided the opportunity for a moment I found full of genderfluid potentiality: the audience cheered uproariously when Jones defeats a male wrestler (Charles, played by longtime Complicite actor Richard Katz). I don't believe I have ever heard a crowd cheer for the physical defeat of a male character by a female actor presenting male in quite the same way before. I admit I was slightly stunned when I heard their response, as it demonstrated for me the potential for an audience to support a nonbinary or transgender character to succeed. Admittedly, I am reading into this potentiality because Jones was not a nonbinary or transgender actor—but what I saw in that moment was the potential for that outcome. I saw not what the Globe staged, but what the possibilities of staging such a scene could be with a cast and crew that wanted to bring it about—not in the future, but in that moment.

Holmes' Globe productions contained both productive and nonproductive failures. Saraf's performance as Ophelia provoked laugher from the audience and did not reflect interpretations of gender that contest established gender hierarchies; rather, the audience's response only reproduced normative power and values. In contrast, Laskey's performance as both Rosalind and Ganymede showed a desire to explore a blending of gender codes. However, Holmes' production also cast no self-identifying genderfluid or transgender actors, instead relying on cisgender actors to imagine nonbinary and transgender experience, a nonproductive failure that also reappears in Simon Godwin's 2017 National Theatre production of *Twelfth Night*.

DISGUISE AND PERSONHOOD IN SIMON GODWIN'S
TWELFTH NIGHT

Casting a Black woman as Viola/Cesario (Tamara Lawrance) and regendering the roles of Malvolio (Tamsin Greig), Feste (Doon Mackichan), and Fabian (Imogen Doel), Godwin's 2017 National Theatre production of *Twelfth Night* was a highly visible London experiment with genderfluid Shakespearean performance.[16] In line with Kemp's critique, in Godwin's production Viola/Cesario's "disguise" is generally successful and no one contests it: Viola/Cesario simply puts on a coat and gets a shorter haircut, as if that is enough to affect a convincing gender change.[17] Nevertheless, the scenes in this production in which Viola/Cesario's "disguise" works can also be productive failures because this acceptance of Viola/Cesario signals the potential acceptance of genderfluid expression.

Moments of acceptance/non-acceptance can incorporate both productive and nonproductive failures. For example, during the early tête-à-tête between Orsino and Viola/Cesario in Godwin's *Twelfth Night*, Cesario boxes with Duke Orsino (Oliver Chris). I have two potential problems with this scene as it is staged. First, is the audience expected to think that Cesario is proficient at boxing because she/he/they are Black?[18] Also second, why does the audience laugh when Orsino knocks Cesario down? My suspicion is that at least some of the audience thought it was humorous for Orsino to knock Cesario down because they know of Cesario's past as Viola, and thus assumed that it would be absurd for a cisgender woman to be capable of boxing with a larger cisgender man. On one hand, this failure of expectations could be thought of as productive—Cesario is not prevented from boxing with a cisgender man on the basis of his/her/their biological sex. On the other hand, the laughter would then also seem to stem from the audience believing that a transgender man could not be expected to compete with a cisgender man (an unfortunate reversal of the scene highlighted above with Jones).[19]

Godwin graciously agreed to an interview in the summer of 2018,[20] and I asked him during our meeting about another scene that I found problematic. Subsequent to several scenes in which Duke Orsino looks visibly nervous about his attraction toward Cesario, at the end of the play when it is revealed that Cesario is also Viola, Duke Orsino looks visibly relieved, which again provokes laughter from the audience. I find that response of both actor and audience a deeply problematic nonproductive failure, because it reads as trans- and homophobic—Orsino is visibly relieved to find out that he is theoretically attracted to Viola and not to

Cesario. When I brought this up to Godwin, he at first said that this moment had "slipped" past him, but then suggested that it should be read as Orsino continuing to be in character as "a bit of an idiot." While I appreciate and prefer Godwin's reading of the scene, it remains problematic that the production provoked a response from the audience that rejected any kind of nonnormative desire.

These scenes draw attention to some of the nonproductive failures of contemporary efforts by well-funded theaters to represent transgender and genderfluid potentiality on the theatrical stage. Lacking both cast members and production team members who were themselves genderfluid or transgender both sends a message that nonbinary voices and bodies are not valued and allows for nonproductive failures like Orsino's rejection of nonheteronormative desire. Nevertheless, mixed with these nonproductive failures were productive failures, and there are three scenes in this production in which genderfluid potentiality is present: Olivia's courting of Cesario, Malvolia's euphoric coming out to the audience, and the final scene in which Cesario is also revealed to be Viola.

The overt expression of sexual desire, homoerotic or otherwise, is heavily gendered as positive for men and shameful for women. Therefore, Olivia's pursuit of Cesario, as a simple reversal of the expectation of the feminine to wait for the masculine character to pursue her, has often felt liberating to me in that it frees both women to pursue their desires and men to accept being pursued without feeling their masculinity threatened as a result. In Godwin's *Twelfth Night*, waifish Olivia (Phoebe Fox) aggressively pursues Cesario's affection, free of those expectations and constraints of cultural propriety around feminine romantic behavior. After she sends a ring to Cesario via Malvolia, she next attempts to seduce Cesario by drawing him into a hot tub while wearing only a bathing suit. When Cesario shows reluctance, Olivia pulls him in bodily. She follows this by shouting in exhilaration, "Why then methinks 'tis time to smile again!" After Cesario continues to reject her, she, more vulnerable, nonetheless resolutely delivers these original lines of text:

> Cesario, by the roses of the spring,
> By maidhood, honor, truth, and everything,
> I love thee so, that, maugre all thy pride,
> Nor wit nor reason can my passion hide.[21]

Of course, all of this does little to move Cesario—who is in love with Duke Orsino—but it will in turn serve Olivia in good stead when she encounters Sebastian. He proves less resistant to her forward and determined romantic charms. Thus, in this play the potential for female desire to engage in the masculine behavior of pursuit will ultimately not be contained but rewarded.

Godwin also chose to regender the ambivalent Malvolio as Malvolia and cast an actor well known to London audiences, Tamsin Greig, to play the part. Godwin described his *Twelfth Night* as full of the "carnivalesque," and Greig described her portrayal of Malvolia as "transgressive." What is more important is what it might mean to read Malvolia's character as a similar performance of desire that is genderfluid like Olivia's in that it ignores prescriptions against free female expressions of desire. In the instigating scene of the subplot, Malvolia, Sir Toby Belch (Tim McMullan) and Maria (Niky Wardley) have conspired to make Malvolia believe that Olivia loves her by dropping a forged letter for her to find. In the play, Malvolia is a frustrated puritan who rebukes Sir Toby for drinking and berates Cesario for refusing her mistress, but once she reads the letter, putting together some clues and interpreting them as Olivia hinting that she is in love with her, she has both an emotional and a sexual awakening. Coming to the realization that she can love Olivia despite their differences in class and perhaps sexuality, she dances in a fountain and splashes water from it all over herself and on some of those in the front rows of the audience. In fact, the set responds to her, the fountain behind her suggestively erupting with water that gushes toward the ceiling when she awakens to, and publicly announces, the love she feels for Olivia. Greig's Malvolia deliberately breaks the fourth wall several times during this scene, acknowledging the audience and essentially inviting the audience to join her in her coming-out party. The ostensibly largely heteronormative audience that I witnessed enthusiastically joined her via applause during and after this shared moment, enacting the potentiality of a world that can acknowledge queer female expressions of desire as normative and to be rewarded rather than punished.

This scene also sets up the finale of the play, in which Viola/Cesario announces her/his/their love for Duke Orsino without changing clothes or reverting back to a different set of gender expectations: even though Orsino asks to see Viola/Cesario in "woman's weeds," Godwin stages a brief extratextual marriage scene in which Viola/Cesario is still wearing the same masculine clothes—with the addition of a bridal veil.[22] Once the possibility for the public expression of genderfluid desire has been established in this play, this particular production makes clear where the possibilities are for an already present acceptance of its genderfluid characters.

Genderfluid representations never feel like something added on to the play. They instead pervade the production, multiplying on themselves: a diminutive Olivia aggressively takes the lead in pursuing Cesario's affection and is aroused by the possibility of a ménage à trois with both Cesario and her twin brother Sebastain (Daniel Ezra). The audience cheers for Malvolia's pronouncement of love; and Viola/Cesario never changes back into her/his/their "woman's weeds."

POTENTIALITY UNFULFILLED

When Viola/Cesario tells Duke Orsino, "I am all the daughters of my father's house, / And all the brothers too," a normative reading of that line would be that this is a statement by Viola/Cesario that she/he/they are the only child left of their father.[23] A more inclusive reading would understand that line to be taken more literally, however: the character, and potentially the actor performing that part, could be, in some ways, both the daughter and the son of their father, both a sister and a brother to Sebastian; that is, she/he/they expressed their gender in such a way as to have claims on an identity that includes all of those familial relationships. Readings like this enable us to see genderfluid potentiality at work and make clear to us the radical possibilities of the thoughtful performances that embrace genderfluidity as an already present reality.

But the limitation of (re)producing plays such as *As You Like It* and *Twelfth Night* on stage with cisgendered actors can also be described as nonproductive failure in that such productions continue to suggest that genderfluidity should be centered on interpretations of cisgendered bodies. The (re)productions that I have analyzed in this chapter are both nonproductive failures in that none of these performances use self-identifying nonconforming genderfluid actors to play the roles of Rosalind/Ganymede, Viola/Cesario, or Malvolio/a. If, however, we exclude nonconforming bodies from our interpretations, we problematically reproduce the issues raised by Kemp and others: although the potentiality for nonbinary and transgender voices and the expression of genderfluid desire has always been present in many early modern plays, the continual casting of heterosexual cisgendered actors in these roles prohibits the full flourishing of its expression by refusing to access the lived experiences of nonbinary and transgender folx. Theatres, however, do not need to continue to engage in this mode of (re)production: by amplifying the voices of activists engaged in the study and practice of feminism, queer theory, transgender studies, critical race studies, disability studies, and their intersections, we better acknowledge and highlight the possibilities for actors to expand our understanding of how classical roles can be portrayed. Despite a largely historical failure to stage transgender bodies as part of Shakespearean performance, potentiality for these plays to be more inclusive already exists. All that is necessary is the desire to amplify that already present reality; the parts are already there, waiting to be accessed.[24] But until the producers and directors of these plays take seriously the call to action by activists to cast nonbinary and transgender actors in these roles,[25] the (re)production of Shakespeare will continue to tease and only reenact nonproductive failures that keep their potential in a far horizon, difficult to see and never fully in view.

NOTES

1. Regina Victor. 2020. "Developing Trans Roles for the Theatre." *American Theatre.* https://www.americantheatre.org/2020/09/23/developing-trans-roles-for-the-theatre. Accessed 2 August 2021.
2. Roles other than Othello and Cleopatra for which actors of color have been cast at large theaters include Tamara Lawrance as Viola/Cesario at the National, which I will be discussing in depth, Ray Fearon as Macbeth at the Globe (Iqbal Khan, 2016), and Paapa Essiedu as Hamlet at the RSC (Simon Godwin, 2016). As noted by Sawyer K. Kemp, the Oregon Shakespeare Festival did cast a self-identifying transgender actor, Bobbi Charlton, as the Forester in their 2018 production of *Love's Labor's Lost.* Sawyer K. Kemp, "Transgender Shakespeare Performance: A Holistic Dramaturgy," *Journal for Early Modern Cultural Studies* 19.4 (2019): 274. As Alexa Alice Joubin notes in the afterword to this volume, London's Transgender Shakespeare Company (established in 2015) includes transgender actors performing Shakespearean roles. See Robin Craig's description of the Transgender Shakespeare Company's work in "Past, Present, Future and the Transgender Shakespeare Company," *TheatreForum* 52 (2017): 6–7.
3. In fact, as noted by Sawyer Kemp, these kinds of false equivalencies perpetuate a distorted sense of the social justice work being accomplished by "inclusive" productions. "Shakespeare in Transition: Pedagogies of Transgender Justice and Performance," *Teaching Social Justice Through Shakespeare*, Hillary Eklund, Wendy Beth Hyman eds. (Edinburgh University Press, 2019), 43–44n2.
4. I am specifically referring to transgender actors here because I cannot be sure about how every actor who has performed on these stages self identifies. I can also find no mention of an actor identifying as nonbinary, genderfluid, genderqueer, nor any of the other various terms transgender folx might use—but as this is a wider range of expression, it is more difficult to state this conclusively. Across this chapter, I discuss a range of gender expressions loosely included

4 "I AM ALL THE DAUGHTERS OF MY FATHER'S HOUSE, AND ALL... 75

within the term nonbinary, which I use as an umbrella term to include any gender expression outside of a strict male/female binary. I also use the term *genderfluid* as a synonym for *nonbinary*, although this term can sometimes have more specific meanings. Many of these terms are highly contested; for example, although I use the term *transgender* to refer to its more specific meaning of someone who desires, is, or seeks to transition away from their gender or sex assigned at birth, the first issue of *TSQ: Transgender Studies Quarterly* famously refused to strictly define transgender, trans, or trans* and insisted that the T in its title should be read as open to self-definition and inclusive of any association with the term. In "Transgender Studies, or How to Do Things with Trans*," Cáel M. Keegan, writes: "The first issue of *TSQ*, therefore, enacts a method specific to transgender studies in which the journal's authoritative stance is placed in immediate tension with the key referent's slippery and open nature. Such paradoxical maneuvers are primary to transgender studies, which grows out of the strategies of resistance and self-fashioning by which trans people have existed both within and against the systems that have classified us" (*The Cambridge Companion to Queer Studies*, edited by Siobhan B. Somerville, Cambridge: Cambridge University Press, 2020: 66).

5. On Richard Robinson, see Simone Chess, *Male-to-female Crossdressing in Early Modern English Literature: Gender, Performance, and Queer Relations* (Routledge, 2016), 17, accessed at https://library.ohio-state.edu/record=b8852216~S7. For details on Mary Frith's life and trial for wearing male attire, see Stephen Orgel's *Impersonations: The Performance of Gender in Shakespeare's England* (Cambridge University Press, 1996) and Chess, 40–41n58, including a discussion of Frith's biography written in 1662, *The Life and Death of Mistress Mary Frith*.

6. Examples include Jean Howard, "Crossdressing, the Theatre, and Gender Struggle in Early Modern England," *Shakespeare Quarterly* 39.4 (1988), 418–40 and *The Stage and Social Struggle in Early Modern England* (Routledge, 1994), Leslie Ferris, ed., *Crossing the Stage: Controversies on Cross-Dressing* (Routledge, 1993), Marjorie Garber, *Vested Interests: Cross-dressing and Cultural Anxiety* (Routledge, 2011), and James C. Bulman, ed., *Shakespeare Re-Dressed: Cross-Gender Casting in Contemporary Performance* (Fairleigh Dickinson University Press, 2008).

7. I focus in this chapter on early modern plays in contemporary performance. *Gallathea* has been performed by Edward's Boys (Perry Mills) and *The Roaring Girl* (Jo Davies) by the RSC, both in 2014.

8. Kemp, 43.

9. Nicholas Ridout, *Stage Fright, Animals, and Other Theatrical Problems* (Cambridge University Press, 2006).

10. Daisy Bowie-Sell. 2018. "What's it like for a Man to Play Ophelia?" WhatsOnStage.com, 16 May. https://www.whatsonstage.com/london-theatre/news/ophelia-as-a-man-hamlet-shakespeare-globe_46579.html. Accessed 1 September 2021.

11. I include all the pronoun options for the characters in these plays, since an actor can choose to represent any of these potentialities. For example, textually Viola/Cesario refers to herself/himself/themselves as both a man and a woman. As Victor's interviews make clear, attention to pronouns is of critical importance to transgender performers. Rather than eliminate or choose a "correct" pronoun, I wish to make space for all the possible options.

12. Understanding laughter as a response in Shakespearean performance is under researched; for a description of how audience laughter can be misread, see John Bruns, "Laughter in the Aisles: Affect and Power in Contemporary Theoretical and Cultural Discourse," *Studies in American Humor* 3.7 (2000), 5–23.

13. My point here is in part to make clear the distinctions between gender, biological sex, and sexuality: that is, there is no automatic correlation between these three categories.

14. The feminine roles were played by Laskey (Rosalind), Nadia Nadarajah (Celia), Catrin Aaron (Phoebe), and James Garnon (Audrey). The six ensemble actors who self-identify as women also played several feminine and masculine roles, none of which were regendered: Bettrys Jones (Orlando), Helen Schlesinger (both Dukes), and Tanika Yearwood (Hymen, Amiens), Nadarajah (Celia), Aaron (Corin/Phoebe), and the Globe's artistic director, Michelle Terry (Adam/William/Jacques de Bouys).

15. As part of The Ohio State Department of Theatre Lab's series, I cast a transmasculine actor, Nicolas Shannon Savard as Rosalind/Ganymede and directed them in several scenes from *As You Like It*. We tried to explore how clothing choices for Ganymede/Rosalind in the scene might reference Savard's one-actor show that explores their challenges traveling across the United States to attend a conference.

16. Shakespeare, William. *Twelfth Night*. Directed by Simon Godwin. Performers Tamara Lawrance, Tamsin Greig, Phoebe Fox. National Theatre, London, UK, National Theatre Live, Gateway Film Center, 25 April 2017. I attended a viewing of this production in a theatre in Columbus and then viewed it again in the NT archives in 2018. It was also made available on the NT Live YouTube page for one week during the coronavirus epidemic in the spring of 2020. NT Live YouTube channel, https://www.youtube.com/channel/UCUDq1XzCY0NIOYVJvEMQjqw. Accessed 26 April 2020.

17. In a later scene in which Olivia woos Cesario in a pool, Cesario does struggle to make sure his/her/their breasts are not revealed. Trevor Nunn's 1996 film version also includes a scene of Viola/Cesario (Imogen Stubbs) unbinding her/his/their breasts, a moment that would potentially have a different resonance if performed by a genderfluid or transgender performer.

18. For a discussion of how boxing is racialized and gendered, see Lucia Trimbur's "Buying and Selling Blackness: White-Collar Boxing and Racialized Consumerism" in *Reconsidering Social Identification: Race, Gender, Class and Caste*, edited by Abdul R. JanMohamed (New York: Routledge, 2011), 177–206.

19. See note 11 on some of the issues that arise in interpreting laughter. For a reading of the benefits of redefining masculinity to include transgender men, see Jack Halberstam's "Raging Bull (Dyke): New Masculinities" in *Female Masculinity* (Durham: Duke University Press, 2019), 267–76, which argues that transgender men who box do not define their masculinity through their capacity to endure pain, a proposition conversely accepted and enacted by Robert DeNiro in his portrayal of Jake LaMotta in Martin Scorsese's 1980 film.
20. Simon Godwin, interview by the author, London, 9 August 2018.
21. Quotations from William Shakespeare, *Twelfth Night*, The Folger Shakespeare, accessed 1 January 2022, https://shakespeare.folger.edu/shakespeares-works/twelfth-night/entire-play, 3.1.133, 3.1.156–60.
22. Kemp describes a similar choice made by a California Shakespeare Festival's 2017 production of *As You Like It*. They, however, went further by also inviting nonconforming actors to apply, designing educational materials for the audience, and redesigning the lobby space and bathrooms to be more accessible to nonbinary patrons. Sawyer K. Kemp, "Transgender Shakespeare Performance: A Holistic Dramaturgy." *Journal for Early Modern Cultural Studies* 19.4 (2019): 279–80.
23. In Godwin's production, Viola/Cesario says, "I am all the daughters," and then catches her/his/their "mistake," quickly correcting it to "all the brothers" in line with her/his/their current masculine gender presentation. This is a clever reading of the text, but one that still seems to insist on an essentialized reading of gender that ignores embracing the genderfluid potentiality of being both masculine and feminine.
24. In the scenes I directed from *As You Like It*, I attempted to explore how gaps in the text can be used to generate new stories with performances by and for nonconforming actors. There is a virtually limitless opportunity for professional and academic production to explore how difference can expand our understanding of the way contemporary productions of classical plays can signify. Of course, there are also limitations, but there are possibilities to explore and expand those limitations as well, including through extratextual means and adaptations. William Shakespeare, *As You Like It?*, New Works Lab, directed by Eric Brinkman, Aubrey Helene Neumann, and Nicolas Shannon Savard, Drake Event and Performance Center, 4–5 March 2019.
25. Several UK theatres, including the Royal Court, Oxford Playhouse, and Royal Exchange have pledged to support the trans casting statement, Lanre Bakare, "UK Theatres Promise to Only Cast Trans Actors in Trans Roles," *The Guardian*, 26 May 2021, https://www.theguardian.com/stage/2021/may/26/uk-theatres-promise-to-only-cast-trans-actors-in-trans-roles, accessed 30 July 2021. I would extend this to include nonbinary parts as well. On considerations for casting trans and nonbinary actors, see also Regina Victor, "Developing Trans Roles for the Theatre," *American Theatre*. 23 September 2020. https://www.americantheatre.org/2020/09/23/developing-trans-roles-for-the-theatre. Accessed 2 August 2021.

REFERENCES

Bakare, Lanre. "UK theatres promise to only Cast Trans Actors in Trans Roles." *The Guardian*, May 26 2021, https://www.theguardian.com/stage/2021/may/26/uk-theatres-promise-to-only-cast-trans-actors-in-trans-roles. Accessed 30 July 2021.

Bowie-Sell, Daisy. "What's it like for a man to play Ophelia?" *WhatsOnStage.com*, May 16 2018, https://www.whatsonstage.com/london-theatre/news/ophelia-as-a-man-hamlet-shakespeare-globe_46579.html. Accessed 1 September 2021.

Bruns, John. "Laughter in the Aisles: Affect and Power in Contemporary Theoretical and Cultural Discourse." *Studies in American Humor* 3.7 (2000): 5–23.

Bulman, James C., ed. *Shakespeare Re-Dressed: Cross-Gender Casting in Contemporary Performance.* Fairleigh Dickinson UP, 2008.

Chess, Simone. *Male-to-female Crossdressing in Early Modern English Literature: Gender, Performance, and Queer Relations.* Routledge, 2016.

Godwin, Simon. Interview by the author. London, August 9, 2018.

Keegan , Cáel M. "Transgender Studies, or How to Do Things with Trans*." *The Cambridge Companion to Queer Studies.* Edited by Siobhan B. Somerville. Cambridge UP, 2020. 66–76.

Kemp, Sawyer. "Shakespeare in Transition: Pedagogies of Transgender Justice and Performance." *Teaching Social Justice Through Shakespeare.* Eds. Hillary Eklund, Wendy Beth Hyman. Edinburgh UP, 2019. 36–45.

Howard, Jean. "Crossdressing, the theatre, and gender struggle in early modern England." *Shakespeare Quarterly* 39.4 (1988): 418–440.

———. *The Stage and Social Struggle in Early Modern England.* Routledge, 1994.

Garber, Marjorie. *Vested Interests: Cross-dressing and Cultural Anxiety.* Routledge, 2011.

Ferris, Leslie, ed. *Crossing the Stage: Controversies on Cross-Dressing.* Routledge, 1993.

Halberstam, Jack. "Raging Bull (Dyke): New Masculinities." *Female masculinity.* Duke University Press, 2019. 267–76.

Orgel, Stephen. *Impersonations: The Performance of Gender in Shakespeare's England.* Cambridge UP, 1996.

Ridout, Nicholas. *Stage fright, Animals, and Other Theatrical Problems.* Cambridge UP, 2006.

Shakespeare, William. *As You Like It.* The Folger Shakespeare, https://shakespeare.folger.edu/shakespeares-works/as-you-like-it/entire-play

———. *Twelfth Night.* The Folger Shakespeare, accessed January 1, 2022, https://shakespeare.folger.edu/shakespeares-works/twelfth-night/entire-play

Trimbur, Lucia. "Buying and Selling Blackness: White-Collar Boxing and Racialized Consumerism" in *Reconsidering Social Identification: Race, Gender, Class and Caste.* Ed. Abdul R. JanMohamed. Routledge, 2011. 177–206.

Victor, Regina. "Developing Trans Roles for the Theatre," *American Theatre*, September 23 2020, https://www.americantheatre.org/2020/09/23/developing-trans-roles-for-the-theatre. Accessed 2 August 2021.

CHAPTER 5

"El español puede ser todo": Bilingual Grassroots Shakespeare in Merced, California

William Wolfgang

Amidst the most significant global health crisis in more than a century, the doors of the traditional theatre closed. Merced, a city of 83,000 in California's Central Valley, was no exception. In March 2020, one day before the state of California entered lockdown, Merced's small grassroots Shakespeare performance organization, Merced ShakespeareFest, assembled for open communal auditions of an original English/Spanish bilingual adaptation of *Richard II*. The organization was embarking on its first attempt at creating bilingual theatre in a bilingual community. The auditions, a product of nine months of collaboration between a team of five, yielded a cast of fifteen local actors. As one of the co-directors for *Ricardo II*, I, along with my colleagues, on the eve of lockdown, confronted the certainty that the play we had envisioned could not possibly continue. Instead of canceling the play immediately, the company reimagined the production into one not restricted by the ephemerality or conventions of traditional American theatre.

W. Wolfgang (✉)
Stevenson University, Stevenson, MD, USA

© The Author(s), under exclusive license to Springer Nature
Switzerland AG 2023
S. Freeman Loftis et al. (eds.), *Inclusive Shakespeares*, Palgrave
Shakespeare Studies,
https://doi.org/10.1007/978-3-031-26522-8_5

79

Months of video conference rehearsals resulted in six days of physically distant filming in June of 2020 at various recognizable locations around the community. By November, twelve subtitled episodes, two hours and forty-five minutes in total, premiered online. Still, *Ricardo II* was set inescapably within the confines of a pandemic, with actors masked and distanced throughout the rehearsal process and to differing degrees in performance.[1] In December 2020, Randall Martin reviewed the production from an ecocritical perspective. He described John of Gaunt's encouragement of Bolingbroke after the proclamation of exile as a "retreat from a plague-ridden country," and he elaborated: "needless to say, John [of Gaunt]'s suggestion to 'suppose devouring pestilence hangs in our air' rings uncomfortably literal as the Covid-19 pandemic continues" (Martin 2021). *Ricardo II* participants similarly identified the production as a respite from the daily grind of the pandemic lifestyle.

However, the production was not centered on the pandemic. For the participants interviewed post-production, this collaborative bilingual initiative created access to a form of inclusive community-based arts they had never experienced. Anthony Yepez Reyes purposefully auditioned for *Ricardo II* because he had never seen an opportunity to do theatre in his first language, and in turn, never felt comfortable participating. He recalled being 'captivated' by the show's audition flyer that announced "una producción bilingüe" (Yepez Reyes 2021). This inclusive mission inspired participants to advocate for future productions, and less than a month after the complete series had premiered online, Merced ShakespeareFest's second bilingual production was in development. The production team concluded that the most inclusive bilingual Shakespeare program also meant embracing the contributions of other playwrights and authors to the English and Spanish literary canons. With this in mind, we selected the work of Shakespeare's Spanish contemporary, Miguel de Cervantes. Once again, the creative team employed a community-based film medium for the production. We developed an adaptation of *Don Quixote* that prioritizes Cervantes's original Spanish text while leaning into the production's locality. However, unlike the unpredictable nature of the Covid-19 situation during *Ricardo II* that forced us to react continually to changing circumstances, we knew our production methodology well in advance. Evident in apparent stylistic differences, *Ricardo II* reads as filmed place-based theatre, whereas *Don Quixote de la Merced* presents as a 'mockumentary' with a delineated structure.

For those of us who engage with this work, we embrace its process-based nature. While we passionately and methodically prepare for performances, we aim to create corresponding dialogues about language, community, and identity through rehearsals. These conversations on the nature of community-based theatre and bilingual identities, not the details of the performances nor its hybridized medium, are the subject of this chapter. Throughout our production, discussions extended beyond the walls or the Zoom boxes of our rehearsal spaces into the community at large. Bristin Scalzo Jones, lecturer of English and Spanish at the University of California, Merced, included *Ricardo II* in her curriculum during the fall 2020 semester. Jones' work with her undergraduate students reveals the academic and personal value of engaging in grassroots bilingual initiatives with participants and audiences. Ultimately, bilingual grassroots Shakespeare generates dialogue as an impetus for continuing multidisciplinary projects deeply rooted in community. I posit that the academy can be a place that nurtures and supports valued communal collaborations. Throughout this chapter, I turn to the perspectives of both the participants and production team members from *Ricardo II* and *Don Quixote de la Merced* to give voice to these experiences.

"Grassroots Shakespeare": Project Origins

My involvement with this bilingual community effort began in March 2019 during research on community-based Shakespeare organizations throughout the United States. At the time, I was a PhD candidate at the University of Warwick, working with my supervisor, Paul Prescott, on Shakespeare in Yosemite, an annual eco-theatre program featuring professional, community, and student actors co-produced with UC Merced. During my Practice-as-Research with Prescott and the group's co-founder, Katherine Steele Brokaw, in Yosemite, I worked with a group of enthusiastic undergraduate students who shared a passion for theatre, Shakespeare, and the ideals of social inclusion. One of these students, Ángel Nuñez, created scene-by-scene summaries in Spanish for the company's production of *As You Like It*. To ensure that as many members of the Merced community as possible could engage with the production, Brokaw asked Nuñez if he would be willing to assemble the summaries for Spanish-speaking members of the audience. Merced is 55 percent Latinx, with 47 percent of the population speaking a language other than English ("Quick Facts: Merced, California, United States"); hence, many appreciated these efforts. Nuñez's Spanish language work with Shakespeare in Yosemite sparked conversations about the nature of grassroots Shakespeare and the paucity of arts opportunities in Spanish, even in a majority Latinx community.

Months later, I served as the dramaturg for Merced ShakespeareFest's *Othello* under the direction of the company's founding artistic director, Heike Hambley. Following this, Hambley asked me if I would be interested in returning as a guest director for the company's 2020 season. I enthusiastically accepted, and she selected the text, *Richard II*. Recalling conversations with Nuñez, I realized that this could be an opportunity to avail Shakespeare to Merced's majority Latinx population through bilingual theatre. Hambley thoroughly supported the project, citing its profound connection with the organization's mission to create "Shakespeare plays that reflect and embrace the diversity of our community" ("About"). I then reached out to Shakespeare in Yosemite alums to compose the production team. Nuñez joined as translator and co-director, Maria Nguyen-Cruz as a co-director and adaptor, and Cathryn Flores contributed as music director. Our team collaborated weekly for six months, carefully editing, adapting, and curating the script for bilingual audiences and participants.

For the production to be rooted in place and connect with the local community, the team set *Ricardo II* in a cantina in 1840s Alta California, during a transitional government after the Mexican-American War. The bilingual community actors were to metatheatrically perform community players enacting Shakespeare's play during this time. We aspired that a narrative rooted in a long-forgotten regional history would encourage conversation about the interconnectedness of California's linguistic heritages. Ricardo's court primarily spoke Spanish, and Henry's forces spoke English. This binary was not prescriptive; the language wavered back and forth, sometimes reiterating specific passages in the other language, coupled with code-switching to support comprehension from monolingual Spanish or English speakers. After the collaborative script work, the production team and artistic director Heike Hambley began publicity work to assure those interested knew how to access the program. However, locating interested individuals would not be our challenge. By March 2020, Covid-19 mitigation measures necessitated an online approach to rehearsal for six weeks. When faced with the decision to cancel the production or continue working online in a video conferencing format, Hambley and I agreed that pushing forward together would be uniquely valuable amid the developing crisis for all involved. We chose to operate rehearsals on an online video conferencing platform. Subsequently, the production team abandoned the original theatrical concept set post-Mexican-American War, began script alterations, and abruptly prepared our participants for a filmed web series. We completed this effort by the end of June, and post-production lasted through November.

The production team anchored the work at the intersection of what I refer to as *grassroots Shakespeare* and the emerging field of "Latinx Shakespeares." My use of the term *grassroots* draws on the work of multiple practitioners and theorists (Wolfgang 2021). First, Robert Gard's eponymous text which coined the term delineates grassroots theatre from community theatre: "There must be plays that grow from all the country-sides of America, fabricated by the people themselves" (Gard 1954). Gard and his predecessors aspired for playwriting to become part of American civic life and to create a movement to find true American drama. Gard's ideal play was locally crafted, home-grown, and deeply meaningful for amateur actor-participants and audiences. Consequently, 'grassroots the-atre' deals with politics, locatedness, and mobilization of the people with its inherent bottom-up imagery. Nearly a half-century later, theatre prac-titioner Dudley Cocke and his colleagues articulate a similar case for the term 'grassroots theatre' in a matrix that includes six tenets: the art of the people, sense of place, tradition, inclusion, collective responsibility, and struggling for equality (Cocke et al. 1993). Like her predecessors, Jan Cohen-Cruz focuses on how the work is produced, differentiating it from community theatre, which she notes is "enacted by people who neither generate the material, shape it, work with professional guidance, nor apply it beyond an entertainment frame" (Cohen-Cruz 2005).

The work explored in this chapter builds on the aforementioned defini-tion of grassroots theatre practitioners. As Cohen-Cruz theorizes, we sought to "'apply' our bilingual theatre effort outside of the realm of 'entertainment'". This form of socially inclusive theatre is the ideal vehicle for continuing studies in the developing field termed by Carla Della Gatta as "Latinx Shakespeares." In *Shakespeare in Latinidad*, Trevor Boffone and Della Gatta interrogate "how a marginalized community in the United States has engaged with the world's most iconic playwright", but first, they emphasize that "Latinx theatre is American theatre" (Boffone and Della Gatta 2021). Therefore, *Ricardo II* and *Don Quixote de la Merced* aid in this effort to redefine perceptions of American theatre. These productions move the field closer to finding, as Gard aspired, local, representative plays "grown from all the countrysides."

"Mɪ español nativo": Participation and Ownership

The production team centered grassroots theatre practices on the equal inclusion of the Spanish language. In interviews, all of the participants in Merced ShakespeareFest's bilingual productions agreed that there is a dearth of Spanish language theatre locally and even regionally in California. Hence, the bilingual nature of *Ricardo II* immediately drew participants to audition. Cynthia Robles recalled being "super excited to be in" the production because it was "actually" in Spanish. Robles continued, code-switching in our bilingual interview, "porque muchas veces teatro en español nomás dice como pocas palabras como 'ey, hermano, Dios, sangre'" ("because often theatre in Spanish just has a few [stereotypical] words like …") (Robles and Yepez 2020).[2] Anthony Yepez Reyes, who "had never seen" an opportunity to participate in a bilingual production, stated that it "brought [him] in" to audition for *Ricardo II* (Yepez Reyes 2021). His experiences in the production prompted him to arrange his final undergraduate semester so he could once again participate, this time as Sancho Panza in *Don Quixote de la Merced*.

Growing up in Merced, actor Claudia Boehm said it would have been "unheard of" to participate in a Spanish-speaking theatrical production. Boehm, who played Queen Isabela in *Ricardo II* and narrator María Zoraida in *Don Quixote de la Merced*, stated "yo siempre pensé que los personajes eran más para las personas blancas" ("I always thought the characters [in Shakespeare] were more for white people") (Boehm and Gutiérrez 2020). She continued, capturing a sentiment shared by many of our fellow participants:

> I would watch productions performed in Mexico in the Grand Theatre, in Guadalajara, or Mexico City through the television dreaming "why can't we have this here," and so it has just been a dream come true to be able to perform in my own language here in California with such amazing people. (Boehm and Gutiérrez 2020)

These experiences parallel the previously noted work of Trevor Boffone and Carla Della Gatta and other studies on Shakespeare in Hispanic communities. Thus, the academy plays a critical role in exploring how bilingual identities intersect with Shakespeare's cultural influence. For example, Ruben Espinosa, who teaches Shakespeare at a Hispanic-serving institution in Arizona, and before that at one in Texas, argues that examining the aforementioned intersections can "generate possibilities for social change" (Espinosa 2019). To meaningfully approach Shakespeare's work for his students, he advocates for "pedagogical practices that allow students to make Shakespeare their own" (Espinosa 2019). Through the equal use of Spanish and English and the constant editing of the script and translations by the actor-participants themselves, *Ricardo II* encouraged Latinx members of the Merced community to take a similar level of ownership of Shakespeare.

Ángel Nuñez translated and co-directed both of Merced ShakespeareFest's bilingual productions. Throughout these projects, he embraced the grassroots theatre ideals of harnessing original work for purposes beyond simple entertainment; "it's something that is your own", he explained, "and it has really changed my perspective on the power of language" (Flores et al. 2020). However, the sense of ownership over the words themselves was not Nuñez's alone. The production sought to increase opportunities for participants to engage with Shakespeare's text and to encourage their responsibility in the process of sculpting a Shakespearean adaptation. In this respect, we endeavoured to follow the matrix of grassroots theatre by having participants create and shape their characters outside of directorial control. Nuñez, Nguyen-Cruz, and I approached the adaptation work on the script with this methodology in mind. After months of independent work, Nuñez opened the translation process to the actor-participants and sought their opinions and experiences. Taking on the role of Henry Percy, cast member Lupita Yepez emphasized the unique intersectionality between personal and collective responsibility in grassroots theatre: "I feel a lot of responsibility when trying to play with words, like Shakespeare does"; Yepez continued by emphasizing that this meant careful attention to specific Spanish pronunciations as well (Robles and Yepez 2020). She stated that the Spanish and English balance in the production was "something that I could really connect to," and she did so on multiple levels (Robles and Yepez 2020). Yepez added that this language, predominantly code-switching between Spanish and English, represented her daily life. Through this, she described an experience markedly similar to Espinosa's students using Shakespeare as a "vehicle" to "register apprehensions" regarding the "burdens of hybridity" along with "daily bi-national, cross-cultural experiences" (Espinosa 2019). She elaborated how this production connected her "two worlds," by presenting an old story in English to people who "only speak Spanish" (Robles and Yepez 2020).

Negotiating these practices meant the group had to maintain the script as a living document, and Nuñez collaboratively led the effort to assure the local dialect was present in the Spanish of *Ricardo II*. Script alterations occurred daily throughout the rehearsal process. This progression was artistically engaging and enlightening for many participants regardless of their command of Spanish or English. The company freely interacted in the two languages, adjusted syntax and grammar, questioned approaches to metaphorical text, and debated the use of arcane words. Co-director Maria Nguyen-Cruz explained how even primarily English speakers "no matter [their] level of familiarity" with Spanish began to "absorb one another's language" (Flores et al. 2020). Nguyen-Cruz's description alludes to the production as a sort of linguistic laboratory. Though the company experimented with particulars throughout the rehearsal process, the production team had established the dialect of Spanish long before any participant read the script at auditions. Claudia Boehm recalled her pre-audition uneasiness as she thought about what Shakespeare's complex language would sound like in Spanish. To achieve this similar linguistic style, she wondered if it would be "un español Castellano" ("a Castilian Spanish") used in translations. "Ahora voy a tener que tratar de aprender un poco más de cómo usan el idioma en España" ("Now I'm going to have to try to learn a bit more about how Spanish is used in Spain"), Boehm remembered (Boehm and Gutiérrez 2020). Accordingly, she was relieved to learn that Nuñez translated the text with the Merced community in mind. These considerations included adaptations for local dialect and a continual balancing act between Latin American Spanish and Shakespeare's English. While these linguistic differences were a challenge for the participants, they also came with rewards. Actor Cynthia Robles, who played three roles in *Ricardo II*, reflected on this complex aspect of the experience:

> I just felt so much more connected. And it was like the language that I always speak with my mom or my whole family, and I grew up with it… It's also a bit intimidating too because I wasn't used to speaking that type of Spanish. (Robles and Yepez 2020)

As Robles suggests, though the dialogue was not Castilian Spanish, it was so closely translated from Shakespeare's text that its composition was still very different from conversational Spanish that participants were familiar with speaking. While admitting that it was "double the work" to prepare for her roles, nevertheless, she recalled feeling more 'grounded' in performance (Robles and Yepez 2020).

The production team aspired to create resonance within the Latinx community through both the translations and minor adaptations of the script. We aimed to delineate relevant themes from the text to align with the production's narrative and our mission of inclusivity and ownership. To realize this, we chose to emphasize a theme that has a stronger meaning for Latinx communities than for America's majority population: displacement. As Thomas Mowbray's response to his banishment poignantly captures the linguistic plight of the immigrant or the exiled, for *Ricardo II*, we assured that through translation and slight adaptation, these lines had added resonance for participants. While the theme of displacement and exile presents throughout the text, from Bolingbroke's exile to Ricardo's loss of self and identity, we focused on Thomas Mowbray's speech after King Richard banishes him from England (1.3.154–73):

The language I have learnt these forty years,	La lengua que yo he aprendido estos cuarenta años,
My native English, now I must forgo,	Mi español nativo, ahora lo dejare:
And now my tongue's use is to me no more	Y ahora el uso de mi lengua es nada más
Than an unstringed viol or harp,	Que un viola o arpa sin cordón,
Within my mouth you have engaoled my tongue,	Dentro mi boca tu has clausurado mi lengua,
Doubly portcullised with my teeth and lips,	Doblemente impedido con mis dientes y labios;
And dull unfeeling barren ignorance Is made my jailer to attend on me.	Y opaca insensible ignorancia Ha hecho mi guarda asistir. (Nuñez et al. 2020)

In the production, Mowbray is exclusively a Spanish-speaking character renamed "Tomás Mercedes". He was one of three characters that Robles portrayed (Robles also played the Bishop of Carlisle and the Duchess of York). For her, as she described in an interview, Mercedes was unquestionably the role with the most personal impact. The textual change from "my native English" to "mi español nativo" reinforced a part of the bilingual identity that participants discussed in interviews. Lupita Yepez acknowledged that Tomás Mercedes' line, "Mi español nativo, ahora lo dejare", was "really poetic", and she stated that it was a role she would like to play: "That whole passage just spoke to me" (Robles and Yepez 2020). Because of these connections, adaptations, and translations, individual ownership of Shakespeare's text instilled a desire for continuing participation in the work.

Mission Billingüe: English y Español

For both of Merced ShakespeareFest's bilingual productions, the company was composed of people with varying levels of fluency with the Spanish language; bilingual and monolingual individuals and those who were somewhere in between all participated. Therefore, some non-native Spanish speakers, at times, had to speak lines in Spanish. While this was difficult, participants and production team members welcomed the challenge. Lupita Yepez recalled working with castmates that "didn't know Spanish at the beginning of the play, [but] were still able to learn" (Robles and Yepez 2020). Ángel Nuñez led Spanish language workshops weekly on Zoom with *Ricardo II* participants to specifically focus on pronunciation and comprehension; he fondly recollected the growth that many of these actors had in their Spanish ability. Likewise, literary advisor to *Don Quixote de la Merced*, Bristin Scalzo Jones, who played the narrator role of Ana Félix, articulated the value she observed in actors with varying linguistic abilities participating together in the production:

> It was very exciting for me to help our actors learn the Spanish words…and to see our lead Don Quixote outside of the play now excited to learn Spanish… It turns the tables on us who grew up with English as a first language to say, listen, it's our responsibility as well to also engage with the Spanish language. (Jones 2021)

As Jones describes, the bilingual productions unconventionally engaged Merced's participants and audiences with the rigors of experiencing two languages within one story. Veteran Merced ShakespeareFest actor Greg Ruelas, who had been performing with the organization for more than fifteen years, took on the role of Henry Bolingbroke in *Ricardo II*. At first, he was unsure of participating due to apprehensions regarding his command of the Spanish language. For Ruelas, reacting to his fellow actors' lines was most difficult. "I think I know what they're saying," he noted as he outlined his process for working with the bilingual text, "and [then] I go back and read the English text to get an understanding (Hambley and

Ruelas 2020). Similarly, artistic director Heike Hambley confirmed that the Spanish language" "mentoring" was part of the production and the organization's mission and, for some, continued in the form of independent Spanish language studies after the conclusion of the productions (Hambley 2021).

Despite the many challenges that inevitably arise, community-based theatre must promote radical and participatory inclusivity. This form of accessibility can be complicated for small grassroots companies often led by dedicated volunteers and limited because of financial and operational capacity. Merced ShakespeareFest had to reach out to new participants when casting *Ricardo II*, as the organization had never previously had a bilingual cast. Co-director Maria Nguyen-Cruz secured a community-partnership grant from UC Merced to assist the organization with promoting the auditions. In order to answer questions about the production and welcome those interested in the process, the creative team organized an informational meeting hosted by Hambley. This session ultimately encouraged those in attendance to audition for *Ricardo II*. Still, some individuals who specifically auditioned because the production was bilingual were unfamiliar with theatre and its processes. Recalling his initial uncertainties, Anthony Yepez Reyes questioned whether he had the necessary abilities to be involved: "You guys know what you're doing. But I was thinking to myself, 'Can I really do this? I don't know. Is it a thing that I should be doing?'" (Yepez Reyes 2021). Both Hambley's desire to have mentoring within the ensemble and support from the cast and production team assuaged Yepez Reyes' apprehensions. After his work concluded on *Don Quixote de la Merced* in 2021, he identified his contributions to Merced ShakespeareFest's two bilingual productions as a "gateway" that helped him find his "own route" (Yepez Reyes 2021). Another first-time theatre participant who attended the *Ricardo II* information session was Alejandro Gutiérrez, Teaching Professor of Engineering at UC Merced. Recalling his expectations going into the audition process, Gutiérrez reflected on his experience:

> It was scary for me because I didn't think I could do it right. When I auditioned I was like, "maybe I'll get a background character or something, and I'll be holding a flag in the background and I'll be very happy." (Boehm and Gutiérrez 2020)

Upon receiving the titular role, Gutiérrez reframed his hopes of playing a supernumerary role into an opportunity:

> So, that's not what happened, and I was scared. But then I started doing it, and it was very therapeutic because with everything else going insane everywhere—I had this. I could regularly practice my lines or do the rehearsals … It was very, very helpful. (Boehm and Gutiérrez 2020)

Like his fellow participants, Gutiérrez took on the role with a profound sense of responsibility despite his unexpected casting. Beyond the intrinsic rewards of playing Shakespeare's ill-fated king, he felt strongly about the production's mission. For him, connecting to both the English-speaking and Spanish-speaking communities was important. Surprised by the perception in the United States that some consider Spanish an inferior alternative to speaking English, Gutiérrez, who immigrated from Venezuela, elaborated, "Para mí, el español es la lengua de la alta cultura" ("for me, Spanish is the language of high culture") (Boehm and Gutiérrez 2020). He then cited the work of Cervantes, Lope de Vega and Rubén Darío among others. For decades, high culture in the United States associated closely with Shakespeare—not influential Spanish writers—and resisted the notion, as Espinosa argues, that Latinxs possess a "legitimate linguistic identity" (Espinosa 2019). In this regard, the mission of Merced ShakespeareFest's bilingual productions was to subvert these deeply ingrained cultural legacies. Gutiérrez mused about what these projects might mean to English-speaking Americans: "el español no es solamente estos latinos inmigrantes que vienen a quitarnos el trabajo" ("The Spanish language is not only these immigrant Latinos who come take away our jobs"); Gutiérrez continued, "sino que también es Shakespeare. El español puede ser todo" ("But it is also Shakespeare. Spanish can be anything") (Boehm and Gutiérrez 2020).

While navigating the extraordinary times of the Covid-19 pandemic, Ruelas, Yepez Reyes, and Gutiérrez overcame their initial reservations and decided to participate in a production that was anything but ordinary. Their inclusion, however, was contingent upon their access to the publicity information announcing the production. Merced ShakespeareFest had extra funding to promote *Ricardo II* 's auditions which occurred on the eve of the lockdown, whereas the auditions conducted for *Don Quixote de la Merced* were in another medium with fewer resources. The production team assembled a talented group of local actors, but auditions were held on Zoom due to the pandemic conditions, limiting accessibility for possible participants. In the coming post-pandemic years, Hambley hopes that new participants will join the organization for bilingual productions. Fully aware that it takes time to develop ongoing community-based arts programs with participants and audiences, especially on a "shoestring budget," she predicted that it would take at least five years before she would be satisfied with the level of community awareness with the continuing bilingual initiatives (Hambley 2021). Hambley also credited the partnership between community-based work and academia as well as an influential regional theatre for inspiring the work. She emphasized that grassroots bilingual theatre is not created in a bubble:

> It was a very lucky, fortunate meeting between a community-based theatre company and a nearby university with scholars, with people who worked on the forefront of all of this... And I've seen lots of good examples: [the] Oregon Shakespeare Festival. That's my big, big role model, for a very small company. And this has helped very much. (Hambley 2021)

Hambley's reflection reinforces the idea that theatre companies of all sizes, from large regional theatres to small grassroots community organizations, can engage with inclusivity and innovation within the field.

For *Ricardo II*, the academic influence was composed of both faculty and students at UC Merced.[3] Involvement in this community-university partnership mutually benefits both entities and the individuals that participate. Furthermore, the shared understanding that the production belongs to the Merced community supports academic study and aids in developing locally relevant pedagogy. As it premiered, several classes at UC Merced viewed the production. Bristin Scalzo Jones utilized *Ricardo II* in English and Spanish literature courses to provide her students with an "example of local and community projects that engage with literature" (Jones 2021). As Jones prepared to teach *Don Quixote* in her Spanish literature course in fall 2021, she looked forward to students once again experiencing this aspect of grassroots theatre:

> It's very exciting for students to see their own places depicted on the screen...for them to see their own city, their own campus, their own favorite cafe in the background in something that's literary and artistic, I think has real value for them. (Jones 2021)

Therefore, according to Jones, the actor-participants are not the only individuals who experience a sense of ownership because of the production; the undergraduate students who viewed *Ricardo II* in class felt this sentiment too. Thus, the interaction serves to enhance the symbiotic relationship between the community organization and the academy.

As with all localized theatre, it is created for and by local viewers, ultimately, to affect their audience. Though these productions are available online for the world to see, the bilingual work represents *their* city, and, as Jones described, students can "see Merced is a place where culture happens" (Jones 2021). Though her students did not have the same participatory experience as the cast members, *Ricardo II* inspired their own local, digital storytelling projects based on Calderón's La vida es sueño. Such creative and academic exercises had an even more significant impact amidst the online learning of the pandemic, as participants and students shared in interviews, reflections, and through anecdotes. Based on the aforementioned pedagogical experiences, Jones noted to me, "local and community art inspire more local and community art" (Jones 2021). Data throughout this case study supports this conclusion. For example, a member of Jones' class auditioned for Shakespeare in Yosemite and then *Don Quixote de la Merced* after viewing and discussing *Ricardo II* in class. Additionally, in my Introduction to Shakespeare course, the *Ricardo II* project and the idea of Shakespeare in translation inspired a first-year student to embark on a semester-long translation project of *Richard III* within his Spanish dialect. This translation, *Ricardo III*, and those like it will undoubtedly continue to cross-pollinate the fruitful and symbiotic relationship between UC Merced and Merced ShakespeareFest.

Ultimately, for the community at large, *Ricardo II* reinforced that theatre was not an exclusive activity. Jones evoked a compelling moment that a student shared with her:

> [My student] didn't know that there was theatre for her, because she always thought theatre was this fancy thing outside, in English. She grew up speaking Spanish. To see and hear a production that was valuing how people spoke where she grew up was really important to her... For me, to feel like she has felt left out of theatre completely, that's devastating. I think that these projects can be a response to that...to say theatre is for you. (Jones 2021)

These experiences were not limited to the classroom at the University of California, Merced or to the geographic limits of Merced county. Participants Lupita Yepez and Cynthia Robles were students at Modesto Junior College during the production, and the value they placed on the work was evident. From work to physically distant rehearsals in Merced, Yepez made a seventy-mile commute to participate. For her, this inconvenience was well worth it: "My parents only speak Spanish. They wouldn't go see me [in a show]; they wouldn't understand what was going on." Yepez recollected, "and now with *Ricardo II*, not only are there subtitles, but also the important parts are translated back into Spanish" (Robles and Yepez 2020). Now, she feels that despite previous apprehension with Shakespeare as an English learner, "if I were to pick up Shakespeare again, I think I would be able to actually enjoy it" (Robles and Yepez 2020).

Participants acknowledged the personal impact of the communal nature of the productions. For some, these initiatives helped to form their careers. Ángel Nuñez indicated in an interview after *Ricardo II* that he hoped the production would "open doors for more of these types of projects, more multicultural art" (Flores et al. 2020). His hopes have materialized on multiple levels. After the community-based work with Merced ShakespeareFest, Nuñez was encouraged to pursue a graduate degree in Arts Administration, and, subsequently, he secured a job as an executive director for a theatre company in Pennsylvania. In yet another example of how these projects build continuity, after *Don Quixote de la Merced*, Nuñez began preparing for a bilingual Cervantes-Shakespeare fusion of *El juez de los divorcios* and *Henry VIII*. Also, Music director Cathryn Flores's production and research experiences with Merced ShakespeareFest have significantly contributed to her desire to pursue a Ph.D., with interest in "interdisciplinary production" and "accessibility and music within Shakespearean studies" (Flores 2021).

Meanwhile, Hambley and Merced ShakespeareFest aspire for permanency for the bilingual programming, and participants introduced to the organization through *Ricardo II* and *Don Quixote de la Merced* continued their involvement even after the projects concluded. In one such instance, after portraying King Ricardo II, Alejandro Gutiérrez accepted an invitation from Heike Hambley to serve on the organization's board of directors. With its new participants and leaders, Merced ShakespeareFest looks toward an optimistic future. The organization's bilingual work exists online and is easily accessible, which fuels Hambley's hopes that the local community's ongoing views "will give us some ideas on how to continue"

(Hambley 2021).[4] In an interview after filming *Ricardo II*, cast member Claudia Boehm advocated for more productions like what she had experienced: "I want all [Shakespeare's] plays, his sonnets, his poems—everything—translated now. Can you guys translate all of them please?" (Boehm and Gutiérrez 2020). Fortunately for Boehm, Merced has the necessary ingredients for the continuation of such an undertaking: an enthusiastic community of local artists and patrons, a nonprofit Shakespeare organization with a mission of inclusivity, and the support of an academic institution composed of dedicated students and faculty.

NOTES

1. For an analysis of the pandemic's effect on *Ricardo II* and the varied uses of technology within the performance, see Wolfgang and Sullivan, "*Ricardo II*: una producción bilingüe de Merced Shakespearefest" in *Lockdown Shakespeare: New Evolutions in Performance and Adaptation* (Wolfgang and Sullivan 2022).
2. Robles is referring to what Della Gatta calls "the West Side Story effect" or the "sprinkling in Spanish words and phrases to signal Latinx culture" (Boffone and Della Gatta 2021).
3. During *Ricardo II*, I was a PhD candidate at the University of Warwick. When the organization moved on to *Don Quixote de la Merced*, I completed my studies at Warwick and began lecturing at UC Merced.
4. The organization held a community premier event at a local theatre for a full-length film version of *Don Quixote de la Merced* in November 2021, followed by a "question and answer session" with the production team.

REFERENCES

"About." Merced ShakespeareFest. https://www.mercedshakespearefest.org/about. Accessed 2 August 2021.

Boehm, Claudia, and Alejandro Gutiérrez. Interview by William Wolfgang. 24 July 2020.

Boffone, Trevor and Carla Della Gatta. "Introduction: Shakespeare and Latinidad." *Shakespeare in Latinidad*. Edited by Trevor Boffone and Carla Della Gatta. Edinburgh University Press, 2021, pp. 1–18.

Cocke, Dudley, Harry Newman, and Janet Salmons-Rue. *From the Ground Up: Grassroots Theater in Historical and Contemporary Perspective.* Cornell University Press, 1993.

Cohen-Cruz, Jan. *Local Acts: Community-Based Performance in the United States.* Rutgers University Press, 2005.

Espinosa, Ruben. "Chicano Shakespeare: The Bard, the Border, and the Peripheries of Performance." *Teaching Social Justice through Shakespeare*. Edited by Hillary Eklund and Wendy Beth Hyman. Edinburgh University Press, 2019, pp. 76–84.

Flores, Cathryn. Personal Interview. 12 August 2021.

Flores, Cathryn, Maria Nguyen-Cruz, and Ángel Nuñez. Personal Interview. 28 July 2020.

Gard, Robert E. *Grassroots Theater: A Search for Regional Arts in America*. University of Wisconsin Press, 1954.

Hambley, Heike. Personal Interview. 11 August 2021.

Hambley, Heike, and Greg Ruelas. Personal Interview. 25 July 2020.

Jones, Bristin. Personal Interview. 16 August 2021.

Martin, Randall. "Ricardo II: Episode 6." *Cymbeline in the Anthropocene*, 8 February 2021, https://www.cymbeline-anthropocene.com/article/17595-ricardo-ii-episode-6. Accessed 9 February 2021.

Nuñez, Ángel, Maria Nguyen-Cruz, and William Wolfgang. "*Ricardo II*—EP. 2: Arpa sin Cordón", *Ricardo II*, YouTube, Merced ShakespeareFest, 11 September 2020, https://www.youtube.com/watch?v=czCQDK0l5FQ. Accessed 11 September 2020.

"Quick Facts: Merced, California, United States." United States Census Bureau, https://www.census.gov/quickfacts/mercedcitycalifornia. Accessed 2 August 2021.

Robles, Cynthia, and Lupita Yepez. Personal Interview. 25 July 2020.

Wolfgang, William. "Grassroots Shakespeare: 'I love Shakespeare and I live here.' Amateur Shakespeare Performance in American Communities." *Shakespeare Bulletin*, 39.3: 355–373, 2021.

Wolfgang, William, and Erin Sullivan. "Ricardo II: una producción bilingüe de Merced Shakespearefest." *Lockdown Shakespeare: New Evolutions in Performance and Adaptation*. Eds. Gemma Kate Allred, Benjamin Broadribb, and Erin Sullivan, Bloomsbury Arden Shakespeare Series 2022.

Yepez Reyes, Anthony. Personal Interview. 10 August 2021.

CHAPTER 6

Shakespearean Madness and Academic Civilization

Avi Mendelson

Foucault's monumental history of insanity, *Madness and Civilization*—a shocking and shockingly broad survey of madness beginning with its symbolic resonances with leprosy in the medieval period and concluding with its asylums in the nineteenth century—does not shy away from taxonomizing Shakespearean depictions of madness.[1] Pairing Shakespeare with Cervantes, Foucault says Lady Macbeth represents "the madness of just punishment" in which mental illness "chastises the disorder of the heart with disorder of the spirit"; Ophelia is an icon for "the madness of desperate passion," which Foucault describes as "love disappointed in its excess, or more commonly a love undone by the inevitability of death".[2] When it comes to Shakespeare, Foucault's primary fascination—at once bleak and morbid—is a supposed link between madness and death:

> Madness, in its empty words, is not vanity: the void that fills it is 'disease beyond my practice' as the doctor says of Lady Macbeth, and it is already the

A. Mendelson (✉)
London, UK
e-mail: amendel@brandeis.edu

© The Author(s), under exclusive license to Springer Nature Switzerland AG 2023
S. Freeman Loftis et al. (eds.), *Inclusive Shakespeares*, Palgrave Shakespeare Studies,
https://doi.org/10.1007/978-3-031-26522-8_6

plentitude that death brings, a madness that does not need a doctor, but divine forgiveness. The sweet joy that Ophelia finds at the end has little to do with happiness, and her senseless song is as near the essential as 'the cry of women' announcing in the corridors of Macbeth's castle that the queen is dead.[3]

Foucault passes over Shakespeare's more joyous, gut-busting portrayals of madness: the slapstick madness of seeing double in *The Comedy of Errors*; Theseus' sourpuss complaints of "The lunatic, the lover, and the poet" (*A Midsummer Night's Dream*, 5.1.7) that interrupt Peter Quince and Bottom's accidentally funny playlet about the perils of erotic melancholy; the Jailor's Daughter's parodying, in *The Two Noble Kinsmen*, of Ophelia's penis song (4.1.107).[4] Shakespeare's depictions of madness were a gasser.[5]

This chapter poses the question of whether, in addition to its kinship with disease, death, and impairment, mental illness can also continue to be associated with joy, fun, and play—as it was in the early modern period. I begin by recounting the thrills and trials of my experience, as an American expatriate living in London, producing theater with a mental health themed drama troupe; this project is one of several—such as Mark Rylance and Ian McKellen performing Shakespeare at the Broadmoor high-security psychiatric hospital, or people with schizophrenia from the Nise da Silveira psychiatric facility staging *Hamlet* in Rio de Janeiro—that have used early modern drama in a mental health context.[6] I then turn to *The Taming of the Shrew* to discuss a representative example of Shakespeare connecting the pleasure of theater to mental illness. Finally, I inquire whether, in an academic setting, it's possible for mental illness to be an enjoyable experience; this section is energized by recent developments in disability studies that critique the lack of access to academia for people with mental illnesses. I argue, however, that Shakespeare may present an occasion to ask these questions in the first place, which is itself a good starting point toward creating a more inclusive environment for neurodiverse students.[7]

THE TALE OF PLEASURE BEDLAM LTD.

In 2018, shortly after relocating to the UK to complete, in the British Library, my dissertation on madness in Shakespeare, I found myself acting in a play staged by a mental health themed theater project at the Arcola Theater. The play was called *No Show* and was about a son's experience, after his mother died, of caring for his mentally ill father; it included true stories from the writer's life, and during rehearsal the actors worked with the leader of a support group for caregivers of people with mental illnesses.[8] The rehearsals were superb; they not only forged communities with people from random walks of life—actors, directors, doctors, teachers, academics, and those who have difficulty maintaining employment due to mental illness—but they also provided a safe place for discussions about the contentious and unspoken topic of mental health. From our group conversations at the start of each rehearsal, I realized that many of the participants either had lived experience of mental illness or were at least interested in compassionate engagement with the subject.

The following year, I performed in the group's next show, *Headlines*, which focused on misrepresentations of mental illness in the media. The story is about an eager, young filmmaker who is making a documentary on mental illness—a movie that is particularly insensitive and makes a spectacle out of profound distress and trauma; for example, while interviewing someone about their suicide attempt, he pushes for more details because doing so might boost his ratings.[9] As the filmmaker was sensationalizing his interviewees' stories of mental illness, statistics were projected onto the back wall of the stage that gave real descriptions of mental illness in Hackney—the borough in which the Arcola Theater is located, and one that has some of the highest rates of mental illness in the UK.[10] Unlike the first play I was in, *Headlines* was directed mostly by psychiatrists and there was one in the cast too. It included personal stories of mental illness from the actors—optionally written to the directors (though anonymous to the cast)—that were later incorporated into the play itself. Though *Headlines* brilliantly offered the audience authentic stories of mental illness alongside facts about mental health in Hackney, a few members of the cast complained that the play was deeply depressing. They asked: to what extent would it be good for a cast—that might consist of several people with chronic depression—to be exposed weekly, during rehearsal, to material that ranges from mildly upsetting to devastating? Could that process exacerbate depression? And are the potential sadness of mental illness and the need to destigmatize the two main interests of those with these health conditions?

A few months after *Headlines*, I was putting the finishing touches on my dissertation, and I proposed, with one of the assistant directors of the previous production, a staging of Middleton and Rowley's *The Changeling*—a play that presents a raucous, satiric take on the early modern mental health industry. Rather than either attempt an accurate depiction of mental illness in the face of misrepresentation or try destig-matizing mental illness by having medical professionals reveal the true facts about it, *The Changeling* both lampoons the first physician who gov-erned Bethlem—London's notorious mental hospital—and, as critic Susan Mayberry notes, interrogates the criteria for mental illness:

> We [the audience] are drawn into a nightmare where people who exhibit unconventional but relatively harmless behavior are deemed insane while those who deliberately lie, deceive, commit adultery and murder but main-tain a conventional appearance are not. The very structure of the drama asks us to question who belongs in the madhouse.[11]

Our production of the play sought to preserve the subversion of tradi-tional valuations of mental health, as Mayberry illuminates it, by pushing an encounter between those with lived experience of mental illness and early modern theatrical representations. Our director, accordingly, did exercises in rehearsal that asked the actors to consider how depictions of madness in *The Changeling* either link to or contrast with modern imagin-ings of mental illness (examples from the play included the relationship between love and madness, money and mental illness, and perceived and actual mental hospital visitation). The actors then devised scenes, based on these drama games, that were interspersed between the scenes from *The Changeling*. Our final play, which we called *The Pleasure of Your Bedlam*, included both Middleton and Rowley's hospital plot and contemporary, dramatically wrought reactions to this plot.[12]

A few weeks after our staging of *The Pleasure of Your Bedlam*, the pan-demic began, and London and all its theaters were shut down. Our crew from *Bedlam*, though, were still buzzing from the production and decided to continue holding meetings, over Zoom, to discuss potential future plays we'd stage. We thought it might be prudent, as we worked quite well together, to fashion a theater troupe based on our mutual interest in the history of theatrical representations of madness and mental health. We called the company Pleasure Bedlam Ltd., named after the title of our last play—which was lifted from one of my favorite quotes in *The Changeling*:

> Isabella (to Lollio)
> Y'are a brave, saucy rascal. Come on, sir,
> Afford me then the pleasure of your bedlam;

You were commending once today to me
Your last-come lunatic: what a proper
Body there was without brains to guide it,
And what a pitiful delight appeared
In that defect, as if your wisdom had found
A mirth in madness. Pray sir, let me partake,
If there be such a pleasure. (3.3.20–28)

Here Isabella—the young wife of the old doctor running the mental hospital (the latter who, ripe with jealousy, imprisons her in the insane asylum to keep her away from other men)—responds to Lollio's (the doctor's right-hand man's) suggestion that she stave off boredom by sleeping with the incarcerated patients: people who either are mentally ill or have learning disabilities. As Isabella makes bold the "bed" inherent in "bedlam," the implied comedy of her response proposes that the mentally ill would naturally develop better bodies, and be better in bed, than the mentally well as a compensatory gesture to the loss of their minds—"what a proper / body there was without brains to guide it." Isabella's response to Lollio, accordingly, subverts humorously (or at least tries to) a cultural assumption that neurodiverse people should be forbidden from sex because they lack the cognitive capacity to understand it; rather than being sexually off limits, Isabella's bedlamites are sexuality incarnate—they are all body—and represent a sexual freedom unavailable to those hampered by the strictures of the rational mind. Though one might question the ethics of Isabella's (a neurotypical person's) eroticizing of neurological difference, her positioning the mentally ill as more sexually alluring than the sane showcases one of the positive associations that madness projects in the early modern cultural milieu—and one that might be overlooked by those who focus intently on the potential difficulty and social stigma accompanying the illnesses: madness was affiliated with pleasure.

During the Zoom meetings of Pleasure Bedlam Ltd., we frequently read plays that depict madness on stage. We discussed performing a double feature of *Sweeney Todd* and *Titus Andronicus* (a kind of "cannibalism in canonical drama" extravaganza), a panto of *Dracula* (a story that depicts the mad Renfield eating spiders in Dr. Seward's asylum), and an ancient Greek play featuring Dionysus (the god of wine, insanity, and—curiously—of theater). We ended up performing a staged reading of *The Bacchae* at the Tower Theater this summer—shortly after the end of lockdown.[13] I'm happy to say that our performance of *The Bacchae* superbly drove home the ethos of Pleasure Bedlam Ltd.: seeking not only the swift dismantling of stigma confining mental health but also the shameless unearthing of positivity echoing in the subterranean history of madness— the ecstasy, the revelry, and the play. *The Bacchae* features a dual depiction of madness, with Dionysus' mind-altering possession of the Maenads lead- ing both to euphoric bliss and to fury-fueled murder. The question, how- ever, that plagued me when working on Euripides' tragedy was "why is the god of alcohol and madness also the god of theater?" Like Bacchus' mythographers, Shakespeare links madness to the pleasure of theater.

MADNESS AND THEATER IN *THE TAMING OF THE SHREW*

Shakespeare draws connections between pleasure, madness, and theater in *Shrew* both by amplifying its source text's brief focus on madness and by making analogies between his own play and the experience of mad- ness. Though important interventions have been made both regarding whether *Shrew* ends with a subversive or complacent Kate and about how "things" or commodities are depicted in the play, little has been written about its representation of madness and mental health.[14] An exception is Wayne Rebhorn's provocative essay on rhetoric in the play, which notes several moments in which *Shrew* describes Petruchio as mad—such as when he's called "mad-brain rudesby" and "mad brained bridegroom."[15] I would add to Rebhorn's sharp observations about the discourse of mental health in *Shrew* that the same language of madness surrounding Petruchio also adheres to Kate: she is called "stark mad" (1.1.69), "rag- ing fire" (2.1.130), "mad herself, [and] madly mated" (3.3.115), and "mad and headstrong" (4.1.189). Given that the mad Kate and Petruchio have significantly more lines than their counterparts, Bianca and Lucentio—Kate has 8% of the play's lines as opposed to Bianca's 3%, and Petruchio has 22% to Lucentio's 7%—the play shows sustained interest in madness.[16]

The theme of madness in *Shrew* reaches a crescendo in 5.1—during a theatrical event of witnessing someone dressing up like another—when Lucentio's father, Vincentio, arrives in Padua only to encounter the Pedant disguised as him. When Vincentio becomes enraged by this identity theft, several characters accuse him of madness and threaten to throw him in jail. The source of this scene, and much of *Shrew*, is Gascoigne's translation of Ariosto's *The Supposes*, a play first performed at the law offices of Gray's

Inn in 1566 (and one that is extremely critical of lawyers). In Gascoigne's translation, a wealthy scholar named Erostrato dresses up as his servant Dulipo and vice versa, so that he can pursue the affections of the noblewoman Polynesta by becoming the servant of her father, Damon. A play full of tricks, intrigues, and identities mistook, *The Supposes* gives a detailed account of the effects of "supposing" someone is another—a gesture ingrained in the experience of theater. The play ends with a pun on supposes/suppository, when Damon tells his servant to transform the chains and bolts that bound Erostrato in jail, into a sizeable, rectally introduced pill: "to make / a righte ende of our supposes, lay one of those / boltes in the fire, and make thee a suppositorie / as long as mine arm, God save the sample" (5.10.61–64). Though *Shrew* does not conclude by asking the audience to applaud an anus joke—a joke so funny that, as *The Supposes* requests, the actors "may suppose you [the audience] are content" (5.10.67–68)—both plays are intrigued by the relationship between madness and theater.

What Gascoigne's play calls a "suppose"—a situation, it argues, that can lead to madness—is akin to the suspension of disbelief, or to the imagining that a person off stage transforms entirely into a different character on stage, that an audience might try to achieve during a theatrical event. His play defines "suppose" in the prologue: "But understand, this our Suppose is no- / thing else but a mystaking or imagination of one thing / for another. For you shall see the master supposed / for the servant, the servant for the master: the / freeman for a slave, and the bondslave for a free / man: the stranger for a well known friend, and / the familiar for a stranger" (Prologue 14–20). *Shrew* self-consciously makes at least a couple of references to "supposes," such as when Lucentio reveals his true identity to Baptista at the end of the play: "Here's Lucentio, right son to the right Vincentio, / That have by marriage made thy daughter mine, / While counterfeit supposes bleared thine eyne" (5.1.96–98).[17] *Shrew* associates the "bleared…eyne" caused by a confrontation with a "suppose" with madness; after Kate supposes Lucentio's father Vincentio for a "young budding virgin" (4.5.37), as Petruchio claims he is, she apologizes to Vincentio for "mad mistaking" due to "mistaking eyes […] bedazzled with the sun" (4.6.46–50). The bleary or mistaking eyes, upon encountering a suppose, reach their fullest expression—as I noted earlier—during a theatrical moment in which a Pedant dresses up as and plays the part of Vincentio; this theme of being potentially maddened through the eyes because of a counterfeit, a mistake, or a suppose pervades both *Shrew* and *The Supposes.*

Shrew, however, is much more emphatic about the connection between theater and madness than *The Supposes.* In the latter play, Erostrato's father Philogano runs into Dulipo (his son Erostrato's servant) disguised as Erostrato and, after accusing Dulipo of falsehood, is declared mad: "What name could you heare me [Dulipo] called by, but my right name ["Erostrato"]? But I am wise enough to stand prating here with this old man; I think he be mad" (4.7.50–53). In *Shrew*'s version of this scene, the father's alleged madness after encountering someone dressed like him is not alluded to just once, but rather becomes the focal point of the scene. Biondello says that Vincentio is "a madman [who] will murder me [him]" (5.1.47); Baptista asks if Vincentio is "lunatic," after which Tranio tells Vincentio, "you seem a sober, ancient gentleman by your habit, / but your words show you a madman" (5.1.60–61); eventually, after the Pedant calls Vincentio "mad ass" (5.1.70), Tranio insists, "Carry this mad knave [Vincentio] to the jail" (5.1.76) and Baptista agrees: "Away with the dotard. To the jail with him" (5.1.87). *The Supposes* only hints that Philogano is mad, whereas in *A Shrew* Vincentio is repeatedly charged with madness and threatened with incarceration. *Shrew*'s preoccupation with links between theatrical events and madness also frames the entire play; *The Supposes* has no equivalent scene to the Sly Induction, which centers on a tinker nearly convinced that he is mad—"What, would you make me mad? Am not I Christopher Sly [?]," he asks his abusers (Induction 2, 16–17)— by being tricked into thinking he is a lord (i.e., he himself imagines he is someone he isn't, just as an audience member is pushed to imagine an actor is someone they are not during a play). Though there is a shadow side to this association between madness and theater—Vincentio is threatened with restraint and imprisonment for being potentially maddened by this playlet—*Shrew* ultimately revels in the link between pleasure, madness, and theater: its climactic scene of comedy before the resolution is a wild dilation of the drama-inspired madness in *The Supposes.*

If we consider *The Taming of a Shrew* (not *The Taming of* THE *Shrew*) to be connected to the main play under discussion in this section, it would add to Shakespeare's promotion of the link between madness and theater.[18] The very end of *A Shrew* depicts a tapster running into the sleeping Sly, and Sly telling him, "I have had / The bravest dream tonight that ever thou / heardest in all thy life" (Scene E. 11–13); that dream: "how to tame a shrew" (Scene E. 16). The dream not only talks about the play's content but also names the play itself. Dreaming and madness in *A Shrew* are considered similar experiences; in the Induction scenes, the Lord instructs his Huntsmen, "Persuade him [Sly] that he hath been lunatic; / And when he says he is, say that he dreams" (Induction 1, 57–61). *A Shrew* even encourages the continual distribution of madness, as the tapster enthusiastically says, "I'll go home with thee [Sly] / And hear the rest that thou hast dreamt tonight" (Scene E. 23). The final message of *A Shrew* is that madness/theater will live on because those who hear about it will desire to hear more.

INCLUSIVITY AND MENTAL ILLNESS IN THE ACADEMY

Though madness may be dreamy in *Shrew*, recent disability scholarship stresses that this is not the case for students with mental illness. It is crucial that universities make efforts to include, in academic conversations, the highly marginalized mentally ill; it is particularly important to do so because some of what in the UK they call "Serious Mental Illness" (SMI), such as schizophrenia and bipolar disorder, emerge when people are of typical university age.[19] Brave disability studies scholarship has recently launched urgent critiques of the exclusion of the mentally ill within the academy: "86 percent of students with psychiatric disabilities," Margaret Price notes in her vital study *Mad At School*, "withdraw from college before completing their degrees."[20] Price, who sees fundamental rifts between madness and the academy at the basic level of rhetoric or discourse, gives this chilling description of what may happen to a mentally disabled academic: "academics [...] with mental disabilities are largely excluded from academic discourse. The instruments of exclusion are not visible or dramatic—men in white coats dragging people away—but quiet, insidious: We flunk out and drop out. We fail to get tenure. We take jobs as adjuncts rather than tenure-track faculty. We transfer schools; we find a way to get a degree elsewhere. Or not."[21]

A handful of bold academics have come forth and disclosed their mental illnesses, pointing out the struggles of navigating academic life while managing a mental health condition. Hilary Clark, for example, talks about the troubles of attempting to pass as neurotypical if one has bipolar disorder:

It seems to me [...] that no one thinks much about the subtle and not-so-subtle exclusions of mental illness from the academy, even while disability advocates are becoming increasingly vocal and politicized, and disability studies are properly taking their place in the curricula of the humanities and social sciences. We are the silent sufferers, whose exclusion or marginalization is rarely recognized. When we identify ourselves, there is discomfort. If we request concessions (extra assistance with marking, for instance, or extra time to write papers) similar to those our disabled students apply for (Braille, note-takers, extra time to write exams), the reaction would undoubtedly be hostile, with the unspoken question, "What are you doing in this job, then, if you can't cut it like the rest of us?"[22]

Clark daringly points out the disparity of treatment between undergraduates with disabilities and professors in a similar situation. Fortunately, some efforts have been made to address mental illness in the university: studies about faculty disclosing mental disability and accessing support services; professors using personal narratives of schizophrenia to combat stigma; and students, faculty, and administrators—at a school with historically high rates of mental illness—pulling together their stories of depression and anxiety.[23]

Shakespeare's obsession with madness, throughout his oeuvre, can initiate discussions about mental health—both its history and, tangentially, its present moment—in surprising ways. Shakespeare is interested, for example, in the relationship between money and mental health; the First Thief in *Timon of Athens* links Timon's reckless spending and his madness, claiming that "[t]he mere want / of gold and the falling-from of his friends drove him into this / melancholy" (4.3.393–395). Madness is also racialized in Shakespeare's plays; in an anti-Semitic speech *The Merchant of Venice*'s Lorenzo suggests that "the motions of his [a Jew's] spirit are as dull as night, / And his affections dark as Erebus [i.e., filled with black bile or melancholy]" because he or she "is not moved with concord of sweet sounds" (5.1.83–86).[24] Though *The Taming of the Shrew* draws positive connections between madness and theater, *The Tempest* depicts plays as malign forces capable of infecting the reasonable faculties; in a metatheatrical moment, Ariel describes the mental effect on the audience after he "perform'd the tempest" (1.2.195): "Not a soul / But felt a fever of the mad and play'd / Some tricks of desperation" (1.2.209–211).[25] Shakespeare's interest in the connection between financial and mental stability, in the racialization of mental disability, and in the mind-altering potential of his own artistic medium are only a few examples of how

Shakespeare can spark awareness and, in turn, create dialogues and communities needed to disrupt the silent expulsion of neurodiverse students and teachers.

NOTES

1. All references to Shakespeare's works, unless otherwise noted, are from *The Norton Shakespeare*, 1st edition, ed. Stephen Greenblatt et al. (New York: W. W. Norton & Company, 2008).
2. Michel Foucault. *The History of Madness* (New York: Routledge, 2006). 37.
3. Ibid., 38.
4. For more on Ophelia's penile ballad, see Harry Morris, "Ophelia's 'Bonny Sweet Robin,'" *PMLA: Publications of the Modern Language Association of America* 73, no. 5 (1958): 601–603.
5. For more on the relationship between laughter and madness in early modern drama, see Bridget Escolme, *Emotional Excess on the Shakespearean Stage: Passion's Slaves* (London: Bloomsbury, 2014), particularly the second chapter. Other studies of madness in early modern drama include Duncan Salkeld, *Madness and Drama in the Age of Shakespeare* (Manchester: Manchester University Press, 1993); Carol Thomas Neely, *Distracted Subjects: Madness and Gender in Shakespeare and Early Modern Culture* (Ithaca: Cornell University Press, 2004); and Kenneth S. Jackson, *Separate Theaters: Bethlem ("Bedlam") Hospital and the Shakespearean Stage* (Newark: University of Delaware Press, 2005).
6. See Murray Cox, *Shakespeare Comes to Broadmoor* (London: Jessica Kingsley, 1992), and Ben Tavener, "From Stratford to Rio: Using Shakespeare to Treat Mental Illness," BBC News, April 12, 2015, https://www.bbc.co.uk/news/health-32241100.
7. By "neurodiversity" I mean, as Wes Folkerth explains, a term "which has come into use within the past two decades as a way of calling for increased awareness and discontinued pathologizing of people who exhibit nontypical cognitive styles. Neurodiversity suggests we consider their difference primarily in terms of diversity rather than lack." See Wes Folkerth, "Reading Shakespeare After Neurodiversity," in *Performing Disability in Early Modern English Drama*, ed. Leslie C. Dunn (New York: Palgrave Macmillan, 2020), 142. My chapter sometimes switches from the language of neurodiversity, to that of mental illness, to older descriptions of madness; I deploy several labels for cognitive difference to honor the variety of self-representation that people experiencing these mental states engage.
8. "No Show," Arcola Theater, accessed August 25, 2021, https://www.arcolatheatre.com/whats-on/no-show/.
9. "Headlines," Arcola Theater, accessed August 25, 2021, https://www.arcolatheatre.com/whats-on/headlines/.

10. As of 2019, Hackney is the borough with the highest rates of depression in London and has the fifth highest rate of Serious Mental Illness (SMI) in England. See Ed Sheridan, "Hackney's Diagnosed Depression Rates Highest of Any London Borough," *Hackney Citizen*, May 14, 2019, https://www.hackneycitizen.co.uk/2019/05/14/hackney-depression-rates-highest-any-london-borough/, and the National Health Service of the UK's report, "City and Hackney Mental Health Strategy," 8, accessed August 25, 2021.

11. Susan Neal Mayberry, "Cuckoos and Convention: Madness in Middleton and Rowley's *The Changeling*," *Mid-Hudson Language Studies* 8 (1985): 22. For additional discussions of madness in *The Changeling*, see Joost Daalder, "Folly and Madness in *The Changeling*," *Essays in Criticism* 38, no. 1 (1988): 1–22; Andrew Stott, "Tiresias and the Basilisk: Vision and Madness in Middleton and Rowley's *The Changeling*," *Revista Alicantina De Estudios Ingleses* 12 (1999): 165–179; Pascale Drouet, "Madness and Mismanagement in Middleton and Rowley's *The Changeling*," *Theta X* (2013): 139–152.

12. "The Pleasure of Your Bedlam," Arcola Theater, accessed August 25, 2021, https://www.arcolatheatre.com/whats-on/the-pleasure-of-your-bedlam/.

13. "The Bacchae," Tower Theater, accessed August 25, 2021, https://www.towertheatre.org.uk/event/lands17/.

14. For discussions about the play's conclusions about gender, see Melinda Spencer Kingsbury, "Kate's Froward Humor: Historicizing Affect in *The Taming of the Shrew*," *South Atlantic Review* 69, no. 1 (2004): 61–84, and Lynda E. Boose, "Scolding Brides and Bridling Scolds: Taming the Woman's Unruly Member," in *The Taming of the Shrew: Critical Essays*, ed. Dana Aspinall (New York: Routledge, 2002), 130–168. Materialist readings of objects in the play include Lena Cowen Orlin's and Natasha Korda's essays in Aspinall's collection (pp. 187–210 and pp. 277–307, respectively).

15. Wayne A. Rebhorn. "Petruchio's 'Rope Tricks': *The Taming of the Shrew* and the Renaissance Discourse of Rhetoric," *Modern Philology: A Journal Devoted to Research in Medieval and Modern Literature* 92, no. 3 (1995): 316.

16. See Jonathan Bate and Eric Rasmussen's RSC edition of *The Taming of the Shrew* (New York: Palgrave Macmillan, 2010), 21.

17. See Albert H. Tolman, "Shakespeare's Part in the '*Taming of the Shrew*,'" *PMLA* 5, no. 4 (1890): 216.

18. *The Taming of a Shrew* was "printed in 1594 and believed to derive from Shakespeare's play as performed"; see Greenblatt et al., *The Norton Shakespeare*, 227. See also Warren Chernaik, "Shakespeare at Work: Four Kings and Two Shrews," *Cahiers élisabéthains* 85 (2014): 21–39.

19. The National Institute of Mental Health (NIMH), in the US, reports that "schizophrenia is typically diagnosed in the late teens years to early thirties." See "Schizophrenia," NIMH, accessed August 25, 2021, https://www.nimh.nih.gov/health/statistics/schizophrenia#:~:text=page%20on%20Schizophrenia.,Age%2DOf%2DOnset%20for%20Schizophrenia,early%20twenties%20%E2%80%93%20early%20thirties.

The National Health Service (NHS), in the UK, says that bipolar disorder "often develops between the ages of 15 and 19 and rarely develops after 40." See "Bipolar Disorder," NHS, accessed August 25, 2021, https://www.nhs.uk/mental-health/conditions/bipolar-disorder/overview/#:~:text=Bipolar%20disorder%20can%20occur%20at,likely%20to%20develop%20bipolar%20disorder.

20. Margaret Price, *Mad at School: Rhetorics of Mental Disability and Academic Life* (Ann Arbor: University of Michigan Press, 2011), 23.

21. Ibid., 6–8. See also Jay T. Dolmage, *Academic Ableism* (Ann Arbor: University of Michigan Press, 2017). For an exposé about a psychiatrically disabled woman (with bipolar type II disorder) who—after her university recommended that she be compassionately expelled from school through medical leave—struggled to pay the bills as a sex worker, see Frances Ryan, "How Austerity is Forcing Disabled Women into Sex Work," *The Guardian*, June 5, 2019, https://www.theguardian.com/society/2019/jun/05/austeristy-forcing-disabled-women-into-sex-work.

22. Hilary Clark. "Invisible Disorder: Passing as an Academic," in *Illness in the Academy: A Collection of Pathographies by Academics*, ed. Kimberly Rena Myers (West Lafayette: Purdue UP, 2007), 128. For additional descriptions of managing academic life alongside mental illness, see Shayda Kafai's and John Derby's essays in *Disability Studies Quarterly* 33, no. 1 (2013).

23. See Margaret Price et al., "Disclosure of Mental Disability by College and University Faculty: The Negotiation of Accommodations, Supports, and Barriers," in *Disability Studies Quarterly* 37, no. 2 (2017); Elizabeth J. Donaldson, "Beyond A Beautiful Mind: Schizophrenia and Bioethics in the Classroom," in *Disability Studies Quarterly* 35, no. 2 (2015); Daniel Jackson, *Portraits of Resilience* (Cambridge: MIT Press, 2017).

24. Becky S. Friedman's powerful talk on *The Jew of Malta* at the 2021 Renaissance Society of America conference, "The 'Evil Affected' Jew of the Early Modern Stage," made me realize that this quote from *The Merchant of Venice*, which I analyzed briefly in my PhD dissertation, was part of a much larger network of imagery that stereotyped Jews as melancholic.

25. For a fantastic discussion of *The Tempest*'s depiction of theatrical violence, see Reut Barzilai, "'In My Power': *The Tempest* as Shakespeare's Antitheatrical Vision," *Shakespeare* 15, no. 4 (2019): 379–397.

REFERENCES

Arcola Theatre. "No Show." Accessed August 25, 2021. https://www.arcolathe-atre.com/whats-on/no-show/

———. "Headlines." Accessed August 25, 2021. https://www.arcolatheatre.com/whats-on/headlines/

———. "The Pleasure of Your Bedlam." Accessed August 25, 2021. https://www.arcolatheatre.com/whats-on/the-pleasure-of-your-bedlam/

Aspinall, Dana E., ed. *The Taming of the Shrew: Critical Essays*. New York: Routledge, 2002.

Barzilai, Reut. "'In My Power': *The Tempest* as Shakespeare's Antitheatrical Vision." *Shakespeare* 15, no. 4 (2019): 379–397.

Boose, Lynda E. "Scolding Brides and Bridling Scolds: Taming the Woman's Unruly Member." In *The Taming of the Shrew: Critical Essays*, edited by Dana E. Aspinall, 130–168. New York: Routledge, 2002.

Chernaik, Warren. "Shakespeare at Work: Four Kings and Two Shrews." *Cahiers élisabéthains* 85 (2014): 21–39.

Clark, Hilary. "Invisible Disorder: Passing as an Academic." In *Illness in the Academy: A Collection of Pathographies by Academics*, edited by Kimberly Rena Myers, 123–130. West Lafayette: Purdue University Press, 2007.

Cox, Murray. *Shakespeare Comes to Broadmoor*. London: Jessica Kingsley, 1992.

Daalder, Joost. "Folly and Madness in *The Changeling*." *Essays in Criticism* 38, no. 1 (1988): 1–21.

Derby, John. "Accidents Happen: An Art Autopathography on Mental Disability." *Disability Studies Quarterly* 33, no. 1 (2013): n.p. Accessed October 12, 2021. https://dsq-sds.org/article/view/3441

Dolmage, Jay T. *Academic Ableism: Disability and Higher Education*. Anne Arbor: University of Michigan Press, 2017.

Donaldson, Elizabeth J. "Beyond *A Beautiful Mind*: Schizophrenia and Bioethics in the Classroom." *Disability Studies Quarterly* 35, no. 2 (2015): n.p. Accessed December 30, 2021. https://dsq-sds.org/article/view/4635/3934

Drouet, Pascale, "Madness and Mismanagement in Middleton and Rowley's *The Changeling*." In *Theta X: Folly and Politics*, edited by Richard Hillman and Pauline Ruberry-Blanc, 139–152. Tours: CESR, 2013.

Escolme, Bridget. *Emotional Excess on the Shakespearean Stage: Passion's Slaves*. London: Bloomsbury, 2014.

Folkerth, Wes. "Reading Shakespeare After Neurodiversity." In *Performing Disability in Early Modern English Drama*, edited by Leslie C. Dunn, 141–157. New York: Palgrave Macmillan, 2020.

Foucault, Michel. *History of Madness*, edited by Jean Khalfa. New York: Routledge, 2006.

Gascoigne, George. *Supposes and Jocasta: Two Plays Translated from the Italian, the first byGeo. Gascoigne, the Second by Geo. Gascoigne and F. Kinwelmersh*, edited by John W.Cunliffe. London: D. Heath & Co, 1906.

Jackson, Daniel. *Portraits of Resilience*. Cambridge: The MIT Press, 2017.

Jackson, Kenneth S. *Separate Theaters: Bethlem ("Bedlam") Hospital and the ShakespeareanStage*. Newark: University of Delaware Press, 2005.

Kafai, Shayda. "The Mad Border Body: A Political In-Betweeness." *Disability Studies Quarterly* 33, no. 1 (2013): n.p. Accessed October 12, 2021. https://dsq-sds.org/article/view/3438

Kingsbury, Melinda Spencer. "Kate's Froward Humor: Historicizing Affect in *The Taming of the Shrew*." *South Atlantic Review* 69, no. 1 (2004): 61–84.

Korda, Natasha. "Household Kates: Domesticating Commodities in *The Taming of the Shrew*." In *The Taming of the Shrew: Critical Essays*, edited by Dana E. Aspinall, 277–307. New York: Routledge, 2002.

Mayberry, Susan Neal. "Cuckoos and Convention: Madness in Middleton and Rowley's *The Changeling*." *Mid-Hudson Language Studies* 8 (1985): 21–32.

Middleton, Thomas, and William Rowley. *The Changeling*, edited by Joost Daalder. London: A & C Black, 1990.

National Health Service (NHS), UK. "City and Hackney Mental Health Strategy." Accessed August 25, 2021. https://www.cityandhackneyccg.nhs.uk/Downloads/news%20and%20Publications/CH%20JOINT%20MH%20STRATGEY_FINAL_OCT%2019.pdf

———. "Overview—Bipolar Disorder." Accessed August 25, 2021. https://www.nhs.uk/mental-health/conditions/bipolar-disorder/overview/#:~:text=Bipolar%20disorder%20can%20occur%20at,likely%20to%20develop%20bipolar%20disorder

National Institute of Mental Health (NIMH), US. "Schizophrenia." Accessed August 25, 2021. https://www.nimh.nih.gov/health/statistics/schizophrenia#:~:text=page%20on%20Schizophrenia.,Age%2DOf%2DOnset%20for%20Schizophrenia,early%20twenties%20%E2%80%93%20early%20thirties

Neely, Carol Thomas. *Distracted Subjects: Madness and Gender in Shakespeare and EarlyModern Culture*. Ithaca: Cornell University Press, 2004.

Orlin, Lena Cowen. "The Performance of Things in *The Taming of the Shrew*." In *The Taming of the Shrew: Critical Essays*, edited by Dana E. Aspinall, 187–210. New York: Routledge, 2002.

Price, Margaret. *Mad at School: Rhetorics of Mental Disability and Academic Life*. Anne Arbor: University of Michigan Press, 2011.

———. Mark S. Salzer, Amber O'Shea, and Stephanie L. Kerschbaum. "Disclosure of Mental Disability by College and University Faculty: The Negotiation of Accommodations, Supports, and Barriers." *Disability Studies Quarterly* 37, no. 2 (2017): n.p. Accessed December 30, 2021. https://dsq-sds.org/article/view/5487/4653

Rebhorn, Wayne A. "Petruchio's 'Rope Tricks': *The Taming of the Shrew* and the Renaissance Discourse of Rhetoric." *Modern Philology: A Journal Devoted to Research in Medievaland Modern Literature* 92, no. 3 (1995): 294–327.

Ryan, Frances. "How Austerity is Forcing Disabled Women into Sex Work." *The Guardian,* June 5, 2019. https://www.theguardian.com/society/2019/jun/05/austeristy-forcing-disabled-women-into-sex-work?CMP=Share_iOSApp_Other&fbclid=IwAR3TWtgfDzVe2%2D%2DQlAbl1kbD3BOmjZUYlSxYVEfYKDNotEkprYGBMCnGQkU.

Salkeld, Duncan, *Madness and Drama in the Age of Shakespeare.* Manchester: Manchester University Press, 1993.

Shakespeare, William. *A Midsummer Night's Dream.* In *The Norton Shakespeare,* edited by Stephen Greenblatt, Walter Cohen, Jean E. Howard, and Katherine Eisaman Maus. New York: W. W. Norton, 2008a.

———. *Hamlet.* In *The Norton Shakespeare,* edited by Stephen Greenblatt, Walter Cohen, Jean E. Howard, and Katherine Eisaman Maus. New York: W. W. Norton, 2008b.

———. *The Comedy of Errors.* In *The Norton Shakespeare,* edited by Stephen Greenblatt, Walter Cohen, Jean E. Howard, and Katherine Eisaman Maus. New York: W. W. Norton, 2008c.

———. *The Merchant of Venice.* In *The Norton Shakespeare,* edited by Stephen Greenblatt, Walter Cohen, Jean E. Howard, and Katherine Eisaman Maus. New York: W. W. Norton, 2008d.

———. *The Taming of the Shrew.* In *The Norton Shakespeare,* edited by Stephen Greenblatt, Walter Cohen, Jean E. Howard, and Katherine Eisaman Maus. New York: W. W. Norton, 2008e.

———. *The Tempest.* In *The Norton Shakespeare,* edited by Stephen Greenblatt, Walter Cohen, Jean E. Howard, and Katherine Eisaman Maus. New York: W. W. Norton, 2008f.

———. *The Two Noble Kinsmen.* In *The Norton Shakespeare,* edited by Stephen Greenblatt, Walter Cohen, Jean E. Howard, and Katherine Eisaman Maus. New York: W. W. Norton, 2008g.

———. *Timon of Athens.* In *The Norton Shakespeare,* edited by Stephen Greenblatt, Walter Cohen, Jean E. Howard, and Katherine Eisaman Maus. New York: W. W. Norton, 2008h.

———. *The Taming of the Shrew,* edited by Jonathan Bate and Eric Rasmussen. New York: Palgrave Macmillan, 2010.

Sheradin, Ed. "Hackney's diagnosed depression rates highest of any London borough." *Hackney Citizen,* May 14, 2019. https://www.hackneycitizen.co.uk/2019/05/14/hackney-depression-rates-highest-any-london-borough/

Stott, Andrew. "Tiresias and the Basilisk: Vision and Madness in Middleton and Rowley's *The Changeling.*" *Revista Alicantina De Estudios Ingleses,* 12 (1999): 165–179.

Tavener, Ben. "From Stratford to Rio: Using Shakespeare to Treat Mental Illness." *BBC News*, 12 April, 2015. https://www.bbc.co.uk/news/health-32241100

Tolman, Albert H. "Shakespeare's Part in *The Taming of the Shrew*.'" *PMLA* 5, no. 4 (1890): 201–278.

Tower Theatre. "The Bacchae." Accessed August 25, 2021. https://www.towertheatre.org.uk/event/lands17/

Accessing Shakespeare in Performance: Northern Michigan University's Stratford Festival Endowment Fund

David Houston Wood

To anyone considering this class: do it. Your mind will be blown, you will make incredible friendships, learn incredible things, witness magic on stage, develop opinions on staging, see world class actors (maybe even meet a few) [;] but be warned: your standards for theater will rise and you may find your local theater doesn't quite measure up to your expectations anymore.— Student A (Double Majors: English Secondary Education/Spanish)

D. H. Wood (✉)
Northern Michigan University, Marquette, MI, USA
e-mail: dwood@nmu.edu

© The Author(s), under exclusive license to Springer Nature
Switzerland AG 2023
S. Freeman Loftis et al. (eds.), *Inclusive Shakespeares*, Palgrave
Shakespeare Studies,
https://doi.org/10.1007/978-3-031-26522-8_7

115

A GIFT BEYOND MEASURE: OUR BENEFACTOR, PROFESSOR BOB DORNQUAST

"The most important theater we ever encounter as individuals is the theater we encounter when we're young." His snowy hair and beard glinting in the sun, the black frames of his glasses resting on his ruddy cheeks, the aging professor once again is holding court. He waves his well-worn pipe in a broad circle in the air, clearly relishing the moment. My group of university students and I fan around him on a grassy knoll outside the Stratford Festival's famed Tom Patterson Theater in Stratford, Ontario, Canada. It is 2009, and, along with my students, I consider these words deeply. This moment took place on the first of what has proved to be more than a decade's run of such annual university trips to the Stratford Festival, each of which has allowed me to do something utterly transformative: to introduce professional theater to university undergraduates who never imagined they would get the chance to encounter it. In this chapter, I plan to explain some of my experiences in this role in the hope that interested faculty in your neck of the woods— maybe even you, whatever your location and your circumstances—might bring about something similar for your students.

Clad in a bright yellow t-shirt splashed with Shakespeare's image, chinos, and distinctive tie-dyed basketball sneakers, it's easy to see that Northern Michigan University (NMU) Professor Emeritus Bob Dornquast is back in his element. Since his retirement in 1998, by his own admission, he'd been flailing a bit. Having accepted an early retirement, he'd realized in retrospect that while this decision had been a wise one financially, it had been a poor one professionally: he felt he still had a lot more teaching to do. As a teacher of rhetoric in our university's Communications Department, for decades he'd led a few lucky students each summer to the Stratford Festival. While not the closest professional theater to NMU, Stratford offers a unique repertory theatrical experience that he felt justified the travel. Some of those trips, he knew, had been the highlights of his career. In 1998, his time at NMU coming to a close, he decided to meet with the university's Foundation Office and, ultimately, to do something remarkable.

Professor Bob (as he insists people call him) made the weighty decision to donate a significant sum of money to NMU, which, in those halcyon days, the Foundation Office agreed to match. Titled the "Stratford Festival Endowment Fund," these monies (along with additional gifts I've solicited from donors in the ensuing years) have grown over the decades into a considerable sum. He wisely housed the Fund in the College of Arts and Sciences rather than in any one academic department. This decision has allowed for the casting of a wider net for student-participants than limiting it merely to students headed into a specific major. Since that summer in 2009, I have honored Bob's original mission, and also, with his permission, developed it a bit: I increased the size of the trip to include ten students, and also found a way to link this annual, week-long trip to formal academic credit.

I operate this excursion based on the premise that the sentiment Professor Bob expressed in 2009 remains absolutely correct: that introducing professional theater to young people who likely would not otherwise access it is most important because it allows such students to develop a baseline for evaluating theater that will last them a lifetime as theatergoers. I continued to enjoy many a performance with Professor Bob over the next few years, until he was forced to cease participation due to health reasons. Appreciating a performance with Bob, as I recall, always began with his perusal of the sea of white-haired people in the audience; he's passionately expressed to me over the years that he fears for the future of the arts. Accordingly, he claims his principal goal is to create a savvy class of youths who will, in time, share their passion for the arts with subsequent generations. As the steward of Professor Bob's wishes, and his Fund, that has been my attempt, as well:

> I remember the energy of the town more than anything else, I've never been to a place like Stratford; it felt so welcoming and connected, the whole town felt excited by the Festival. Very cool energy! (Student B, Double Majors: Medicinal Plant Chemistry/German)

Where We're Coming From: Our Region, Our University, Our Students

Like so many "directional" state universities across the United States, NMU serves as what is familiarly called a "regional comprehensive" institution, with nearly 7000 students (mostly undergraduates). Nestled midway along the southern shore of our inland sea, Lake Superior (containing 10% of the world's surface fresh water), the university enjoys a dramatic location in Michigan's Upper Peninsula (the U.P.), on the northern fringe of Marquette, a friendly town of some 23,000 residents. Enjoying a measure of recent, tourism-driven economic growth, Marquette neverthe-less continues to remain remarkably isolated. Not unlike the stony islands off its shoreline, the town is surrounded by hundreds of square miles of wooded wilderness, which span in large part the whole of the U.P. The traditional home to the indigenous Anishanaabe people (now roughly 4% of the population), the region has also attracted, over the last three centu-ries, numerous European immigrants seeking employment. These groups include individuals of French Canadian, Cornish, German, Italian, and, especially, Finnish descent. The U.P. includes the largest grouping of Finns outside of Finland, in fact. Statistically, the region comprises 33% of the state of Michigan's land mass, but contains only 3% of its people.

Contributing to this sense of isolation, the region finds itself buried each winter under hundreds and hundreds of inches of snow, which its residents enjoy to the full in terms of both recreation and self-identity: Yoopers ("U.P.-ers"), as the people of our region term themselves, are remarkably proud and independent. The region has been famous since the seventeenth century for a series of extraction industries, including fur, lumber, copper, and iron ore. However, little to none of that extracted wealth has remained in the U.P.: in fact, as a region, the U.P. remains one of the poorest rural areas in the US, with a poverty rate, in 2020, of 15.6%.[1] Beyond a handful of towns of any size (Marquette, Houghton, and Sault Ste. Marie) endemic poverty among its rural residents is perva-sive. NMU was founded in 1899 as a normal (teaching) university, and has played a key role since its founding in educating the youth of the region, though in recent years it has seen an increase in out of state students. The school attracts a certain type of student: outdoorsy, adventurous, quietly inquisitive, and generally quite career-minded. First-generation college students at NMU comprise fully 35% of the population.

Since I began my position in the English Department at NMU in August 2007, I have made access and inclusion of these bright, first-generation students a main priority in my teaching. To my great joy, they tend to take themselves and their educations very seriously. In addition to my training as a scholar of English Renaissance drama, I've also developed over the years a helpful array of life experiences that contribute to this trip. Back in the late 1990s, for example, I earned a Commercial Driver's License (CDL) during a period in which I served as a tour guide for the Northern Alaska Tour Company, based in Fairbanks, Alaska. That training comes in handy in alleviating student (and parental) concern regarding our transport to Ontario, Canada—which, of course, features me at the wheel. As any map will inform you, Marquette is a remarkable distance from Stratford, Ontario. Students often chuckle when I point out that we actually face a ten-hour drive *south* in order to arrive at our destination in Canada:

> [I]t was really refreshing to be in an environment where all of the students were totally engaged with the material and ready to provide a lot of feedback and talking points. I can remember some really amazing discussions my classmates and I had over dinner at various Stratford eating establishments. Post-trip, I still love to talk about Shakespeare, and I try to see new productions whenever possible. I don't know if that habit is entirely due to my Stratford experience, but I do know that Stratford gave me more confidence in myself to interact with the theater and with other theater-goers. If anything, I think Stratford has led me to pay more attention to how others perceive the theater. (Student C, Major: Political Science; Minor: Religion)

THE MECHANICS OF THE TRIP

The mechanics of the trip are rather simple. In the autumn, when the Festival announces its theater schedule for the upcoming year, I meet up with the trip's Co-Leader, Dr. Chet DeFonso, NMU Associate Professor of History, with specialties in British and Canadian history. We debate the Festival's theatrical offerings for the period of our visit, always during the third week in August. Recently singled out in *The New York Times* as one of the finest repertory theater experiences in North America, the Festival offers four different theaters of various size and scope, simultaneously running two different plays per day.[2] Not only can our group enjoy six different plays during this three-day window, that is, but we can also include two popular tours: the first, of the Festival Theater, featuring a thrust stage designed by Tyrone Guthrie in the 1950s; and the second, of the Wardrobe Warehouse, a new space containing three football fields of space crammed full with all sorts of theatrical costuming and set pieces. After we come to an agreement regarding our schedule— as an example, in 2017: "Well, if we see Euripides' *Bakkhai* on Wednesday at 2pm, we'll be able to catch *Twelfth Night* at 8pm; and if we see *Timon of Athens* on Thursday at 2pm, we'll still be able to catch Middleton & Rowley's *The Changeling* at 8pm, which we missed in order to see Moliere's *Tartuffe* at 2pm on Tuesday"— I purchase the tickets in December through the Festival's helpful "Groups & Schools Department," and begin to promote the course to prospective students in January.

As for selecting our student-participants, I've come to believe that Professor Bob's directive for doing so, however counterintuitive, is genuinely inspired. Rather than look to prospective students' academic majors or minors, or even to their GPAs, Professor Bob requests that the only consideration we should heed is our reaction to their responses to a rhetorical exercise: all applicants have 500 words in which to make the case, in writing, for what this trip will mean to them now and to their possible, future selves. That's it. The plus here is that students of all majors have a relatively equal shot at succeeding in their applications. For every theater or English major accepted for the trip, that is, we've had a slew of pre-med students, education majors, geology majors, nursing majors, and Spanish majors. Good writers, after all, come in all sorts of packages, and so do students attracted to such a unique cultural opportunity.

There are many incentives for students to join a trip like this one. Based upon Professor Bob's financial backing, the trip is as close to free for the students as we can possibly make it. The Fund fully covers all theater tickets (in the finest A+ and A seats), all lodging, and all travel costs. In addition, we also employ the Fund to cover at least two formal meals, including a luncheon banquet we host at a terrific restaurant, The Parlour, at which we formally toast our Benefactor, Professor Bob (whether he's present or attending only in spirit). Since 2011, the success of our trip has also attracted several of NMU's theater-minded, governor-appointed Trustees to join us (who, in turn, have contributed financially to the Fund). Some of my fondest Stratford memories involve the Trustees' reactions to our students' incisive comments regarding a specific performance we've all just encountered, or to a specific student's excitement regarding an upcoming show. At least in some measure, the reason for the students' insights hinges on the meticulous preparation for the trip that I demand of them as the sole Instructor for the academic portion of the course, and to what ends their work is ultimately headed: a 20-page research paper, based upon both text and performance:

> This trip allowed me to see world class theater that many people do not get the chance to see, and the class allowed me to truly analyze and appreciate it. To complete the class, I wrote a 20-page paper on the agency of the female characters in *The Merry Wives of Windsor*. Never before did I think that I could write 20 pages on a topic that was completely out of my usual realm as a Biology major, but for the rest of my life I can proudly say that I wrote a 20-page paper on Shakespeare. And, not only did I write it, but I under-

stood it and found it quite interesting. I think this class is worthwhile for any student in any major as long as they are curious and excited to learn. I am so grateful for this experience and will carry it with me through my life. (Student E, Major: Biology)

The Mechanics of the Course

Due to this travel course's odd fit in the academic calendar, it was recently singled out for special analysis in a visit by the US Higher Learning Commission (2018). Ultimately, the trip and its associated classes were strongly praised— and it's not hard to see why, honestly. Once we select the ten student-participants, each one signs up for a Fall semester, full-credit course in either of two ways: (1) as "English 385: the Stratford Festival Experience"; or (2) as "Honors 495: the Stratford Festival Experience." While neither class specifically fulfills any university Gen Ed credit, the first can contribute toward undergraduate coursework credit in drama, for English majors; and the second as Upper Division Honors coursework, within our NMU Honors Program. As an additional bonus, situating the courses within the fall semester means that participating students need not pay additional summer school fees.

In the months preceding our trip, our group engages in two organizational meetings: the first in March, with NMU's International Programs Office (even from Michigan, travel to Canada is international in scope, of course); and the second in April, to establish the academic components of the class. Our meeting with International Programs can be eye-opening for our students, most of whom have never traveled before and certainly not abroad. NMU levies a $150 fee for travel insurance from each student, and the International Programs representative proceeds to discuss behavioral matters and other such topics, including the process by which students will attain their first passports. It is crucial for us to do so: over the years, at least a few of our students have fully dropped out of this experience simply because they were too nervous to complete the passport process until it was too late.

At our second meeting, in April, I distribute the course syllabi, each of which we discuss at length. I follow up this meeting in early summer by sending the students a series of multi-page reading worksheets (one for each play), and links to secondary readings including both scholarly essays (for Shakespeare plays, the relevant chapters in Marjorie Garber's *Shakespeare After All* are always insightful), and a series of reviews from other theatrical stagings of the plays that we will be encountering.[3] One of the things we've learned is the importance of setting the students' expectations regarding the vibrant range of adaptative possibilities of live theater. Given this preparatory work, once we meet up for our trip in August, the students are hyper-prepared, excited as can be, and itching to talk all about it.

The trip itself is unique to our geographical circumstances, of course. We depart on Monday morning of our travel week, driving six hours to Birch Run, MI. At our midway point on this leg of the drive, we cross the Mackinac Bridge— a.k.a., the "Mighty Mac"— which connects Michigan's Upper and Lower Peninsulas, and I'm always astounded at the number of my students who've never yet crossed this bridge: one year, it was fully half the van. After our group dinner in Birch Run, we meet up for a multi-hour discussion of the two plays we'll encounter on Tuesday. The following morning, we drive the final four hours to Stratford, and at the midway point of this second leg, we cross the border at Port Huron/Sarnia. Once we enter Canada, student excitement builds and builds. Arriving in Stratford, we grab lunch at Bentley's, a downtown restaurant where it's easy to reserve a big table in the back for our full crew. As we dine, I present to each student a copy of the season's Stratford Festival Visitor's Guide, which the Festival scatters freely across Stratford's various downtown establishments. It helpfully contains key information on every play that season, ads for regional cafes, restaurants, and used bookstores, as well as an array of useful maps pertaining to the town and its theaters. By 1:30, we're heading off to our first production. Here is a sample itinerary for our 2022 trip:

Monday, August 22: Depart Marquette, MI (11am); drive to Birch Run, MI (arrive c.5pm). A quiet hour, then dinner, followed by multi-hour class session in the hotel Business Center regarding the two plays we will be encountering on Tuesday. Students then write a 500–750-word essay, to be turned in next morning at breakfast.

Tuesday, August 23: Depart Birch Run, MI (7am); arrive in Stratford, Ontario (c.11am, depending on our border-crossing experience). Continue our discussion informally throughout the day, including at lunch when we arrive in Stratford. Then view Moliere's *The Miser* (2pm), followed by a discussion of this adaptation. Dinner on your own, and then view the hit musical *Chicago* (8pm). Another class discussion, followed by students writing their 500–750 word essays to be turned in next morning.

Wednesday, August 24: Continue our discussion of the previous day's events and anticipate today's over conversation during breakfast, followed by a 1-hour Festival Theatre Tour (9:30am). Then some down time with lunch on your own in Stratford. Then view *Richard III* (2pm), followed by class discussion of this adaptation. Dinner on your own, and then view *Hamlet* (8pm). Another class discussion, followed by students writing their 500–750 word essays.

Thursday, August 25: After breakfast, a 1-hour Wardrobe Warehouse Tour (10am). Then a formal lunch at 12noon at The Parlour, joined by four NMU Trustees. Conversation, and a toast to our Benefactor. Then view Alcott's *Little Women* (2pm), followed by a class discussion of this adaptation. Then dinner on your own, and then meet up to see Soyinka's *Death and the King's Horseman* (8pm). Another class discussion, followed by students writing their 500–750 word essays.

Friday, August 26: Continue our discussion of the previous day's events as we start our long drive back to Marquette.

This trip was the experience that ultimately led me to choose a second study abroad experience in college. I always had felt like such trips would be out of my reach financially and didn't align with my Chemistry major, but Stratford got my foot in the door and led me to see myself as having the ability to travel much more. I stopped limiting myself and what I felt like I could complete after the trip. Stratford also shifted what I had an interest in seeing in other countries and cities! This trip was one of the most transformative experiences in my early college years and it was the best thing I could have done for myself. I met so many amazing people and had so much fun; it was a big step for me and it felt a little scary. It pushed me out of my comfort zone in all of the ways that I needed to be pushed and helped me grow: I wouldn't trade the experience for anything else! (Student B, Majors: Medicinal Plant Chemistry/German)

SOME TRAVEL TIPS FOR STRATFORD, AND OUR RETURN TO NMU

Two things worth noting: for student groups, the cheapest lodging in Stratford can be found at the Stratford General Hospital (SGH) Residences. The SGH rooms are quite spartan, befitting a budget experience, but the fees for the Residences include both a fine breakfast and access to a leafy courtyard, which can be a great space for holding discussions on a trip like this one. Frankly, though, Stratford is full of such spaces. Over the years, I've held talks outside each and every theater (often joined by other intrigued theatergoers), and at a number of outdoor parks, especially those which surround the bucolic grounds of the Festival Theater.

The second item worth noting involves the students' nightly writing assignments. I insist that students complete these assignments for three reasons: (1) so that I can see what they are thinking about the day's events (how did the day's plays thwart their expectations? for example); (2) so that the students will have a written record of their initial impressions of these dramatic experiences, which, in time, will become crucial components of their research projects; and (3) so that I can keep them relatively busy each night … and thus, ideally, out of trouble. Given the draining excitement of the day, and that nightly writing assignment, we've honestly never had any behavioral problems on this trip.

As for the remainder of the course: once we return to the NMU campus, we begin the fall semester with weekly, formal class meetings for a month or so, during which students recount their reactions and develop specific areas of interest for their research projects. Over the subsequent two months, each student and I engage in a series of one-on-one tutorials, in which they hone their theses, develop their evidence, and engage in thoughtful analysis of it. By this point, each essay is often juggling the play-text, the student's memories of the Stratford performance (bolstered by their journal entries), an array of secondary scholarship on the play, possible film adaptations, and formal theatrical reviews of that performance and perhaps of other productions. Throughout this process, the students come to sense the thrill of shaping their ideas, with some guidance, into their substantial research projects.

Over the years, I've garnered some keen student reactions to specific productions. One student, an English major with a minor in Film Studies, shares his experience:

Being able to attend the festival through NMU gave me not only the opportunity to see world class theatre, but also to consider it in ways that I hadn't before; whether it be Robert LePage's *Coriolanus* that still blows my mind when I think about it (the only way I've been able to aptly describe it is as "live-action cinema"), or the subdued yet powerful performance of *Long Day's Journey into Night*. Ultimately, I felt that attending the Stratford Festival was one of the first times that I felt I was able to truly see such a dynamic and diverse array of what theatre has to offer.

Another student, a Biochemistry major, was also impressed with that same LePage production:

That production of *Coriolanus* is one of the plays that pushed the boundary of what I understood theater can be. It felt like it was remaining honest to the text while the special effects (some of which I still remember so vividly) felt so innovative in a way that didn't feel like a gimmick to modernize and reinvent the story. I remember leaning forward out of my seat throughout almost the entirety of the play because it felt so exciting to watch and to be a part of that audience. The minute it was over, I immediately felt like I would have loved to sit through it all over again.

Another student, a Pre-Dental major, observes of a very different play:

When I think back to Stratford, I can still feel how hard I laughed at the 2019 performance of *The Merry Wives of Windsor*. It took me by surprise— after all, I had read the play already, analyzed the jokes on paper. But the moment an aggressively exaggerated French accent rebounded through the theatre, my fate was sealed. I physically covered my mouth with my hand, unbearably yet eagerly awaiting the next lines. How could reading with my own inner voice ever compare with such a performance?! I could have attended that play with my eyes closed and still treasured the experience.

Of another play which she found especially fascinating, the same student notes:

The performance of *The Front Page* stood out the most to me— enough to make me desire to write a 20-page essay on it! The Stratford performance took the original script—which I admittedly loved before even arriving in

Canada—and created a female-centered version of it, amazingly. I remember I both adored and questioned these changes. I was intrigued enough to seek out other variations of the script and watched two movies based on it in order to write my research paper.

Another student, a Chemistry major, observes:

While in Stratford, we saw a performance of *Oedipus Rex* that transformed the story for me and allowed me to connect to it in a way that I hadn't ever before. There was a moment where Oedipus himself bursts onto the stage, covered in blood and completely nude, and delivers his final monologue. This scene, just as powerful as it was shocking, allowed me to fully understand his desperation in these last moments, and to this day, this is one of my favorite theater performances of all time.

CONCLUSION

But the very first thing we do upon our return from Stratford to the NMU campus is in some ways the most important. I arrange, through NMU Catering, a formal luncheon to which I invite our students, the participating NMU Trustees, the NMU President, the NMU Provost, and, chiefly, our Benefactor: Professor Bob himself. At this event, during which everyone beams as the students buzz about their Festival experiences, Bob is surely the most pleased of all. Each year, like clockwork, he shares the sentiment he'd uttered in 2009 on the importance of providing young people with access to professional theater, and now he goes a step further: "Through my gift, I have done you this service. But it is my fervent wish that years and years from now, in your own unimaginable futures, you too will do the same for others. I know you will."

It's hard to put into words how much this annual Stratford Festival experience has meant to me both professionally and personally over the years. It's worth noting that during this same period I've led students on countless other theatrically-oriented trips, some closer in proximity to Marquette than Stratford, to be honest (to the Guthrie Theater, in Minneapolis; the Chicago Shakespeare Theater at Navy Pier; the Milwaukee Repertory Theater; the Milwaukee Symphony; and the Milwaukee Opera Company), and some much further afield (to the Royal Shakespeare Company and Shakespeare's Globe Theater). Each of these trips offered experiences for my students that were undoubtedly amazing. In retrospect, though, I largely consider such trips one-offs. I guess I've found that only a proper repertory theater experience, like that offered at the Stratford Festival, justifies the long drive and the immersive week-long trip I most want to lead.

In the end, I encourage you— as university faculty with a bent toward drama of any sort—to consider your own interests and abilities: to befriend your school's Foundation Office in search of a donor or two, however modest; to survey a map to locate some national, regional (or, if you're lucky, local) professional theatrical prospects; and to meet with your Department Head, Dean, and even your university's Provost in order to harness additional institutional support. Professor Bob's donation continues to provide access to professional theater for young people who quite reasonably might never have considered it a possibility in their lives. His Fund has helped me shepherd into the world more than 120 veterans of his Stratford Festival Experience, each of them excited about live theater and ready to pay that love forward. It is an honor for me to continue to celebrate the goals of our Benefactor, Professor Bob, by stewarding at my university his impossibly generous gift.

NOTES

1. See Murembya (2020). For more on the Upper Peninsula and the results of its extraction economy, see Bellfy (2021).
2. See Isherwood (2016).
3. See Garber (2004).

REFERENCES

Bellfy, Phil. 2021. *U.P. Colony: The Story of Resource Exploitation in Upper Michigan: Focus on Sault Sainte Marie Industries.* Ann Arbor, MI: Ziibi Press.

Garber, Marjorie. 2004. *Shakespeare After All.* New York: Anchor Books.

Isherwood, Charles. 2016. "In Praise of Repertory Theater: Macbeth at the Matinee; Miller at Night." https://www.nytimes.com/2016/08/14/theater/repertory-theater.html. *The New York Times.* August 11.

Murembya, Leonidas. 2020. "2020 ANNUAL PLANNING INFORMATION AND WORKFORCE ANALYSIS REPORTS: UPPER PENINSULA." http://milmi.org_docs/publications/PlanningReports2020/Region_1.pdf

PART II

Inclusive Shakespeares in Pedagogy

Blackfishing Complexions: Shakespeare, Passing, and the Politics of Beauty

Kelly Duquette

When white feminists catalogue how beauty standards over time have changed, from the "curvier" Marilyn Monroe ... to the synthetic-athletic Pamela Anderson, their archetypes belie beauty's true function: whiteness... Whiteness is a violent sociocultural regime legitimized by property to always make clear who is black by fastidiously delineating who is officially white. It would stand to reason that beauty's ultimate function is to exclude blackness.—(Cottom 2019: 44–45)

When Ophelia DeVore hit the New York fashion scene in 1938, the sixteen-year-old model had no plans of becoming the Vogue School of Modeling's first African American graduate. Toward the end of her studies there, she was shocked to learn of the school's refusal to admit another Black candidate. It was only then that she realized the institution's error: Vogue School misidentified DeVore's race, mistaking her light skin for

K. Duquette (✉)
Georgia Institute of Technology, Atlanta, GA, USA
e-mail: kduquette3@gatech.edu

S. Freeman Loftis et al. (eds.), *Inclusive Shakespeares*, Palgrave Shakespeare Studies,
https://doi.org/10.1007/978-3-031-26522-8_8

131

white. "I didn't know that they didn't know," she admits, "I thought they knew what I was" (Gainer 2012).

Racial "passing" in America is a response to white supremacy, an ideology engineered to make spaces inhabitable for people of color. Passing has a painful and complex past; it is a state akin to exile. As historian Allyson Hobbes explains, this exile is "sometimes chosen, sometimes not... To pass as white was to make an anxious decision to turn one's back on a black racial identity and to claim to belong to a group to which one was not legally assigned" (Hobbs 2014: 4–5). A sense of loss often accompanied such impossible decisions. James Weldon Johnson, for example, once described racial passing as "sell[ing] one's birthright for a mess of pottage" (Johnson 1995: 100; Hobbs 2014: 6). Yet many Black Americans saw passing as the only chance to survive slavery or escape the oppression of the Jim Crow South.

Racial passing in early modern literature is well documented (Thompson 2011; Espinosa 2021; Corredera 2015; Iyengar 2004). Images of beauty in Shakespeare's sonnets, I argue, helped create a world where whiteness is an assumption, where fair complexions are "vogue." Images of cosmetic fairness, like those in the sonnets, inform a world where I and other white cisgender women like me have rarely—if ever—felt excluded walking the makeup aisles of a drugstore. Black-owned beauty lines like Sharon Chuter's UOMA Beauty, singer Rihanna's Fenty Beauty, and the 2021 relaunch of Fashion Fair Cosmetics, originally created by Ebony and *Jet* magazine's co-founder Eunice Johnson, are changing the industry to be more inclusive, ensuring that Black women, like former international model, Kimberly Kearse-Lane, do not have to "mix three different colors" in order to achieve shades close to their natural skin tones (Kearse-Lane 2022). While DeVore's racial passing was not a conscious act of concealment, her story reveals the complex challenges unique to racially ambiguous individuals making their way in an exclusive world of fashion dominated by white standards of beauty. In this chapter, I argue that attending to scholarship emerging out of the 1960s Black is Beautiful Movement offers students of Shakespeare a new understanding of racism in the discourse of beauty. Dating back to at least Shakespeare's day, the cosmetic industry's Eurocentric marketing schemes have marginalized women of color all over the world. The work of advocate-entrepreneurs like Ophelia DeVore and Caroline Jones resisted these efforts to define "Black beauty" as an emulation of whiteness.

Recently, there has been an alarming increase of Black cultural appropriation among white women in the form of "race fishing," or "Blackfishing," which sociologist Shirley Anne Tate defines as an engagement in "racial cosplay for material and social gain," or staking a "false claim" to Blackness (Tate 2012: 212). Because beauty's "ultimate function" is to exclude Blackness, as Tressie McMillam Cottom reminds us, Blackfishing not only commodifies and fetishizes Black beauty but also risks erasing histories of feminist resistance and Black liberation (Cottom 2019: 45). Scholars of early modern literature should position Shakespeare within more inclusive contexts of beauty movements led by women of color. We must responsibly attend to histories of white supremacy that have excluded Blackness from notions of beauty and, at the same time, elevate the voices of its most persistent critics.

To what extent, then, might the 1960s Black is Beautiful Movement be characterized as inclusive? On the one hand, Black activists and artists rejected or excluded white standards of beauty to create safe spaces for all shades of Blackness to be embraced as beautiful. In this way, the Movement appropriated beauty itself as form of Blackness. On the other hand, it celebrated Blackness in its many forms to expand and revise a previously exclusive notion of beauty, subsuming Blackness into existing norms of beauty. I argue, as many others have before me, that any assessment of inclusivity must be rooted in stories of Black feminist resistance. For to be Black and beautiful is not only a question of race but also gender. When Shakespeare critics and teachers insist, as Kim Hall has suggested, on protecting Shakespeare and his poems as "universal" or as praise of an abstract "beauty," rather than as "specific cultural productions that manage fairness," they produce the "invisibility that fuels white hegemony" (Hall 1998: 80–81). The sonnets, as Hall has argued, can teach students about the complicity of cosmetics in the pre-modern creation of racial and gender categories, and more precisely, artificial productions of whiteness (Hall 1996). Positioning this history alongside a modern context of Black aesthetic liberation, then, can enable students to identify how "Blackfishing" and similar performances not only rehearse harmful tropes dating back to the early modern period but also risk whitewashing historically politicized notions of Black beauty.

EARLY MODERN COSMETICS AND RACE

Early modern scholarship on cosmetics facilitates our understanding of race in the period. As Farah Karim-Cooper explains, the social meaning of cosmetics in the early modern period was subject to the status of the woman wearing it (Karim-Cooper 2019: 37). Cosmetic paints were a material link between the private and public domain. A woman painted herself or was painted within the secret walls of her chamber, and she showed her face in the public sphere (Karim-Cooper 2019: 37). The paradox of cosmetic paint, Karim-Cooper suggests, is that it simultaneously conceals and displays. In her research, Kimberly Poitevin takes up this paradox of cosmetic practice and examines the ways whiteface conceals and displays racial tensions in ordinary life and on stage (Poitevin 2011: 59). Poitevin considers the ways in which women used cosmetics to create racial identities in early modern England, a nation that, throughout the sixteenth and seventeenth centuries, was increasingly defining itself through contact with foreign peoples. She argues that "just as blackface performances by actors on early modern stages worked to fuse blackness with racial difference in the English imagination, so too did the whiteface cosmetic practices of women in daily life promote a notion of white English identity that would eventually be embraced by both sexes" (Poitevin 2011: 59). Domestic manuals, dramatic works, and anti-cosmetic tracts often likened English women who used makeup to foreign others. In Thomas Tuke's *A Discourse Against Painting and Tincturing of Women* (1616), for example, women who use cosmetics are considered "barbarous people, which delight in painting their skinne" (Poitevin 2011: 66; Tuke 1616: 17). In Tuke's estimation, an effort to conceal a dull complexion displays a woman's proximity to otherness. This kind of cosmetic concealment, as Frances Dolan has argued, was often read by Tuke and others as an act of "transgressive female creativity" (Dolan 1993: 232).

Skin color in the early modern period had become an increasingly important signifier, not just of beauty, but of class, nation, and race. In descriptions of women's uses of cosmetics, the colors red and white dominate. Poitevin explains that when Dudley Carleton expressed his displeasure at Queen Anne's performance in Ben Jonson's *The Masque of Blackness* (1605), he suggested that the paint covering the ladies' skin "became them nothing so well as their red and white" (Herford et al. 1950; Poitevin 2011: 69). Although there are some exceptions, domestic manuals for manufacturing cosmetics for the most part instructed women how to look whiter than their peers. Thomas Jeamson's book, *Artificial Embellishments* (1665), for example, promises that women who follow his advice will "with a radiant luster outshine their thickskind companions, as so many browner Nymphs" (Jeamson 1665: A4; Poitevin 2011: 70). The "browner nymphs" may have referred to sun-tanned or sunburned English (white women whose social status forced them to work outside), African women with whom travelers and city-dwellers had increasing contact, or potentially the African nymphs impersonated by Queen Anne in Jonson's *Masque of Blackness*. Jeamson's book goes on to suggest that every English woman needs his cosmetic products to be truly beautiful. She must be rosier than her pale-skinned sister and whiter than her brown ones: the perfect in-between can only be achieved with makeup. In addition to creating an idealized image of beauty using the colors red and white, racial purity or "blue-bloodness" could also be signified by painting veins on the surface of the skin. In Thomas Heywood's *The Fayre Mayde of the Exchange* (1607), the character Mall is accused of "Painting the veins upon thy breasts with blew" (1.1) (Heywood 1607). Doctor Plasterface in John Marston's play *The Malcontent* (1604) is said to be skilled "in the most exquisite... forging of veines" (2.4) (Marston 1604). In painting their faces white, their cheeks red, and their veins blue, Poitevin argues, early modern women reproduced long-standing associations of beauty with whiteness and helped solidify associations between racial difference and skin color.

"Black beauty's successive heir": Shakespeare's Sonnets

In the opening scene of Ben Jonson's *Epicoene* (1609), Truewit and Clerimont debate women's use of makeup. Clerimont admonishes cosmetics as "adulteries of art" (1.1.97), but Truewit loves "a good dressing" and suggests that women ought to "practise any art" to amend their appearance (1.1.105–106) (Jonson 1609). However, enhancing one's beauty must be executed behind closed doors: "The doing of it, not the manner ... must be private" (1.1.108, 123). The use of cosmetics is sanctioned only when done privately. In drawing the curtain back on how femininity is produced, Jonson's play inadvertently calls attention to how race happens in the early modern period. Lightening one's complexion to look more "feminine" and thereby more beautiful is desirable, so long as no one witnesses the act of whitening the complexion. It would follow that differentiating race based on skin color, or the production of whiteness, is an act meant to be concealed behind closed doors.

As Tuke and Jonson's characters allege, a fair complexion becomes "false" or deceptive when the act of "making-up" crosses out of domesticity and into the public realm. However, unlike Jonson's play and early modern cosmetics manuals, Shakespeare's sonnets afford today's instructors a unique opportunity to interrogate the long and problematic history of "fair beauty," the notion that whiteness and beauty were poetically and etymologically synonymous. Sonnet 127, specifically, provides an alternative to the exclusive models of beauty and domesticity set forth in the manuals. The poem acknowledges the artificiality of beauty along racial lines in contrasting fairness with "false beauty," ascribed to trends in women's fashion, which Shakespeare deems a "shifting change" (20.4) (Shakespeare 2015). The tension between fair and false beauty participates in a contemporary poetic conceit: cosmetic enhancement fairs the "foul" with "art's false borrowed face" (127.6) (Shakespeare 2015). A painted complexion, so the argument goes, augments reality. Makeup tricks the white male gaze.

When we read the sonnets as an ecology of beauty standards, the poems interrelate to critique relationships between race and beauty. From its opening lines, for example, Shakespeare's Sonnet 127 resounds with racial categorization:

> In the old age black was not counted fair,
> Or if it were, it bore not beauty's name.
> But now is black beauty's successive heir,
> And beauty slandered with a bastard shame. (1–4) (Shakespeare 2015)

Unsurprisingly, this exclusive ecology is centered around whiteness. For Shakespeare's speaker, the fact that Blackness is "vogue" is a source of tension. As Kim Hall has observed, Sonnet 127 brings into play the "dark/fair binarism" (Hall 1998: 75). The poet, here, praises Blackness as "beauty's successive heir" because white women's use of cosmetics undermines natural fairness. The use of cosmetics is deceptive, augmenting the appearance as something it fundamentally is not:

> For since each hand hath put on nature's pow'r,
> Fairing the foul with art's false borrowed face,

> Sweet beauty hath no name, no holy bow'r,
> But is profaned, if not lives in disgrace. (5–8) (Shakespeare 2015)

Sonnet 127 reiterates the fact that cosmetics are associated with artificial fairness and by default, a white complexion. Fairness is undesirable when it is achieved with cosmetics. The sonnet offers a notion of beauty which includes Blackness and excludes whiteness artificially achieved.

Because a white complexion is an unstable marker of beauty, as Hall argues, fairness is associated with the "duplicity of femininity" (Hall 1998: 75). It is the connection between duplicity and complexion that I emphasize here and which is vital to understanding Shakespeare's sonnets in a longer history of race and cosmetics. In Sonnet 20, the poet alleges the protean whims of feminine fashion:

> A woman's face with Nature's own hand painted
> Hast thou, the master mistress of my passion;
> A woman's gentle heart, but not acquainted
> With shifting change, as is false women's fashion. (1–4) (Shakespeare 2015)

The sonnet implies that a fair complexion, like women's fashion, is ever-changing and, more significantly, duplicitous—because it augments what "Nature's own hand painted." Because whiteness is an artificial production achieved through the use of cosmetics, it is no longer desirable. Blackness, as beauty's "successive heir," only attains that title by default. In the sonnets, Black is beautiful only when whiteness is undermined. The misogynistic tenor of the sonnets reveals the complex interplay between race and commodification. In many ways, this interplay resembles what Black feminist scholar Moya Bailey terms "misogynoir," the uniquely "co-constitutive racialized and sexist violence that befalls Black women as a result of their simultaneous and interlocking oppression at the intersection of racial and gender marginalization" (Bailey 2021: 1). The white male speaker, no longer the racial gatekeeper of fair beauty, attempts to control and limit Blackness, declaring it beauty's "heir." As Bailey adds, "Black women's bodies are never their own" (Bailey 2021: 5). The sonnets, then, set the precedent that complexions are features which can be in or out of style—they enable a reading of beauty wherein what's "beautiful" is determined by a white, male observer.

THE POLITICS OF BEAUTY: OPHELIA DEVORE AND THE MOVEMENT

While Shakespeare's sonnets subtly present race—in the form of both dark and light complexions—as shifting trends in women's fashion, the political environments of segregation and the Civil Rights Movements bear this line of thinking out in more explicit ways. Revisiting the "Black is Beautiful" movement of the 1960s, and its foundations in the 1940s, helps us understand the commodification of complexion in social media and popular culture today. The narratives of America's first Black models and fashion industry pioneers are stories of resistance and liberation. For scholars and teachers of Shakespeare, it is crucial that we acknowledge that in many ways, this liberation means freedom from the standards of white beauty rooted in English literature produced hundreds of years earlier.

Ophelia DeVore was born in Edgefield, South Carolina, in 1922. She never aspired to fashion stardom but rather stumbled upon it during her studies in New York when friends encouraged DeVore to pursue the field. She enrolled in the Vogue School of Modeling in 1938, an era when the fashion industry, schools, and jobs were overwhelmingly closed to Black women (Fox 2014). In 1946, when a second Black student sought admission to the Vogue School and was refused, DeVore realized that she had passed as white inadvertently. It wasn't her "mission" to be a model. DeVore's vision was bigger than that: she committed herself to presenting Black women "in a way that was not stereotyped" (Touré 2014). In addition to learning the modeling trade at the Vogue School, DeVore also learned how to run a school like it, one that could cater specifically to the needs of aspiring Black models.

After graduation, DeVore worked primarily for *Ebony* magazine and in 1946 founded the Grace del Marco Modeling and Talent Agency with four of her friends. Grade del Marco Models represented such notable figures as Diahann Carroll, Richard Roundtree, Cicely Tyson, and Helen Williams, often described as the first Black supermodel. Two years later, DeVore expanded the business to include a charm school, offering courses on elocution, movement, and presentation (Ophelia DeVore-Mitchell Papers, 1920–2010 1920–2010). In addition to learning ballet and social graces, among other skills, students at the charm school engaged in a curriculum designed to "bolster them inwardly, offering a counterweight to the tradition of internalized self-hatred that was many Black Americans' legacy" (Fox 2014: 21). DeVore's persistence, entrepreneurial spirit, and keen understanding of aesthetics enabled her and other Black models to undermine anti-Black attitudes in the fashion industry. Modeling was "just a vehicle" DeVore used to "communicate a positive image of [her] people... [she] wanted everybody to be accepted as human beings" (Touré 2014: 42).

Beyond her school and modeling agency, DeVore also developed a cosmetics line, produced the first beauty pageant for African American women, and served as a consultant in sales and marketing for companies targeting minority communities (Ophelia DeVore-Mitchell Papers, 1920–2010). Yet despite her work and impact on the Black is Beautiful Movement of the 1960s, popular culture attempted to whitewash and minimize DeVore's contributions to the beauty business. In October 1969, *Life Magazine* published a feature on the "Black Model Breakthrough," which failed to acknowledge DeVore's influence on the industry decades earlier. The *Life* story prioritized white modeling agencies like Ford Model Agency, many of which poached models from Grace Del Marco and other Black agencies. *Life* cited "pressure" of the Civil Rights Movement in the 1960s as the source of recent trends in ad agencies and fashion houses hiring Black models (Yale 1969: 34; Ophelia DeVore-Mitchell Papers, 1920–2010). DeVore sued *Life* in 1971 for "rewriting" the history of Black models in the fashion industry, telling *Jet* magazine the same year that the white agencies featured in the spread had "not devoted the years of struggle and sacrifice to train, develop, guide and direct Black models for business contacts" like DeVore had done for twenty-five years (Gainer 2012).

DeVore's business savvy paved the way for beauty movements in the 1960s. Her actions proved to the world that "Black is beautiful" long before Stokely Carmichael declared as much in 1966. Of course, by Carmichael's time the political environment differed quite significantly from DeVore's fashion forays of the 1940s. Black aesthetics were often mobilized in the name of political resistance or protest. The Afro, for example, originated in the United States as a style worn by Black women as a symbol of racial pride in the mid-1960s. The style, a rejection of "white" beauty standards at the height of the Black Power movement, was as fashionable as it was political (Walker 2000: 536–537). "Hair," Paulette Caldwell explains, "seems to be such a little thing. Yet it is the little things, the small everyday realities of life, that reveal the deepest meanings and values of a culture" (Caldwell 1991: 4; Taylor 2016: 106). In a 1998 article, Angela Davis, for example, lamented the Afro's status as nostalgic "hairdo," a development, she argues that, "reduces a politics of liberation to a politics of fashion" (Davis 1998: 23). Davis pointed to a 1994 fashion spread in *Vibe*, featuring an actress dressed as a "revolutionary" Angela Davis of the late 1960s. Davis argued that her likeness was used as a "commodified backdrop for advertising," because the spread neglected to cite the historical and political context that gave the image meaning and power (Walker 2000: 537).

The commodification of Black beauty and style also risks erasing the contributions of figures like Caroline Jones, who sought to increase representation of natural hair in advertising. In 1965 while working at J. Walter Thompson, Jones, one of the first female African American advertising figures, created a hypothetical campaign for a women's cosmetic line. The campaign emphasized products that could bring out the natural beauty of Black skin, rather than attempt to manipulate it with lightening products. Central to the campaign was also the idea of freedom: "freedom to wear natural hair, freedom from trips to the beauty salon, and the freedom that comes from no longer trying to emulate white beauty standards" (John W. Hartman Center for Sales, Advertising & Marketing History). However, freedom to express Black style was not as simple as embracing the Afro. Michele Wallace, for example, embraced natural hair as a commitment to "Blackness" and of her "emancipation from commercial beauty standards" (Walker 2000: 558). However, her intersectionality as "Black" and "woman" complicated these goals: "No I wasn't to wear makeup but yes I had to wear skirts that I could hardly walk in. No I wasn't to go to the beauty parlor, but yes I was to spend countless hours controlling my hair" (Wallace 2015: 36). The "Black is Beautiful" Movement was, in many ways, not entirely liberated from misogyny. Women were expected to be beautiful, Wallace asserts:

> Whatever that was ... So I was again obsessed with my appearance ... worried about the rain again—the Black woman's nightmare—for fear that my huge, full, Afro would shrivel up to my head ... Whether one felt compelled to wear the big full Afro of feminine Black consciousness or followed the latest spectacular Afro trends promoted by the beauty industry, natural hair offered little escape, it seems, from the admonition that Black women needed to work hard—and spend money—to be beautiful. (Wallace 2015: 36)

For Black women, beauty is politicized. For DeVore, inadvertently passing as white got her through the doors of the Vogue School, but she leveraged this power to assert her Blackness and lift up other Black women. Michele Wallace's reflections demonstrate the near-impossible expectations of Black beauty at the height of the Black Power movement. Black women liberated themselves from white standards of beauty, such as straightening or relaxing their hair or lightening their skin but faced tremendous pressure to still embody patriarchal ideals of femininity.

Cultural Appropriation and the Shakespeare Classroom

White cultural appropriation of Black aesthetics threatens to erase the long and difficult road Black activists have paved in asserting that "Black is beautiful." Today, the subtle, yet insidious, performances of "Blackfishing" in music videos, magazine spreads, and social media should be cause for concern not merely among scholars of race and racial equality activist groups but also for Shakespeare scholars and teachers. To connect Shakespeare's critique of augmented beauty to its modern analogue, "catfishing," we may look to our students and their peers for expertise. Teen Vogue writer, Adryan Corcione, explains that catfishing is the act of creating a false identity in order to lure people into relationships online, wherein "catfish" refers to the "predator" who creates the false identity (Corcione 2020). The catfish might pose as an entirely different person using images acquired on the Internet or, alternatively, virtually augment or manipulate their appearance using photo filter enhancements.

Merriam-Webster Dictionary has even updated its "catfish" entry to accommodate this trendier sense of the word: "a person who sets up a false personal profile on a social networking site for fraudulent or deceptive purposes" (Merriam-Webster.com Dictionary, s.v. "catfish"). This practice was the subject of Nev Schulman's 2010 documentary-turned television show, *Catfish*, now in its eighth season running on MTV. In the ever-evolving world of social media, the concept of "catfishing" has even undergone its own transformation. The white Australian rapper, Iggy Azalea, and her contemporary, British pop star, Jesy Nelson, for example, have recently come under fire for cosmetic "Blackfishing" in their music videos, a term used to describe non-Black people attempting to appear of Black ancestry. High school and university students are among Blackfishing's most vocal critics. In an op-ed in *Teen Vogue*, Raven Smith points out that Blackfishing is "subtler than cultural appropriation" and yet just as harmful to young, Black women, especially:

> Cherry-picking our culture—adorning the palatable aesthetics without the sticky Black-adjacent issues of lack of opportunities, low income rates, and less access to education—is theft. Blackfishing embodies the look of Blackness without the racism, the discrimination, the chronic negative expectations of Black people, making Blackness something to put on. It allows white women to live Black, or at very least racially ambiguous lives, without the inherited mess of literal Blackness. Reducing Blackness to a series of aspirational body parts diminishes the Black experience, offering a blanket denial of multifaceted Blackness … Blackfishing is, in essence, a celebratory blackface, one that admires rather than ridicules. It is esteemed minstrelsy. (Smith 2021)

Here, I want to suggest that catfishing, or more precisely, Blackfishing, is a modern but more destructive analogue to Shakespeare's images of cosmetic conceit. When the white women of Shakespeare's sonnets enhance a fair complexion with the use of cosmetics, the elevation of whiteness debases Blackness, and the poet responds by attempting to control the color of beauty. Cosmetic augmentation is duplicitous because it tricks the white, male gaze. Our modern analogue, however, risks erasure of a long history of the politicization and commodification of Black beauty. The challenges Ophelia DeVore, Caroline Jones, Angela Davis, Michele Wallace, and countless others have faced in asserting that "Black is beautiful" comes under attack when white women appropriate Black style. Given that racial passing for many Black Americans meant survival, white passing as Black in popular culture is a harmful and concerning new trend in anti-Black racism. When we put the narratives of these women in conversation with Shakespeare, instructors and critics can help students understand how these insidious acts of appropriation reinforce white hegemony.

REFERENCES

Cottom, Tressie McMillam. 2019. *Thick, And other Essays*. New York: The New Press, 2019.
Gainer, Nichelle. 2012. "Ophelia DeVore: Bold Beauty and Brains." *Ebony Magazine*, March 16, 2012. https://www.ebony.com/style/ophelia-devore-bold-beauty-and-brains/. Accessed December 31, 2021.

Hobbs, Allyson. 2014. *A Chosen Exile: A History of Racial Passing in American Life*. Cambridge: Harvard University Press.

Johnson, James Weldon. 1995. *The Autobiography of an Ex-Colored Man*. New York: Dover Publications.

Thompson, Ayanna. 2011. *Passing Strange: Shakespeare, Race, and Contemporary America*. Oxford, England: Oxford University Press.

Espinosa, Ruben. 2021. *Shakespeare on the Shades of Racism*. London: Routledge.

Corredera, Vanessa. 2015. "Complex Complexions: The Facial Signification of the Black Other in Lust's Dominion." *Shakespeare and the Power of the Face*, edited by James K. Knapp, 93–112. Surrey, Burlington: Ashgate.

Iyengar, Sujata. 2004. *Shades of Difference: Mythologies of Skin Color in Early Modern England*. Philadelphia: University of Pennsylvania Press.

Kearse-Lane, Kimberly, interviewee. 2022. *The Beauty of Blackness*. Directed by Tiffany Johnson and Kiana Moore. Vox Media. https://www.hbomax.com/feature/urn:hbo:feature:GYhpakgyYVMLCwwEAAAAk, 00:07:03.

Tate, Shirley Anne. 2012. "'I do not see myself as anything else than white': Black resistance to racial cosplay blackfishing." *The Routledge Companion to Beauty Politics*, edited by Maxine Leeds Craig, 205–214. New York: Routledge, 2012.

Hall, Kim. 1998. "'These bastard signs of fair': Literary whiteness in Shakespeare's sonnets." In *Post-Colonial Shakespeares*, edited by Ania Loomba and Martin Orkin, 64–83. London: Routledge.

Hall, Kim. 1996. "Beauty and the Beast of Whiteness: Teaching Race and Gender." *Shakespeare Quarterly* 47, no. 4, 461–475.

Karim-Cooper, Farah. 2019. *Cosmetics in Shakespearean and Renaissance Drama*. Edinburgh: Edinburgh University Press.

Poitevin, Kimberly. 2011. "Inventing Whiteness: Cosmetics, Race, and Women in Early Modern England," *Journal for Early Modern Cultural Studies* 11, no. 1, 59–89.

Tuke, Thomas. 1616. *A Discourse Against Painting and Tincturing Women*. London.

Dolan, Frances E. 1993. "Taking the Pencil out of God's Hand: Art, Nature, and the Face-Painting Debate in Early Modern England." *PMLA* 108, no. 2, 224–239.

Herford, C.H., Percy Simpson, and Evelyn Simpson, eds. 1950. *Ben Jonson*. Oxford: Clarendon.

Jeamson, Thomas. 1665. *Artificial Embellishments*. Oxford.

Heywood, Thomas. 1607. *The Fayre Mayde of the Exchange*. English Verse Drama Full-Text Database. Cambridge: Chadwyck-Healey, 1994.

Marston, John. 1604. *The Malcontent*, edited by W. David Kay. New York: Methuen, 1999.

Jonson, Ben. 1609. Epicoene, or The Silent Woman, edited by Roger Holdsworth. New York: Bloomsbury.

Shakespeare, William. 2015. *Shakespeare's Sonnets and Poems*, edited by Barbara A. Mowat and Paul Werstine. New York: Washington Square Press.

Bailey, Moya. 2021. *Misogynoir Transformed: Black Women's Digital Resistance*. New York: New York University Press.

Fox, Margalit. 2014. "Ophelia DeVore-Mitchell, 91, Dies; Redefined Beauty." *New York Times*, March 13, 2014. https://www.nytimes.com/2014/03/13/nyregion/ophelia-devore-mitchell-91-dies-redefined-beauty.html. Accessed December 15, 2021.

Touré. 2014. "Teaching America that black was beautiful." *New York Times Magazine*, December 28, 2014. https://www.proquest.com/magazines/ophelia-devore-mitchell/docview/1640813180/se-2?accountid=10747. Accessed December 15, 2021.

Ophelia DeVore-Mitchell Papers, 1920–2010. Stuart A. Rose Manuscript, Archives, and Rare Book Library, Emory University. https://findingaids.library.emory.edu/documents/devore1224/?keywords=devore. Accessed December 15, 2021.

Yale, Joel. 1969. "Black is Busting Out All Over." *Life Magazine* 67, no. 16.

Walker, Susannah. 2000. "Black is Profitable: The Commodification of the Afro, 1960–1975." *Enterprise & Society* 1, no. 3, 536–564.

Caldwell, Paulette. 1991. "A Hair Piece: Perspectives on the Intersection of Race and Gender." *Duke Law Journal* 40, no. 2, 365–396.

Taylor, Paul C. 2016. *Black is Beautiful: A Philosophy of Black Aesthetics*. Hoboken: Wiley.

Davis, Angela. 1998. "Afro Images: Politics, Fashion, and Nostalgia." *Soul: Black Power, Politics, and Pleasure*, edited by Monique Guillory and Richard Green, 23–31. New York: NYU Press.

John W. Hartman Center for Sales, Advertising & Marketing History. "Black is Beautiful" in the Race and Ethnicity in Advertising Exhibition at Duke University Libraries. https://exhibits.library.duke.edu/exhibits/show/-black-is-beautiful-/-black-is-beautiful%2D%2Dafrocentr. Accessed December 31, 2021.

Wallace, Michele. 2015. "A Black Feminist's Search for Sisterhood." *All the Women Are White, All the Blacks Are Men, But Some of Us Are Brave*, edited by Gloria T. Hull, Patricia Bell Scott, and Barbara Smith, 35–40. New York: Feminist Press.

Corcione, Adryan. 2020. "9 Signs You're Being Catfished." *Teen Vogue*, January 21, 2020. https://www.teenvogue.com/story/signs-youre-being-catfished. Accessed January 1, 2022.

Merriam-Webster.com Dictionary, s.v. "catfish". https://www.merriam-webster.com/dictionary/catfish. Accessed December 15, 2021.

Smith, Raven. 2021. "The Problem with Blackfishing." *Teen Vogue*, October 13, 2021. https://www.vogue.com/article/the-problem-with-blackfishing-jesy-nelson. Accessed January 1, 2022.

CHAPTER 9

Intersectionality, Inclusion, and the Shakespeare Survey Course

Maya Mathur

On March 14, 2020, as colleges across the United States shifted from in-person to online instruction, the musician, Rosanne Cash, tweeted, "Just a reminder that when Shakespeare was quarantined because of the plague, he wrote *King Lear*" (Cash 2020). Cash's tweet went viral, inviting both agreement and backlash to her claim that a period of enforced isolation during a global pandemic might generate a period of productivity on par with that of England's most famous poet. Cash's offhand words, written prior to the pandemic's devastating toll on lives and livelihoods, also initiated conversations about the similarities between "the bleakest tragedy Shakespeare wrote" and the fractured social relations of our time (Dickson 2020). In higher education, the pandemic highlighted the ongoing inequities that are often masked by the seemingly egalitarian framework of the college classroom, including access to the Internet and space in which to study or take classes. The murder of George Floyd on May 25, 2020, which led to months of protest against systemic racism in the United

M. Mathur (✉)
University of Mary Washington, Fredericksburg, VA, USA
e-mail: mmathur@umw.edu

S. Freeman Loftis et al. (eds.), *Inclusive Shakespeares*, Palgrave Shakespeare Studies,
https://doi.org/10.1007/978-3-031-26522-8_9

States and inspired movements for social justice around the world, drew renewed attention to the lack of racial diversity in higher education and generated calls for the adoption of inclusive curriculum and anti-racist pedagogical practices (England and Purcell 2020).

These calls for changes to the curriculum inform the intersectional approach that I used to redesign my survey courses on Shakespeare. While I have taught specialized courses on race, gender, and sexuality in early modern drama, the two-part survey courses at the public liberal arts institutions where I teach have traditionally focused on genres and themes in Shakespeare's early and later plays. My redesigned courses drew on Kimberle Crenshaw's description of intersectionality to combine established modes of literary analysis with investigations of gender, sexuality, race, and disability in a selection of Shakespeare's plays. In her seminal essays on the subject, Crenshaw uses the term intersectionality to describe the specific forms of injustice that Black women experience because of their race and gender (1989, p. 140). The term has come to define those overlapping systems of oppression that disproportionately affect members of marginalized communities. Crenshaw's work has influenced a number of fields, including that of premodern critical race studies, whose proponents have emphasized the importance of adopting inclusive and anti-racist approaches to teaching in order to combat the erasure of BIPOC voices in the early modern classroom (De Barros 2020). Kimberly Ann Coles, Kim F. Hall, and Ayanna Thompson make a persuasive case for inclusive teaching in a recent issue of Profession, where they call on faculty to center "systems of power and epistemologies of race, indigeneity, gender and sexuality" to attract new students to the study of early modern literature (2019). Katherine Gillen and Lisa Jennings likewise advise educators to "decolonize" the classroom by addressing Shakespeare's colonial legacy, attending to the racism and misogyny in his plays, discussing responses to the plays by BIPOC artists and critics, and creating assignments that privilege students' cultural knowledge (2019). These scholars offer valuable lessons on how to make Shakespeare more accessible to new generations of students, especially those students who do not feel like their lives and experiences are reflected in his work.

AN INTERSECTIONAL APPROACH

The issues of access and inclusion that these scholars discuss are less acute in the predominantly white institution (PWI) where I teach. My courses are composed primarily of students who have grown up reading or performing Shakespeare. While the students who attend my classes may be interested in studying Shakespeare, they have little experience with examining representations of gender, sexuality, race, or disability in his plays. An intersectional approach can encourage students well versed in Shakespeare to find new meaning in his plays and enable students who may not have engaged with Shakespeare in the past to bring their lived experience to bear on the process of interpretation. An intersectional pedagogy can enhance engagement for both groups of students by providing them with new vocabularies for reading the plays and connecting his work to their identities and interests.

This methodology not only opens up new conversations about Shakespeare to students who are familiar with his work but also offers a point of entry to those who may be acquainted with discussions of race or disability but lack significant experience with Shakespeare's plays. An intersectional lens may also produce greater buy-in from those students who believe that premodern writers do not speak to their interests. As Wendy Beth Hyman and Hillary Eklund note in the volume, *Teaching Social Justice Through Shakespeare*, "Prioritizing modes of inquiry over the unquestioned veneration of celebrated objects (like Shakespeare, the First Folio, or any other thing) allows humanists across the disciplines to address issues of justice—to confront racism, misogyny, and lack of diversity in the canon, and more broadly to open up the richness of the past ass a prod to action in the present" (2019, p. 6). Adhaar Noor Desai writes in the same volume, "Pairing Shakespeare's texts with contemporary issues was a way to make clear to students that our task was to dig in rubble and try to make sense of it together" (2019, p. 31). An intersectional approach can create a bridge between the past and the present by exploring the inequities that Shakespeare chronicles in plays and those that exist in our own time.

While the work of premodern scholars, particularly scholars on race and disability, informs course content and design, the methodologies for examining and assessing student learning discussed in this chapter are based on the Scholarship of Teaching and Learning (SoTL). SoTL work, first conceptualized by Ernest Boyer, has historically been more popular in the fields of social science and education but has much to offer scholars in the humanities (1990, p. 27). SoTL-oriented research frames student learning as a central area of inquiry; analyzes the practices that enable such learning; conducts empirical research in partnership with students by following the tenets of human subject research; and encourages researchers to share their pedagogy with a wider audience (Felten 2013, p. 122). Literary scholars are especially suited to conducting SoTL research since our training relies on "closely reading, interpreting, and analyzing written texts" (Chick et al. 2009, p. 405). This chapter follows the tenets of SoTL work by drawing on class discussion boards and an end-of-semester survey to demonstrate how an intersectional approach can enhance student engagement with Shakespeare.

An intersectional approach invites students to examine the systems of power in Shakespeare's plays and deconstruct the forms of dominance and marginalization that they enable and perpetuate. Intersectional modes of analysis can thus be used to unpack moments of race-making, hegemonic masculinity, heteronormativity, and ableism in the text as well as those moments where these discourses are destabilized. As Ambereen Dadabhoy notes with regard to premodern race studies, educators must challenge the pervasive belief "that the Renaissance and early modern England were raceless or race unconscious, and…that this period was not sullied by the brutality of the trans-Atlantic slave trade, the plantation economy, and the destruction and degradation of black bodies, people, and culture that followed" (2020, p. 230). Students are better prepared to examine color-coded imagery and racialized discourse in Shakespeare when they are aware of the history of whitewashing that has gone hand-in-hand with narratives about his superiority. Allison Hobgood and David Houston Wood make similar claims about discourses of disability, suggesting that students can produce "innovative critical interventions" once they are aware of the inherited ideas and representations of disability in the plays (2013, pp. 187–88). The most productive responses to Shakespeare occur in the intersections between these historically discrete fields. Courses designed with these intersections in mind can not only introduce students to emerging areas of scholarship but also provide them with valuable tools for literary analysis (Shaw 2019; Hobgood 2020).

PRACTICING INTERSECTIONALITY

I introduce students to the benefits of an intersectional approach at the beginning of the semester by assigning essays on the four methodologies that will be used to frame class discussion. These essays outline scholarly approaches to gender, sexuality, race, and disability in early modern drama and offer frameworks for reading that can be used to examine the selection of plays assigned for class. Students also read critical essays from one approach alongside each play in order to deepen their knowledge of how that text might be interpreted through a specific theoretical lens. Class discussion of each play begins by outlining how different modes of inquiry might frame the play and focuses on analyzing specific passages through these frames. For instance, during class discussion of *Two Gentlemen of Verona* (c.1589–1593), students investigated the homoerotic relationship between Proteus and Valentine, the play's lovelorn heroes; the racialized language used to describe Sylvia and Julia, the objects of Proteus and Valentine's affection; as well as the figurative connections between love and blindness in the text. Students were also asked to choose one or more of these approaches in their written responses to the plays, which they submitted to a class discussion board.

I introduce students to the concept of intersectionality through Mari Matsuda's phrase, "asking the 'other' question," which highlights the importance of forging connections between different minoritized groups and communities (Liu 2020). In her work on feminist coalition-building, Matsuda writes:

> The way I try to understand the interconnection of all forms of subordination is through a method I call 'ask the other question.' When I see something that looks racist, I ask, 'Where is the patriarchy in this?' When I see something that looks sexist, I ask, 'Where is the heterosexism in this?' When I see something that looks homophobic, I ask, 'Where are the class interests in this?' Working in coalition forces us to look for both the obvious and non-obvious relationships of domination, helping us to realize that no form of subordination ever stands alone. (Matsuda 1991, p. 1189)

While Matsuda focuses on the importance of recognizing marginalized subject positions, her invitation to ask the "other" question is also generative for literary analysis. Her description can remind students of the range of interpretive possibilities that are available to them and prompt them to read Shakespeare's characters both in terms of those identities that may be explicit, such as gender and race, and those that may be implicit, such as sexuality or disability.

Students demonstrated their engagement with these modes of inquiry by posting written responses to a selection of the following texts: *Two Gentlemen of Verona, Henry V, Richard III, Julius Caesar*, and *Titus Andronicus*. Given the demographics of the class, which consisted primarily of white women, few of whom had disclosed disabilities, I expected the majority of student responses to the text to center on gender and sexuality, with some discussion of race and disability. While approximately 42% of the responses focused on gender and sexuality, disability was an equally important area of analysis, making up 33% of responses, while race and class constituted 11% and 14% of responses, respectively. In what follows, I review those plays in which a singular approach dominated as well as those texts in which students pursued multiple axes of inquiry.

The plays where one approach dominated include *Richard III* and *Julius Caesar*, which students examined primarily in relation to disability. Their responses reflected their reading of essays on disability in these plays by Katherine Schaap Williams and Allison Hobgood from the collection "Disabled Shakespeares" (2009). Students drew on Williams's discussion of Richard's performative use of disability to trace those moments in the play where his opponents use ableist language to demonize him, with one student commenting, "the constant abuse Richard faces from his able-bodied counterparts forces him to respond in an antagonistic way." In a similar vein, students were interested in exploring the ramifications of Caesar's "falling sickness" after reading Hobgood's work, with one student tracing different attitudes toward Caesar's epilepsy to arrive at the conclusion that "Overall, while some members of society hold deeply negative attitudes toward Caesar's disability, others possess generally positive views…which defines the nature of his disability as socially constructed." It is worth noting that while we read and discussed essays on disability in relation to both plays, these readings made up only part of the broader discussion, which touched on issues of divine right, the place of women in matters of state, and the importance of citizens to the monarchy. The students' responses suggest that they were more interested in exploring different models of disability in the play than in pursuing other modes of analysis.

While students tended to use one mode of analysis to study *Richard III* and *Julius Caesar*, they explored multiple models for examining *Two Gentlemen of Verona* and *Titus Andronicus*, the plays that were assigned at the beginning and end of the semester. Several students built on class discussion of gender and sexuality in *Two Gentlemen*, by exploring the nexus of disability and masculinity in the play. One student wrote of the figurative connections between love and disability: "Valentine's and Proteus's loves disable them by making them incapable of rational thought ('blindness') while simultaneously disabling others, Valentine's love 'deforming' Sylvia and Proteus's love disabling his relationships with Valentine and Julia." Another student suggested that Valentine and Proteus use the language of disability to issue "warnings" about love to each other, since "being love-sick was often associated with a loss of self-control which can be seen within the characters as the story progresses." Students also considered the ramifications of being a disabled woman in their examinations of Lavinia in *Titus Andronicus*. One student wrote, "Lavinia's disabilities are portrayed as hindrances that lead to her character being infantilized and ostracized by others while she, herself, finds a way to retain her agency." This student was invested in exploring how Lavinia's tools for communication are overlooked and her choices diminished by the men in her life. While students examined metaphors for disability and their effect on definitions of masculinity in *Two Gentlemen of Verona*, they moved beyond the study of language to address the intersections of patriarchal power and ableist attitudes in *Titus Andronicus*.

Students also combined discussions of race, gender, and sexuality in their reading of these plays. One student drew attention to the framing of Sylvia and Julia in the comedy by noting:

> One of the ways that Shakespeare seems to be showing the hierarchy between the two women is through the language of race…he chooses to refer to Silvia as "fair", but Julia gets referred to as an "Ethiope," signifying that she would essentially have darker skin than Silvia. Proteus is saying that because of her darker skin, she doesn't particularly fit the beauty standard during this time. It is also interesting to point out that Proteus says it is heaven that makes Silvia so fair because this, of course, implies that only someone of a lighter skin tone can be blessed.

This student draws attention to race-making in Shakespeare's early comedy by connecting references to Sylvia's white complexion with paeans to her interior grace and divinity. Their response indicates that early discussions about the construction of race in Shakespeare and color-coded imagery in the sonnets were a productive point of entry into studying race and gender in the plays.

The responses offered equally important insight into race, especially constructions of racialized masculinity in *Titus Andronicus*. As one student noted in their examination of Chiron and Demetrius, "Another way the Goths are raced is through their hyper-sexuality. Each of the main Gothic characters exhibit not only increased sexual desire, but also violent and/or immoral desire." This student was able to draw on essays about sexuality from the beginning of the semester in order to highlight the intersection between race and sexuality in the construction of the Goths in *Titus*. Another student was influenced by David Sterling Brown's essay on domesticity in *Titus Andronicus* (2019) to consider the intersections of gender and race in the play, writing, "Roman masculinity rests on the idea of supporting your country and defending your honor while the Moors have a focus on kinship and protecting one's family." These responses suggest that, by the end of the semester, students were comfortable adopting multiple perspectives in their examination of the play and combining scholarly interpretation with their investigations of the play.

Students were also required to reply to at least one response posted to the discussion board by mentioning what they had enjoyed, asking questions, or adding to their peers' writing. These replies helped build a community outside the classroom where students could exchange ideas about the reading, learn from their classmates, and receive validation for their work. For instance, a student replied to a response on love and disability in *Two Gentlemen*, "I sometimes struggle with identifying the language of disability and its significance in the text, but I feel like I now have a better understanding of it…It seems like the disparity between homosocial and heterosexual relationships is intensified by the use of the language of disability." Another student comments on their peers' discussion of race in *Two Gentlemen*, "I appreciate that you brought in the beauty standards of the time. I wish that we had actually spent some time discussing this in class because women actually painted their faces white to appear to be lighter-skinned. This was a trend in many cultures, but it was prominent at the time that this play was written." The student added important historical information to their classmate's response and pointed to areas of class discussion that might have been developed further in the process. Another student responded to a post on *Julius Caesar*, "I enjoyed reading your response very much. Interestingly, I had not considered the medical and religious models for framing Caesar's epilepsy, but your articulation of the ways those models manifest is good. Literature like *Julius Caesar* can help us understand how people with disabilities are represented and discussed, thereby encouraging us to consider whether those representations are positive, negative, accurate, realistic, hopeful, etc." The replies to the responses helped address gaps in students' knowledge as well as signal areas of inquiry that interested them, which could be pursued further during class discussion.

REFLECTING ON INTERSECTIONALITY

An overview of the results from the end-of-semester survey also offers insight into which perspectives the students turned to most often and why they did so. The survey asked students to discuss the approaches they found most engaging and then invited them to reflect in greater detail on which plays they enjoyed reading from a specific perspective. The survey also encouraged students to consider which frames enhanced their thinking about Shakespeare. The 11 students who responded to the anonymous survey included 9 seniors and 2 students in their junior year.

Their written responses echoed the patterns of interest that emerged in the discussion boards. While a majority of students responded by mentioning their interest in a disability-focused approach to Shakespeare, several students discussed their investment in a combination of approaches. Their reasons for engaging with a particular perspective ranged from critical interest in the approach to a personal connection with an approach that they had previously overlooked. Seven respondents mentioned having some or moderate experience with Shakespeare before they took the class, while eight mentioned having some or moderate experience with using intersectional approaches for the study of literature. Ten of these students either agreed or strongly agreed that an intersectional approach had enhanced their reading of Shakespeare.

When responding to the question about the approach they drew on most frequently, a few students expressed an interest in using multiple approaches, noting, "Honestly, all of the perspectives were engaging, especially when we read the essays/articles to help further understand these perspectives and their relevance to the plays." Other students wrote of their preference for a specific approach that gave them new insight into the plays. For instance, one student noted in regard to race, "There were many reasons that I did not ever think to look at Shakespeare through a racial lens and I really liked being able to figure out what I can read to learn more on this," while another wrote that their interest lay in studies of disability because "I had never really encountered discourse like this before and I feel like it has broadened my understanding of disability discourse in terms of all literature." Another student responded to the survey by noting that an intersectional framework helped them combine familiar approaches with new areas of inquiry:

> I usually find that studying Shakespeare through the lens of gender and sexuality to be the most engaging and is the lens that I find I am most experienced with at this point, but I think that this semester our discourse on disability and how that relates to race discourse is what I found the most compelling simply because have never taken a course that talked about discourse in literature so extensively and it was so prevalent throughout his plays that it made me question how I read Shakespeare since I had never noticed it before.

As these reflections indicate, respondents to the survey were drawn to the study of race and disability because they had rarely used these approaches to study literature and because they had never considered that they could interpret Shakespeare using these modes of analysis.

In their responses to those approaches that they had found most interesting for reading specific plays, students meditated on how the frames of disability and race had helped them engage with Shakespeare in ways they had not anticipated. As one student noted about a disability-centered reading of *Julius Caesar*, "I have actually read this play multiple times for previous courses but never studied it from this angle, and I felt that it added a lot to my understanding of the characters. Being able to look at the social aspects and different opinions of Caesar's illness was surprisingly interesting to me." Students took similar approaches to the discussion of race, noting that the approach had enhanced their reading of specific plays. One student wrote that they were most interested in Titus Andronicus in terms of race because of the way Shakespeare deviated from his habitual elevation of whiteness in the play: "While Shakespeare more often than not depicts differences between races negatively, specifically elevating characters with light-colored skin, Aaron challenges the racial stereotypes he knows the other characters in the play embody, especially when the nurse brings him the biracial child he has had with Tamora." Another student expressed their surprise at finding discussions of race in the history plays, writing, "In terms of race, I enjoyed reading *Henry V*. I think this is because I probably wouldn't have considered the soldiers in Henry V's camp in terms of race, otherwise." These responses suggest that introducing students to new approaches, especially those of race and disability, which are adopted less frequently in courses on Shakespeare, can both expand their critical vocabularies and help them engage with familiar texts in new and important ways.

Finally, some students spoke to the personal impact of specific approaches, particularly those involving gender, sexuality, and disability. One student wrote about the power of seeing their life and struggles reflected in the text, "I found the gender and sexuality perspectives most engaging because they are both topics that are important to me. I struggle with my gender expression and have spent much of my formative years struggling with accepting my sexuality. To be able to analyze using those perspectives felt therapeutic, in a way." Another discussed how paying attention to sexuality made reading Shakespeare more approachable, "Shakespeare's dalliances with sexuality in his plays were a game changer for me. As a member of the LGBTQ+ community, it was so much fun to notice such intricacies within relationships. It brought Shakespeare out of the untouchable stratosphere and into my hands. I felt as if Shakespeare was finally something I could read and enjoy to its fullest." Students with disabilities shared similar stories of connection, with one student reflecting on their interest in the roles of Hamlet and Ophelia, "As someone whose anxiety can border into the paranoid, it was very fascinating to watch two mirrored characters struggle so much with it" and another suggesting, "Of all the plays, this one felt the most intimate in terms of mental disability and actually delving deep into the psyche of the main character." For these students, discussions of gender, sexuality, and disability provided new avenues for exploring Shakespeare and allowed them to forge intimate connections to his work.

While conversations about pedagogy may not be on par with producing another *King Lear*, the intersectional frames that I discuss in this chapter offer one point of entry into ongoing conversations about teaching early modern texts in an inclusive way. Intersectional frames can help students examine forms of race-making that idealize whiteness and debase blackness; recognize ableist language and constructions of disability; and explore gender roles and queer desires in Shakespeare's plays. An intersectional approach can have a positive impact on student learning by providing analytical tools and critical vocabularies that can be used to unpack the text. Focusing on a set of core perspectives that are used for each play can also help students build interpretive communities through which they can teach and learn from one another. Intersectional modes of teaching and learning can help dispel myths about the "universal Bard" by demonstrating that Shakespeare's value lies not in his timelessness but in his ability to speak to contemporary lives and interests.

REFERENCES

Boyer, Ernest L. 1990. *Scholarship Reconsidered: The Priorities of the Professorate.* 15–25. Princeton, NJ: Carnegie Foundation for the Advancement of Teaching.

Brown, David Sterling. 2019. "Remixing the Family: Blackness and Domesticity in *Titus Andronicus.*" *Titus Andronicus: The State of Play.* Edited by Farah Karim-Cooper. Bloomsbury. 111–134.

Cash, Rosanne. Twitter post. March 14, 2020, 1:35 a.m. https://twitter.com/rosannecash/status/1238700345548627969?lang=en. Accessed 10 Jan 2022.

Chick, Nancy L, Holly Hassel, and Aeron Haynie. 2009. "Pressing an Ear against the Hive: Reading Literature for Complexity." *Pedagogy: Critical Approaches to Teaching Literature, Language, Composition, and Culture.* 9 (3): 399–422. https://doi.org/10.1215/15314200-2009-003.

Crenshaw, Kimberle E. 1989. "Demarginalizing the Intersection of Race and Sex: A Black Feminist Critique of Antidiscrimination Doctrine, Feminist Theory and Antiracist Policies." University of Chicago Legal Forum 1: 139–167.

Coles, Kimberly Anne, Kim F. Hall, and Ayanna Thompson. 2019. "BlacKKKShakespearean: A Call to Action for Medieval and Early Modern Studies." *Profession.* https://profession.mla.org/blackkkshakespearean-a-call-to-action-for-medieval-and-early-modern-studies/

Dadabhoy, Ambereen. 2020. "The Unbearable Whiteness of Being in Shakespeare." *Postmedieval: A Journal of Medieval Cultural Studies* 11 (28 August): 228–235. https://doi.org/10.1057/s41280-020-00169-6.

De Barros, Eric L. 2020. "Teacher Trouble: Performing Race in the Majority-White Shakespeare Classroom." *Journal of American Studies* 54 (1): 74–81. https://doi.org/10.1017/Soo21875819002044.

Desai, Adhaar Noor. 2019. "Topical Shakespeare and the Urgency of Ambiguity." *Teaching Social Justice Through Shakespeare.* Edited by Wendy Beth Hyman and Hillary Eklund. 27–36. Edinburgh, Edinburgh University Press.

Dickson, Andrew. 2020. "Shakespeare in Lockdown: Did he write *King Lear* in plague quarantine?" *The Guardian* 22 March. https://www.theguardian.com/stage/2020/mar/22/shakespeare-in-lockdown-did-he-write-king-lear-in-plague-quarantine. Accessed 18 Jan 2022.

England, Jason, and Richard Purcell. 2020. "Higher Ed's Toothless Response to the Killing of George Floyd." *Chronicle of Higher Education.* June 8. https://www.chronicle.com/article/higher-eds-toothless-response-to-the-killing-of-george-floyd. Accessed Jan 15, 2022.

Felten, P. 2013. "Principles of Good Practice in SoTL." *Teaching & Learning Inquiry: The ISSOTL Journal* 1 (1): 121–125. https://doi.org/10.20343/teachlearninqu.1.1.121.

Gillen, Katherine and Lisa Jennings. 2019. "Decolonizing Shakespeare? Toward an Antiracist, Culturally Sustaining Praxis." *The Sundial*. November 26. https://medium.com/the-sundial-acmrs/decolonizing-shakespeare-toward-an-antiracist-culturally-sustaining-praxis-904cb9ff8a96. Accessed Feb 1, 2022.

Hobgood, Allison P. 2009. "Caesar Hath the Falling Sickness: The Legibility of Early Modern Disability in Shakespearean Drama." *Disability Studies Quarterly*, 29, no. 4. Edited by Allison Hobgood and David Houston Wood. https://doi.org/10.18061/dsq.v29i4.

Hobgood, Allison P. 2020. "Crip Sexualities and Shakespeare's *Measure for Measure*." *Shakespeare/ Sex: Contemporary Readings in Gender and Sexuality*. Edited by Jennifer Drouin. 75–98. New York, Bloomsbury.

Hobgood, Allison P. and David Houston Wood. 2013."Shakespearean Disability Pedagogy." *Recovering Disability in Early Modern England*. The Ohio State University Press. www.muse.jhu.edu/book/23952.

Hyman, Wendy Beth and Hillary Eklund. 2019. "Introduction: Making Meaning and Doing Justice with Early Modern Texts." *In Teaching Social Justice Through Shakespeare*. Edited by Wendy Beth Hyman and Hillary Eklund. 1–27. Edinburgh, Edinburgh University Press.

Liu, Helena. 2020. "Teaching Intersectionality: Activities and Resources." *Disorient*. Nov 18. https://disorient.co/teaching-intersectionality-activity/. Accessed Jan 17, 2022.

Matsuda, Mari J. 1991. "Beside My Sister, Facing the Enemy: Legal Theory out of Coalition." Stanford Law Review 43, no. 5. 1183–1192. https://doi.org/10.2307/1229035.

Shaw, Justin P. 2019. "'Rub Him About the Temples': Othello, Disability, and the Failures of Care." *Early Theater* 22.2

Williams, Katherine Schaap. 2009. "Enabling Richard: The Rhetoric of Disability in *Richard III*." *Disability Studies Quarterly*, 29, no. 4. Edited by Allison Hobgood and David Houston Wood. https://doi.org/10.18061/dsq.v29i4.

CHAPTER 10

Making First-Generation Experiences Visible in the Shakespeare Classroom

Katherine Walker

Divine Instinct

Near the middle of *Richard III*, a group of citizens gather in the streets of London to discuss the recent death of King Edward and the political consequences of an England ruled by the King's young son. In this brief moment, a respite from the high-pitched violence throughout the play, the citizens are seeking and making knowledge. While the events in the drama render the fallout of Edward's death largely a matter that takes place in court or upon a battlefield, the citizens remind us that these events will produce "a troublous world" (2.3.6).[1] The Third Citizen astutely warns his companions that the factions at court, those of Elizabeth and Richard, will prove disastrous for all the citizenry; the violence "[w]ill touch us all too near" (2.3.28). He leaves us with a forewarning of the collective woe that is bound to ensue:

K. Walker (✉)
University of Nevada, Las Vegas, Las Vegas, NV, USA
e-mail: katherine.walker@unlv.edu

S. Freeman Loftis et al. (eds.), *Inclusive Shakespeares*, Palgrave Shakespeare Studies,
https://doi.org/10.1007/978-3-031-26522-8_10

> Before the times of change, still is it so:
> By a divine instinct men's minds mistrust
> Ensuing dangers; as by proof, we see
> The waters swell before a boisterous storm.
> But leave it all to God. (2.3.43–47).

This "divine instinct" is from God, but located and expressed in the bodies of the English populace. They keenly intuit that they too are stakeholders in the political games that are largely represented in the spaces of gentility in the play. As the Citizen goes on to compare this instinctive mistrust to an ecological event that all can observe and gather knowledge from, he draws upon multiple sources of understanding, before concluding with a providential determinism that rings hollow given the tenacious feelings of dread that each Citizen in this brief scene articulates. In short, this collective knowledge is more than just commentary on the forthcoming downfall of the York line. Rather, it represents a rebuttal to the machinations of all those at court, an embodied and learned aspect of participating in the political and epistemological world of the play.

In this moment, the Citizens interpret and respond to a world that, at least initially, appears inexplicable. They use their prior experiences and their situated understanding to comment percipiently on the future. They are therefore part of the energies of *Richard III* that contribute to Richard's own dethroning. Indeed, it is highly likely that these same citizens play the soldiers at Bosworth, and therefore, they embody a wide range of experiential knowledge that is represented both through language and action, figures of dissent both actually and through the forms of knowledge they articulate. In my Shakespeare courses at the University of Nevada Las Vegas, I begin the semester with this moment. I begin with this analogy because, as I emphasize to students in my Shakespeare courses, we have to foreground social class, gender, sexuality, race/ethnicity, and disability in our discussions of plays if we aim to have anything like a productive conversation that brings in, rather than excludes, diverse perspectives. This chapter thinks through the strategies available on that all-too-influential first day as a means for setting the tone of rebellion that allows students to "talk back" to Shakespeare—and in talking back, I hope, our study of Shakespeare together occurs in a mode of intellectual curiosity that is permissible rather than formulaic or unidirectional.

I like to frame our semester with this short scene from *Richard III* because it demonstrates how to confront, and therefore challenge, the presumed authority of a singular or monolithic form of knowledge. To focus on the citizens in this scene serves a larger point that I underscore in teaching Shakespeare—moments in which marginal characters contribute new knowledge are everywhere in early modern drama. The types of knowledge that figure in Shakespearean plays evince an impressive range that is never located in a single character but also enable students to identify with a range of socially marginalized figures who are almost always better readers of their environment than the plays' protagonists.[2] Whether gathered from oral traditions, experiences, or instinctive deductions, these forms of knowledge are sources of rich opportunities for students' entry-way into a text. My course design charts out the ways in which early modern dramatic characters who often get less critical and performative attention nonetheless produce real knowledge; this knowledge seriously informs political and cultural potentials, both in and outside of the text.

In my courses, I call this "dethroning," which refers to the destabilizing of existing structures of power and thought that can restrictively homogenize accepted knowledge itself. The aim is to facilitate students' critical engagement with Shakespeare on terms that enable their own voices to be heard amid a conversation that might feel, to them, imposing or unwelcoming. In this I take my cue from Ayanna Thompson's reading of Shakespeare and race in contemporary America. As Thompson emphasizes, "Shakespeare (again I stress the multivalent meanings of this name) ... was never and, therefore, is never coherent, stable, fixed, and defined" (Thompson and Strange 2011). This destabilized Shakespeare then enables students to redefine their relationship to his works, opening up his plays to multiple entryways and elevating diverse articulations of knowledge practices instead of replicating familiar readings. Where I teach, the University of Nevada Las Vegas, one of the most diverse universities in the United States, most of my students are both first-generation and racial/ethnic minorities. UNLV is a Minority Serving Institution, an Asian-American and Native-American, Pacific Islander-Serving Institution, and a Hispanic Serving Institution. Because I ask my students to disclose, if they are comfortable, their backgrounds to me in an opening letter during the first weeks of class, I have learned that they are primarily without a long-standing relationship to Shakespeare established in their families or education.

My perspective on strategies for promoting first-generation student participation in an equitable and inclusive classroom is informed by several questions. How do you provide first-generation students with a forum to "talk back" to Shakespeare? How can we as instructors encourage our students to dismantle the Shakespearean mythos in order to engage—honestly and creatively—with his plays? The burden of a conjured image of Shakespeare as an "elite" author is a particular concern for students from first-gen, low-income, and/or minority backgrounds. They might feel trepidation at the language or remain silent rather than acknowledge that they do not understand something in the text. They might also feel the need to reproduce readings of the play in the vein of what criticism has largely deemed to be important—ideas like kingship or character motivations that students might have no interest in but feel the need to echo.[3]

I also have a slightly more iconoclastic aim in mind, which I explain during our first meeting of the semester—that is, my goal in "Shakespeare" is to enable my students to dethrone the Shakespearean mythos. This mythos includes the accumulated assumptions, laudations, or privilege associated with the works of Shakespeare.[4] To be clear, Shakespeare the playwright is not the Shakespearean mythos. Bardolatry has had exclusionary consequences, to put it lightly. What I am proposing is a type of irreverence in our own pedagogy. To move toward a more equitable and inclusive Shakespearean classroom, we would do well to remind ourselves that Shakespeare's works are not just one thing—one style, genre, or even single-authored text—and that characters frequently contemplate the possibilities inherent in acts of dismantling. To "talk back" to the Shakespearean mythos, I believe, gives students a more intimate and thorough knowledge of not only early modern literature but also the practice and possibilities of literary scholarship. To dethrone the very subject of our course then opens up the potential for first-generation scholars to see themselves as knowledge-makers. They are by no means the Citizens of *Richard III*; however, they are able to ask questions about not only the motivations of characters in the play but also what it means to take their own forms of prior knowledge and experiences seriously in reading and reforming Shakespearean texts. In other words, the analogy is one that works if we question the very idea of what constitutes "knowledge" in the academy and in Shakespeare's plays. Pedagogically, to underline dethroning consequently underlines epistemological alternatives. And it speaks to a new generation of potential early modern scholars. We are helpfully reminded by Ayanna Thompson and Lauri Turchi that "[t]he more culturally responsive approach we promote recognizes that students bring their own perspectives and identities to their experience of Shakespeare's plays—just as audiences have for more than 400 years" (Thompson and Turchi 2016).

By foregrounding discussion in ideas of rebellion and knowledge-making, first-generation students are given the license to "talk back" to Shakespeare. Such an emphasis does not erase the affective resonances of Shakespeare's language for our students, nor the responses that his characters and plays can evoke. But it does offer one method for students to interpret Shakespeare's works and language in more permissible, or emboldened, terms. As Cassie Miura proposes in an essay that brilliantly details involving students in discussions of canon formation, "first-generation students are uniquely equipped to participate in the ongoing reappraisal of Shakespeare in the field of early modern studies and doing so can furnish them with the critical skills and conceptual vocabulary needed to articulate their own positionality within the university and to interrogate other forms of symbolic power" (Miura 2019). My aim here is to build off of this insight by considering additional conceptual frames for Shakespearean pedagogy. It is also framed by the conviction that our professoriate is in dire need of a more accurate reflection of the pluralistic society we actually inhabit. Kyle Grady puts this issue aptly: "Despite some of our best efforts to foster inclusivity, our field's demographics and culture are still quite far away from representing the racial and cultural diversity of the world outside of most traditional spaces of higher education" (Grady 2019). For first-generation students or students of color, the Shakespearean classroom might seem to largely replicate the homogeneity that the Shakespearean mythos automatically conjures.

First-Generation Students

First-generation students are those whose parents have not obtained a degree from an institution of higher learning. Many first-generation students are also low-income. The Department of Education has reported that 41% of Black students and 61% of Latinx students, compared to 25% of white and Asian-American students, are first-gen. Without the tacit knowledge gained through parental higher education, these students are often left to navigate the college transition entirely or almost entirely on their own. In 2007, Saenz et al. demonstrated a high correlation between parental education level and attending college (Saenz et al. 2007). Students whose parents have not obtained a higher education degree are less likely to even attend college, let alone to graduate (Cataldi et al. 2018). This point is important to stress because it means that our first-generation scholars have already overcome significant barriers to be sitting in our

Shakespeare classrooms in the first place. Those prior challenges, however, continue to inform their experiences, while a plethora of continuing stressors loom large in their ability to move toward gaining their degrees.

First-generation college students often lack the implicit codes of behavior that govern college culture, particularly the expectations of discussion within a seminar setting and the resources available for additional study, social, or financial support. They also often operate with Stereotype Threat and Imposter Syndrome at the same time.[5] Importantly, first-generation students have been disproportionately affected by the global pandemic. The socio-economic pressures that resulted from rapidly shifting college housing plans, canceled on-campus employment, and the need for advanced technology and Internet capabilities to participate in their courses meant that many underprivileged students were at an immense disadvantage compared to continuing-education peers who did not confront food, housing, and financial insecurities.[6] At the same time, the onset of the COVID pandemic witnessed some professors increasing their demands upon students, with swollen workloads and, in a move that was highly ableist, a requirement that students keep their screens on during virtual meetings. On top of all of these problems in equity and access, the question of where these and other marginalized students belong in a Shakespeare classroom is an important one.

It is a key question because we have the opportunity to think through structural inequalities and to question the structures of normalizing knowledge practices because of the abundant acts of questioning and challenging evident in the material we teach. In navigating the monolith that higher education often seems or is, instructors of Shakespeare likely witness these issues on a smaller scale in courses on early modern literature. I want to suggest that the challenges first-generation students in the classroom confront can and should be underlined in a course in Shakespeare because, in an unfortunate parallel, Shakespeare often represents a similar type of colossus of ideologies, stereotypes, and assumptions regarding "high culture" that can intimidate, not to mention explicitly exclude, students who lack role models in the academy.

If more than a third of college students are first-generation, then it behooves us; indeed, it is our job's imperative to think through how to ensure these students are encountering Shakespeare in an inclusive and equitable manner. We must facilitate their participation in Shakespearean scholarship in a way that enables them to envision themselves as legitimate makers of knowledge. That project will entail more than one chapter or edited collection, but we should aim for creating a repository of resources and materials. Alongside the tacit knowledge that continuing-education students possess, one of the central forms of knowledge comes with what Shakespeare represents. Some first-generation students also share these assumptions. On the first day of our semester, then, after thinking about divine instinct, knowledge, and rebellion in *Richard III*, I turn to the collective knowledge that Shakespeare represents for students. Students freewrite a list and then volunteer some of their own instinctive responses to who or what Shakespeare and his works are. In a largely first-generation, low-income, minority student classroom, the answers are both insightful and productive. The aura of Shakespeare, for my students, has conjured the following: "skull," "tomes," "theaters," "elite," "genius," "professors," or even "fancy." It is worthwhile to interrogate the stakes of these terms alongside their sources. The very terms that have historically been used to describe Shakespeare—genius, universal, and so on—are worth interrogating. Indeed, in one class session we study the etymologies of these very terms. Such an analysis reveals the contingency and capaciousness of words of praise in the seventeenth century. I like, for example, the fact that "genius" primarily signaled not innate intelligence or poetic disposition, but hearkened back to the figure of the genii in Greek and Roman mythology, the external tutelary god who prompts a human to make moral choices ("genius, n. and adj" 2021). If we reconfigure genius to represent an external divine force at work in human lives, suddenly Shakespeare is no longer alone. Where, I ask my students, did they gather this knowledge? Often it arises from high-school experiences or cultural osmosis. The latter, that cultural awareness arising from hearsay, film and television, or social media, can also be a source of anxiety for first-generation scholars because it largely reifies Shakespeare as one of elite culture's treasured own. It goes without saying that this elite culture is white, upper class, and versed in a form of scholarly discourse that heavily polices its boundaries.

My own stakes in the experiences of first-generation scholars of Shakespeare arise from several sources. As a white, first-generation assistant professor, I narrate, on the first day of class, an experience I had at a visit to a prospective graduate program for my PhD. Meeting with a potential advisor, a white male well known in the field of early modern studies, I enthusiastically asked questions about his research. When he in turn, finally, queried my own interests, I accidentally began with a non-standard dialect version of "well" that sounded distinctly Southern. After my misplaced "whelle" as a transitional phrase, I paused, mortified. The white male professor grinned, and following the embarrassed silence reassured me, "don't worry, that will go away with more education." Needless to say, I decided not to attend that program, and the moment prompted some serious consideration on my part on whether I would ever be able to move in the world he inhabited, let alone whether I should. I tell my students this painful story simply to establish that one of the first rules of our classroom is to throw out any notion of what pronunciation or dialect is "standard" in our classroom.[7] As I demand, "Whelle, why should it?"

My hope is that this moment humanizes me, and I welcome laughter while I recount the anecdote. More importantly, it addresses upfront the socio-economic disparities that are evident throughout the academy and the invisibility of first-generation status. In providing a brief snippet of my own narrative, I also invite (but do not demand) my students to consider their narratives and knowledge as central parts of our shared rebellion against the Shakespearean mythos. At once, I declare that there is no "right" way to pronounce character names or difficult terms in the text. I highlight that the expectation is not that one come prepared to speak or discuss Shakespeare "trippingly on the tongue" (*Hamlet* 3.2.2).[8] Rather, what if we threw out all of those rules and instead interrogated what Shakespeare means today, and what it could, in a more equitable and adventurous mode, mean in the future?[9]

REBELLION AND KNOWLEDGE

Breaking down Shakespeare's texts through the lens of knowledge-making, paradoxically, enables my students and I to craft a more nuanced narrative of the role early modern drama might play in our own moment, an incredibly vexed one at that. There is a plurality of knowledge-forms in Shakespeare's texts. The "divine instinct" of the citizens in *Richard III* is one example. Another arises from the folkloric understanding of the supernatural that both the guards and Horatio share in the opening of *Hamlet*. Marcellus initially rebuts Horatio's skepticism regarding "our fantasy" (1.1.22) of the actual appearance of the Ghost; after the harrowing encounter that provides Horatio with "the sensible and true avouch / Of mine own eyes" (1.1.56–56), Marcellus also recounts a form of folkloric understanding of the behavior of supernatural beings, beginning his explication with "Some say" (1.1.157) to narrate the power of a crowing cock to prevent malefic beings from arising during Christmas Eve. In short, Marcellus's "Some say" and his objection to Horatio's distanced skepticism are both powerful and valid challenges to the knowledge that Horatio, as scholar, holds. In Hamlet's Denmark, soldier, scholar, and prince are on an equal epistemic footing. Each brings to the Ghost a frame of knowledge that relies upon experience, folklore, or even emotions.

In *Hamlet*, as in most of Shakespeare's plays, marginal figures confront and often challenge the existing forms of knowledge that the protagonists hold. I typically pair *Hamlet* with *Julius Caesar* because these plays echo each other in important ways, establishing knowledge that flits between dramatic texts. For example, we spend ample time on Calphurnia's dream and the knowledge that she, the Roman populace, the Soothsayer, and Cinna the Poet articulate in their growing unease and response to the supernatural. We take seriously the knowledge formation that occurs throughout the play as a way of rebelling against Caesar's self-assured fatalism or Brutus's moral security.

For all of his bravura, Caesar attempts to interpret these omens after his own fashion, to make them in this one case "general" rather than specific. Calphurnia, however, insists upon Caesar's singularity, which comes across quite forcibly in her dream of his statue spouting blood. Caesar relates the dream to Decius, who has come to fetch him to the Senate: Decius, however, interprets the dream after his own fashion:

> This dream is all amiss interpreted.
> It was a vision, fair and fortunate.
> Your statue spouting blood in many pipes
> In which so many smiling Romans bathed
> Signifies that from you great Rome shall suck
> Reviving blood, and that great men shall press
> For tinctures, stains, relics and cognizance.
> This by Calphurnia's dream is signified. (2.2.83–90)[10]

Notable in Decius's interpretation is the swapping of gender, in which Caesar will be the breast-feeding mother to the Romans, albeit pouring forth blood instead of milk. There is no hint in Decius's interpretation that Caesar would be a living body in this image—others will press forward to snatch a relic (thought to have magical and spiritual powers) from this statue/body. This is exactly what Antony will play upon to the Roman crowd, suggesting that they will desire a handkerchief dipped in Caesar's blood for their own reliquaries. The suggestions of Caesar as savior, or as alchemical tincture, are much more ominous, but Caesar has been flattered. At this moment, I encourage students to narrate how they come across and process information in their everyday lives. How, for example, do past experiences refract their encounters with performances? How does it shape how and what types of understanding they seek? Who, in this moment from *Julius Caesar*, do they trust, and why?

Elizabethan audiences would have been familiar with the many prodigies that occurred the night before Caesar's assassination. Shakespeare returns to these events in *Hamlet*, in which Horatio, having encountered the Ghost of Hamlet, uses history to attempt to interpret his current moment:

> In the most high and palmy state of Rome,
> A little ere the mightiest Julius fell,
> The graves stood tenantless and the sheeted dead
> Did squeak and gibber in the Roman streets:
> As stars with trains of fire and dews of blood,
> Disasters in the sun; and the moist star
> Upon whose influence Neptune's empire stands
> Was sick almost to doomsday with eclipse:
> And even the like precurse of fierce events,
> As harbingers preceding still the fates
> And prologue to the omen coming on,
> Have heaven and earth together demonstrated
> Unto our climatures and countrymen. (1.1.112–124)

This is an environment, then, that requires interpretation. Both *Julius Caesar* and *Hamlet*, in dialogue with each other, also present opportunities for examining acts of rebelling against received knowledge. It is also useful to ask first-generation students at this moment what they know about the supernatural, and I receive anecdotes from family life in Cuba to recent popular TV series like *The Haunting of Hill House*. Of course, I also contextualize a historical understanding of supernatural beings but such context does not foreclose comparative readings across cultures and languages that underscore the role of knowledge. Instead, this perspective legitimizes a closer examination of the creation of knowledge, broadly conceived, on the part of Shakespeare's characters. Student responses and essays then examine how marginalized figures rebel, both actually and epistemically, against the dominant systems in the worlds they inhabit.

While we read plays variously focused on rebelling against knowledge and offering new forms of knowing, we primarily examine what rebellion against Shakespeare might look like in the modern classroom and, by extension, in contemporary performances and adaptations. This then opens up the door for studying Shakespeare alongside texts, performances, and art that confronts Shakespeare's legacy. For example, we recenter Cinna the Poet in *Julius Caesar* by watching the RSC's *I, Cinna* and then students "fix" the play, or talk back to it, by rewriting their own portions. I, *Cinna*, written and directed by Tim Crouch and performed by Jude Owusu, offers important interrogations of the status of poetry in a crisis-ridden world.[11] In this production, Cinna is hungry, waiting for bread, and yet also forcibly displaying a desire for knowledge. How, the performance asks, does one move through a world of conflicting signals, including signals for who has the right to speak? Such a powerful performance, which we watch together, allows for students to again ask: What does Cinna know? And what do we know? In the play itself, Cinna is compelled forward by an unknown force, a type of instinct perhaps that drives him out into the streets, with dangerous consequences: "I have no will to wander forth of doors, / Yet something leads me forth" (3.3.3–4). Crouch's production models a form of explicating this instinctive move forward, and it leads to a discussion on how Crouch and my own students might rethink minor characters to take seriously their unique perspectives. Many of my lessons center on rewriting Shakespeare and highlighting alternative responses to his works from contemporary artists and scholars, and the frames of rebellion—does Cinna rebel against the idea of Caesar/ Shakespeare in Crouch's production, for instance—alongside new knowledge means that my UNLV first-generation scholars are able to witness how their own narratives could dethrone the image, those tweed jackets with elbow-pads, of the modern Shakespearean. Why not examine, then, the quieter voices in the text or seek a fuller affective landscape in drama through those often ignored—clowns, poor gardeners, the "crowd or mob"—who offer perspectives on the foibles of the protagonists?

Conclusion

This chapter has made brief proposals for why we should make visible the experiences and ideas of first-generation scholars in our teaching of early modern works. I have called this "dethroning Shakespeare," and I shape my pedagogy around the idea that if we allow for alternative narratives—particularly those of students without college-educated parents—then we can provide pathways for a new, more diverse generation of scholars. From the beginning, I propose to my students that we undercut Bardolatry altogether. With this framework, students at UNLV are active participants in a thorough and eclectic, but ultimately productive, deconstruction of "Shakespeare" and the sometimes overbearing, and certainly intimidating, accounts of what it means to study Shakespeare's works today. I acknowledge that my attitude throughout this chapter has been one of irreverence and optimism. It is contingent on my experiences as a first-generation, low-income scholar who now teaches students who, at first, express curiosity but also trepidation at reading Shakespeare. There are much larger changes to be made, but thinking through how to render explicit the assumptions that follow the Shakespeare colossus allows my students and I to reconsider new ways of producing knowledge when interpreting early modern texts. Marginal figures in Shakespeare provide models that merit our closer appreciation for their willingness to juggle with multiple possibilities. Pushing against the absolutism of figures like Macbeth or Romeo, the citizens, scholars, healers, or everyday folk in Shakespearean drama give us a glimpse into a more equitable intellectual landscape, one that first-generation scholars might find inviting.

We are all aware, hopefully, that teaching in an equitable and inclusive classroom is an ongoing practice, necessarily open to revision. To make that revision visible, a good idea is to be forthright with students about how our own pedagogies evolve. Here, I have only had space to map out a few related emphases in my Shakespeare courses—rebellion, knowledge, and rebelling against received knowledge about who is allowed to talk to Shakespeare. There are other approaches that can help to undercut this false shibboleth of a singular genius toiling away in a study, removed from the popular influences of a street-level view. One such point is to highlight for students that early modern theater was fundamentally a collaborative practice. Such an emphasis acknowledges the role of musicians, printers, script-doctors, theatrical stakeholders, censors, and audiences, among many others, in "putting on" a play in sixteenth- and seventeenth-century London. Another, as Perry Guevara underscores, is ensuring that "[i]nclusive pedagogy, while open to many voices, must also empower those without a voice, those who are struggling to find it, and those who are not allowed to speak" (Guevara 2019). Often, as Guevara and others have demonstrated, our first-generation students are those who are initially struggling to find a voice, and therefore a place, in an early modern classroom. Understanding and valuing first-generation prior knowledge, and demonstrating how such knowledge also functions across Shakespearean drama, can serve to challenge, productively, what it is that "Shakespeare" represents for our students.

We have to be responsive to the structural inequalities that drastically shape our students' experiences prior to entering early modern literature classrooms. A significant element to those experiences includes first-generation students' assumptions that Shakespearean study is too elite, or perhaps arcane, for them to add anything new. Therefore, we have to open up interpretative access to Shakespeare, and one method for doing so is to unpack the problems with "universality" that have accreted onto just one author from one historical period. Again, such an emphasis does not undercut the power of Shakespearean drama to move audiences or students—but measurable action in the premodern literature class is needed, particularly as we continue to learn about the ramifications of the pandemic on the lives of our students.

What I have aimed to articulate here is a pedagogical framework that should be bolstered by the important work in critical race studies and scholarship on queer, trans, disability, and feminist approaches. Universities can be sites of dissonance for first-generation scholars, particularly those with intersectional identities, and bringing further attention to disjunctions in the material we teach and the knowledge our students already possess has the potential to radically alter the narrative of our own field and, by a crucial extension, to revise the homogeneity of our profession. My students want to learn to read Shakespeare. They are perhaps daunted by the confusing syntax and the Shakespearean mythos, but they are also enthusiastic and tenacious. My courses attempt to make room for intellectual vulnerability by making visible my first-generation experiences and acknowledging that there is still much work to do. I try as often as possible to articulate why my pedagogy is motivated by the idea of pushing back against a monolithic image of a lone genius who speaks for all of us. Rather, my students can speak for themselves. Analyzing Shakespeare's text presents one opportunity for them to do so.

Notes

1. All in-text citations are from *Richard III*. Edited by James R. Siemon. Arden Third Series. New York: Bloomsbury, 2009.

2. I am aware, however, that this must be done without fetishizing, uncritically, an ethos of the crowd, a caution that Denise Albanese articulates in "Identification, Alienation, and 'Hating the Renaissance,'" in *Shakespeare and the 99%: Literary Studies, the Profession and the Production of Inequity.* Edited by Sharon O'Dair and Timothy Francisco. New York: Palgrave Macmillan, 2019: 19–36.

3. To be clear, such a claim does not support a mode of "deficit thinking," and all types of students, including this author at times, have felt the pressure to mirror arguments and even language to what they perceive as important to the field or discourse. On this concept, see Richard R. Valencia, who writes "Deficit thinking refers to the notion that students (particularly low income, minority students) fail in school because such students and their families experience deficiencies that obstruct the learning process (e.g. limited intelligence, lack of motivation and inadequate home socialization)." *The Evolution of Deficit Thinking: Educational Thought & Practice.* London and New York: Routledge, 1997.

4. On the business of Bardolatry, see Graham Holderness, 'Bardolatry: or, The Cultural Materialist's Guide to Stratford-upon-Avon', in *The Shakespeare Myth*, ed. by Graham Holderness. Manchester: Manchester UP, 1988.

5. On Stereotype Threat, see Claude M. Steele and Joshua Aronson, "Stereotype Threat and the Intellectual Test Performance of African Americans," *Journal of Personality and Social Psychology* 69, no. 5 (1995): 797–811. On Imposter Syndrome, see Leary, M., Patton, K., Orlando, A., & Wagoner Funk, W. (2000). "The Impostor Phenomenon: Self-Perceptions, Reflected Appraisals, and Interpersonal Strategies." *Journal of Personality*, 68(4), 725–756.

6. These are only a few of the many stressors first-generation college students experience. The list also includes mental health issues and scarcity in healthcare access.

7. See Kyle Grady, "Why Front? Thoughts on the Importance of 'Nonstandard' English in the Shakespeare Classroom," *Pedagogy* 17, no. 3 (October 1, 2017): 533–40.

8. All in-text citations to the play are from *Hamlet*, edited by Ann Thompson and Neil Taylor. Arden Third Series. New York; London: Bloomsbury, rpr. 2014.

9. Here I am inspired by the methodological approaches modeled by the collection *Teaching Social Justice through Shakespeare: Why Shakespeare Matters Now*, edited by Hillary Eklund and Wendy Beth Hyman. Edinburgh: Edinburgh University Press, 2019. As the editors powerfully argue, "we humanists must counter the forces that denigrate knowledge-based discourses, threaten humane values, and whitewash historical events" (2). A

focus on knowledge acquisition and valuation in Shakespeare, I believe, can complement the important topical frames discussed by contributors in the collection.

10. All in-text citations are from *Julius Caesar*. Edited by David Daniell. Arden Third Series. New York: Bloomsbury, 1998.
11. Found at the following link: https://www.youtube.com/watch?v=6xQ Ar5le0UU.

REFERENCES

Emily Forrest Cataldi, Christopher T. Bennett, and Xianglei Chen. "First-Generation Students: College Access, Persistence, and Postbachelor's Outcomes." U.S. Department of Education. 2018.

"genius, n. and adj.". OED Online. September 2021. Oxford University Press. https://www-oed-com.ezproxy.library.unlv.edu/view/Entry/77607?redirect edFrom=genius (accessed November 08, 2021).

Kyle Grady, "'The Miseducation of Irie Jones': Representation and Identification in the Shakespeare Classroom," *Early Modern Culture* 14 (2019): 32.

Perry Guevara, "Toward Speech Therapy: Affect, Pedagogy, and Shakespeare in Prison." *Early Modern Culture* 14 (2019): 59.

Cassie Miura, "Empowering First-Generation Students: Bardolatry and the Shakespeare Survey," *Early Modern Culture* 14 (2019): 46.

Victor B. Saenz, Sylvia Hurtado, Doug Barrera, De'Sha Wolf, and Fanny Yeung. *Fist in My Family: A Profile of First-Generation College Students at Four-Year Institutions since 1971*. Los Angeles: Higher Education Research Institute, 2007: 8–10.

Ayanna Thompson, *Passing Strange: Shakespeare, Race, and Contemporary America*. Oxford: Oxford University Press, 2011. 17.

Ayanna Thompson and Lauri Turchi. *Teaching Shakespeare with a Purpose: A Student-Centered Approach*. New York; London: Bloomsbury, 2016: 4. I first encountered this text when I began to teach Shakespeare, and its influence on my pedagogy is impossible to overstate.

CHAPTER 11

Shakespeare Goes to Technical College

John Gulledge and Kimberly Crews

You can find Shakespeare just about anywhere. That's especially true in higher education, where the study of Shakespeare is both commonplace and deeply contested. At traditional four-year institutions, as well as smaller liberal arts colleges, students and faculty expect to find his works. At Technical Colleges, however, he appears to be missing. Why is that? More importantly, what happens when Shakespeare does show up in the vocational classroom? While writing about Shakespeare curricula in community college nearly three decades ago, Dora Tippens sums it up as "a sort of 'As You Like It,' a something-for-everyone menu" (Tippens 1984, pg. 653). Because community college is meant to spread across general education as well as specialized career training, Tippens brings forward how the inclusion of Shakespeare would have to be both broad and specific—an obvious but difficult undertaking. This need for transfer is even

J. Gulledge (✉)
Wittenberg University, Springfield, OH, USA
e-mail: gulledgej@wittenberg.edu

K. Crews
Atlanta Technical College, Atlanta, GA, USA
e-mail: kcrews@atlantatech.edu

more urgent in technical education, where the curriculum is more "hands-on" in preparing students for professional life, or, as is often the case, for a transition from one career to another. At Atlanta Technical College (ATC), a predominantly Black institution in the heart of metro Atlanta, Georgia, we have a shared vision to "transform" the lives of students in preparing them for the global workforce and community leadership.[1] Thus, embedded in the language of what constitutes technical education is transformation. In this chapter, we focus on the role of transformation, as well as its linguistic cousins "transfer" and "translate," to reflect on the ways Shakespeare finds his way into a technical curriculum. Further, we argue that vocation-centered education reveals Shakespeare as a pedagogical tool, not some sacred font of human existence.

Students at a technical college are particularly keyed into questions relating to their own contemporary lives when reading early modern texts. Rather than ending at a meta-analysis of the theater, our experiences teaching at a technical college have taught us that students seek to understand connections between the plays and their everyday lives. Deploying Shakespeare in this way reveals a level of utility belonging to the humanities that we often ignore. Not reducing or confining the teaching of Shakespeare to a tool for specialized labor, nor a mere cultural touchstone, we posit that the study of Shakespearean drama prepares students to live among others and to survive in an age of (mis)information overload. Before the COVID-19 pandemic, for example, several of John's students at Atlanta Technical College developed a mantra that they would shout at him across campus: "Eyes open, Mr. G!" The maxim first came about during one of his Introduction to Humanities classes in the spring of 2019. He and his students were studying Hamlet's play within a play as a way to think about information literacy and contemporary media. "The Mousetrap" scene is used to spy and discern guilt, of course, and involves various levels of deceit and rhetorical manipulation. Indeed, the performance is meant to accomplish something. At every turn, parties involved must distinguish between fact and fiction while modulating their own performances. Halfway through a semester, it is not uncommon for a student to confess that they found unreliable sources for their end-of-term research paper, and another student will proudly remind them: "Eyes open."

What this brief anecdote begins to untangle are our three primary claims. First, approaching Shakespeare on our students' terms, and in ways that make sense for them, opens the text rather than forecloses its possibilities. Second, teaching Shakespeare at a technical college has illuminated his works for us, and teachers would benefit from focusing more attention on how Shakespeare speaks across cultural and socio-economic backgrounds. In fact, Shakespeareans do not discuss Shakespeare in technical or vocational college curriculum nearly enough. Our purpose is to highlight how the study of early modern drama and the vision of technical education are catalysts of change, of transformation, for each other. A logic of elitism would have us hold these two pedagogical spheres apart, but once intertwined, both adapt and translate alongside each other. Here, there is a production of a shared creative content. Our hope is that more research and interest will take foot in the shared vision of vocational education and Shakespeare Studies to trace the production of agency and how educational outcomes are transformed by career-ready students through the pedagogical use of Shakespeare in the technical classroom.

Indeed, most research on teaching Shakespeare at the college level centers around traditional four-year university contexts.[2] Shakespeare remains a synecdoche for the study of English literature in and out of the English classroom, and this mythos, we contend, perpetuates yet another myth: somehow, we have come to agree (without much agreement) that Shakespeare is best suited for students pursuing bachelor's degrees at institutions with strong backgrounds in the liberal arts. Behind this implicit consensus lurks the fiction that Shakespeare is not for the working class— that somehow an actor-turned-playwright born to a working-class father in the sixteenth century represents only the "elite" among us now. Despite Sharon O'Dair's blistering impeachment of the colonial elitism within Shakespeare Studies roughly two decades ago, attention to the affordances and limitations of Shakespeare at technical colleges has gone largely unmentioned (O'Dair 2000). What's more, the counter belief that students attend two-year institutions only to prepare for the workforce arises from a similar place of privilege.

WHERE IS SHAKESPEARE?

Though scholarship and pedagogical discussion surrounding Shakespeare in technical and vocational school settings is scarce in comparison, we find a strong corollary in the work done on including Shakespeare in community college curricula. This work signals the vital importance of transfer, not simply as a practical use-case, but in the sense that we are willing both to entrust our students with transforming the content and developing their subsequent transformation for having done so. Writing with Timothy

Francisco, O'Dair once again addresses the pervasive elitism of Shakespeare studies, giving a blueprint for what college teachers can do now while working toward long-term goals of radical inclusivity:

> Those in the 99 percent of the profession must, first and foremost, continue to explore pedagogies grounded in the realities of our students' lives... doing the best to mitigate the inequalities of higher education by equipping our students with the intellectual agility that might actually translate to some real social mobility. (Boutry 2019, pg. 15)

The technical college is nothing short of the standard bearer for the ninety-nine percent in higher education. The emphasis on translation in Francisco and O'Dair's instruction above corresponds with the mission of Atlanta Technical College and its emphasis on transforming students' lives.

What's more, "Non-traditional" students are already equipped with life experiences of adaptation and, through this resourcefulness, creative transformation. In her discussion of teaching Shakespeare at an urban community college in Los Angeles, Katherine Boutry reminds us that "a professor who intends to capture and hold the intellectual interest of this demographic must be prepared not only to teach and to entertain, but also to reassure and to inspire" (Davidson 2017, pg. 124). In short, the driving question behind teaching Shakespeare does not assume the value of reading and discussing his works, but, instead, challenges the instructor to reveal that value in how the class is designed and facilitated. For Boutry, creativity became the key to doing this.

The construction of the liberal arts as the premier pathway to social mobility and personal fulfillment (Benedicks 2007), and Shakespeare's long-standing correspondence with that program, may give us some clue as to why little has been written on the technical college in Shakespearean circles. Crystal Benedicks usefully teases out the tension between what has come to be called a "liberal education" and "general education" and the assumed social and cultural implications of each. She warns us, for example, to remain aware of the cultural access that Shakespeare promises students and to examine the role of the instructor both in empowering students to engage with said market, while questioning and confronting such mythos (Forrester 1995a, pg. 182). Like Benedicks, we "find it difficult to believe that knowledge of Shakespeare's writing is transformative in and of itself" (Forrester 1995a, pg. 183). Rather, the transformation occurs in our students' working through, with, and sometimes against the texts. Put simply, they are the agents of their transformation. Conversely, Ann Forrester's perspective in 1995 emphasized the inherent "goods" on offer by teaching Shakespeare, focusing on the perceived merit of the literary and historical material for any given "educated person" (Mareneck 2018). Our technical students have been real-world counterexamples to this "traditional" take.

In addition to what Shakespeare might offer working-class students at technical or vocational institutions, we should continue to explore what this diverse student body may offer the study of Shakespeare. In her reflection on teaching acting at Bronx Community College, Ellen Mareneck distinguishes between a "culturally biased" and "culturally based" view of theater education. She candidly describes the need to move beyond her own ideas and assumptions about what theater, acting, and teaching were in order to join her students in creative transformation (Koon 2007, pg. 3). As with Boutry's observation of students' adaptation, Mareneck's first encounter with teaching community college led to personal and pedagogical insight: "Here were these students," she writes, "who had learned to play transforming roles long before enrolling in a theatre class with amazing stories to tell, yet when they entered my classroom, I had no clue how to support, acknowledge and welcome them into academic discourse" (Koon 2007, pg. 8). By centering the technical college's emphasis on "transformation," teachers of Shakespeare across institutional lines have an opportunity to prepare students to be agents of change rather than containers of arcane knowledge.

To clarify, "transformation" is built into the very mission of technical college and thus explicitly informs our approach to teaching Shakespeare. Many of our students come from trade backgrounds or are seeking to enter new trades. It is common for students in our English and Humanities classes to be working on degrees in welding, cosmetology, culinary arts, nursing, and cybersecurity—there are no Physics, English, History, or Pre-Med students. In other words, our students come to us with a unique set of tools and unique language built around their chosen career paths. These are the primary tools with which our students see themselves as agents of transformation. What a Shakespeare pedagogy built around transformation requires, then, are creative ways of enabling students to approach and feel their way around a text using their own strategies for knowledge-making and creative re-working. A student in cybersecurity, for example, has approached the unauthenticated, often misleading missives in Shakespeare as "phishing" attempts. By exploring an early modern drama built around "phishing," this student was able to draw out new tools not only for understanding his future employment but as a member of future communities: what rhetorical tactics have prevailed over 400 years, for instance, and how far might the consequences stretch? Students ultimately transform the text—both for themselves and each other—and create new strategies and tools relevant to the future they desire. If we take it that reading, writing about, and performing Shakespeare is in any way transformative, it should come as no surprise that a demographic inundated with life challenges and diverse backgrounds should sense and unlock those parts of his works that academics tend to forget.[3] Although she is not a Shakespeare scholar, Kimberly has born witness to a historically underserved and disadvantaged community of students who fashion Shakespeare's work into applicable knowledge. She has witnessed Shakespeare's work shapeshift into a more accessible narrative, because, as an example, a cosmetologist within our technical college system has the opportunity to reveal another level of beauty, dress, style, and chemistry analysis from Shakespeare's body of work.

TECHNICAL CURRICULA

Technical education, also known as vocational education, is not a new concept globally. World War II elevated this traditionally local training program into a federal mission and mandate. Federal legislation, funding, and local to state governance transformed traditional vocational objectives from war initiatives to objectives that holistically trained students and prepared them to enter a competitive workforce. Technical education, specific to the state of Georgia, evolved through several iterations, from Trade and Vocational Schools to the Department of Technical and Adult Education, to its current name and mission of Technical College System of Georgia (TCSG) (Carleton 2002).

Historically, the state of Georgia elevated the production, acreage, and market value of cotton in the United States. In the wake of 1917, the cotton labor and market economy steadily decreased, prompting the passage of the Smith-Hughes Act, legislation often called the "magna carta" of education that created an avenue for Georgians to retool and retrain in order to reboot Georgia's economy [pg. 63].[4] Education became the key to combat growing and glaring inequities. TCSG's mission, then, is to "build a well-educated, globally competitive workforce through technical education, adult education, and customized training for Georgia's businesses and industries."[5] Here, students may find a space to regroup, retrain, and experience a transformation into a new field or onto a new pathway through customized business and industry training. This caveat is where technical education diverges from its university counterpart. Whereas the typical accredited four-year university, or the two-year community college, hones a student's ability to research and produce scholarly work, the technical or vocational school is designed to train students for workforce development specific to career preparation.

In 2015, fifteen technical colleges in Georgia, including Atlanta Technical College, created a new program to bridge the gap between higher academia, the workforce, and the economic development of students. At Atlanta Tech, we call the program "Interdisciplinary Studies," and it is meant to "develop the core academic competencies necessary for student success in college and in the global workplace."[6] Atlanta Tech is among the handful of colleges that have opened the program to all students, not merely focusing on dual enrollment students, or rather high-school students enrolled in college courses. The wealth of knowledge and experience instructors bring to the general education programs, but specifically to Arts and Sciences, enables their ability to translate scholarly works and research into relatable and applicable tools and material for the life and work of the technical student. In the meetings and working sessions that led to the creation of this program, Kimberly notes that our students (and essentially our program) required faculty and leadership to think and present materials from a flexible posture. If our success is directly linked to the workforce development of our students, their community, and the "economic well-being of our state," then we needed to innovate and bend toward means which make our students equally, if not more, competitive than their traditional counterparts (Adams 1992). In 2019, we created a Center for Workforce Innovation at Atlanta Tech to further advance our community and business partnerships throughout Atlanta, redoubling our efforts to support the economic well-being of our students and the State of Georgia.[7] The shift, then, was less about mirroring four-year or more traditional two-year institutions—rather, it was to meet the needs of our students and community partners.

In order to meet those expectations from program and industry partners, Arts and Sciences at Atlanta Tech integrates those two pillars in its curriculum, career preparation projects, and research ventures. Here, faculty are heavily encouraged to bring their industry experience, field experience, and/or classroom experience to ensure that the curriculum meets transfer expectations. Our degree-level English courses have the Student Learning Outcome of Writing and Research, writing being the primary outcome. After successfully completing the course series, the student is ready, at the sophomore level, to participate fully in writing tasks within the workforce. This training is paired with opportunities for professional development and practical hands-on experience in that field. TCSG, and more specifically Atlanta Tech, is known for its ability to lean heavily on turning abstractions into practical, hands-on experience. Shakespeare's works garner an opportunity for Atlanta Tech's English and Humanities faculty to make real transformation. But we also deploy Shakespeare's works to challenge the dominant, hegemonic culture as it is often taught— to appreciate and analyze his wit, while interrogating his language and how that language is crafted (or perhaps interpreted) through a classist or ethnic lens.

TEACHING SHAKESPEARE AT ATC

We each started teaching at Atlanta Technical College at different points. John started in 2018, first with English composition and eventually the current course he now teaches, Introduction to Humanities. While his specialization is in Shakespeare and early modern literature, these courses had a lot more content to cover, and the expectations of ATC students could not be simply mapped onto those expectations familiar to John from teaching at a traditional four-year university. The inclusion of Shakespeare, he knew, would benefit his students and help them to meet the expectations of their future employers. However, over the last several years, and roughly twenty classes later, the how to this belief has become clearer, marked by as many missteps as successes. Moreover, the inclusion of Shakespeare in a technical college context has illuminated facets of the plays and their afterlives that he had not heard in great circulation among Shakespeareans, if at all. For instance, the generic features of the sonnets as precursors to "diss tracks" or the rhetorical "sales pitch" of characters like Portia in *The Merchant of Venice*.

The richness of a technical college lies in its students: they come from diverse backgrounds, at varied stages in life, and with unique interests. The myth that Shakespeare is somehow "good for all" is tested here; assumptions about what matters most in Shakespeare's plays are likewise under scrutiny and often found wanting. For example, while teaching the "To be or not to be" speech from *Hamlet* 3.1, John has the students read the speech aloud, and he also show clips of past productions. Though he has included this in almost every iteration of his Introduction to Humanities course, his approach and understanding of the speech have changed dramatically. Initially, his emphasis was on parsing the language, treating the speech like a language puzzle to be "figured out." The result of such an exercise, he expected, would lead to discussion about life and death, the nature of contemplation, and human agency in the face of felt-obligations. These conversations were the usual suspects. His students at ATC, however, challenged the speech at face value. "Does he not have a job to be doing?" one student asked. The rest of the class joined in shared puzzlement. Due to time constraints, they had not read the play in its entirety: they had read a short summary and had briefly discussed the plot and major character points of the play before turning to the speech. The students understood that the Prince of Denmark has a serious issue with taking definitive action and that the play has been read time and time again as being about indecision and the postponement of doing. What they wondered was powerful in its simplicity: how does he have all this time? Their lives are on tight budgets, especially in relation to time, where a once or twice a week class is sometimes the one place they are free to sit in total contemplation.

Though in varied shades, our students react similarly to this play every semester. The discussion that follows is one whereby students access the figure of Hamlet as a foil to their own lives. They begin to wonder about their own labor and the ethics surrounding the demands made by external forces on their time, skills, and creativity. The pangs of life are made concrete, given flesh by the embodied, complicated lives of the students. John now begins every post-speech discussion with the question: "Do you see yourself in Hamlet?" Before, he would have tried in earnest to show them potential connections, no matter how tenuous or generalizing. Now, their answer of "not really" opens the text to serve as a tool to discovering more about who they are and who they want to be. It matters little about who Hamlet is, of course, and their engagement with what at first appears to be a thoroughly opaque text and character orients them toward self-reflection in relation to their current work and life situations, as well as to future career aspirations. This is so, not because *Hamlet* is universal, but precisely because the play is not. Students at ATC revised assumed understandings of Hamlet, the character, making clear their distinct ability to transform the assumed boxes put before them. The belief that vocational training— what in our class looks like ethics, argumentation, creative problem solving, interpersonal skills, and so on—is somehow divided from intellectual enrichment and self-discovery holds little water in these moments.

Importantly, we want our students to see Shakespeare as a single figure along a literary line, rather than the line itself. Doing so achieves at least two important aims we view as critical to technical education. On the one hand, it casts a light against the looming cultural shadow of Shakespeare, empowering students to see themselves as potential co-creators in the making of history. On the other, it emphasizes the creative components of vocational training; students are encouraged to see the creative process as collaborative—not a process of singular "genius" but rather one of community. One example of this is when John spends a week on the sonnet and its tradition. We trace this tradition through four poets, beginning with Shakespeare. From the sixteenth century, we turn to John Keats in the early nineteenth century, then to Gwendolyn Brooks during the Harlem Renaissance of the twentieth century, and finally end with Rita Dove. This timeline is a product of course constraints, and at first glance, it would be easy to suspect that it tells a disingenuous story of how Shakespeare made possible the rest and so on. Another seductive but equally deceptive story would be that each poet's iteration was an improvement on the form. Our students aren't interested in these kinds of narratives, however, and so reductive discussions of this sort are easily avoided. Instead, we focus on the significance of remix and revision. Dove's "Hades' Pitch" and "Persephone, Falling" (though not a sonnet itself) are great models of this and invite students to think both creatively and strategically about resisting oppressive, otherwise imperial, forms. At her best, Dove is a masterful allusionist, remaking the world through transformation rather than destruction.

FUTURE DIRECTIONS

Our goal has not been to suggest that the inclusion of Shakespeare in vocational curricula is easy or straightforward. Many internal and external customers and interest groups find Shakespeare to be "highbrow" and unrelated to vocational needs. In the Arts and Sciences division at ATC, Shakespeare has a presence, albeit small, but a sure presence in varying English and Humanities courses. During semesterly meetings or curriculum review and grading alignment sessions, faculty and leadership review textbook readings and workshop assignments creating a "Strengths, Weaknesses, Opportunities, Threats" (SWOT) analysis to decide what's working well and what's not. This leadership firmly believes in meeting the system competencies but also providing a space where faculty can do the work of shaping a holistically trained student, using whichever tools are necessary. Shakespeare, thus, is a tool wielded in our classrooms. Most instructors who have used Shakespeare in either English or Humanities courses use his work and life as a jumping off point, a bridge to other materials, thoughts, or present-day issues (e.g., the transitory nature of language and the politics behind it). Inspired by Jeff Adams's pathbreaking work in the 1990s, we see a future for technical education that combines disciplines in more meaningful ways. This type of "cluster teaching" integrates more traditionally "academic" fields with vocational departments, turning Shakespeare into a truly hands-on learning experience.[8] Theater is a prime vehicle for this path because it involves many collaborators: those responsible for set design, hair and makeup, historical research, acting, marketing, and so on.

Additionally, in our combined years of teaching, we have never encountered a student who did not struggle with Elizabethan works. Students, at the introduction or reintroduction of Shakespeare, consistently struggle with the language. In Kimberly's class, for example, after an in-class activity concludes with students highlighting vocabulary about which they are confused, the true lesson begins. Students then learn that some of the words they use today were first used in writing by Shakespeare, words like *swagger*[9] or phrases like *green-eyed with jealousy* (Leggatt 1992). This close attention to the material history of words and meaning is often eye-opening for our students. Many remain under the assumption that words in the English language have always existed and are not continuously created, tested, and revised. We have the pleasure of teaching them that they have the potential to impact history by creating and expanding the English language, just like Shakespeare, and just like many of the Hip-Hop and Pop artists of today. The lesson continues with a group discussion about Shakespeare penning his works in a common tongue, and how this trend did not change even when playing for royalty. At this point, our students begin to make several realizations: (1) Shakespeare lived by a similar code as they do: FUBU, or "for us, by us," both a clothing brand and also a community attitude for many of our African-American students; (2) their home and community language is valid and generative and with it they can create something beautiful and timeless; and (3) they have the opportunity to become their own versions of a lyricist, authors of their own ingenious wordplay, and they might use these tools to feed their families. With additional time and leeway, faculty and students would have the chance to deeply engage with Shakespearean works, to challenge his assumptions, and open the work to include varying human experiences, more specifically from vocational-centered students, more akin to his original audience (Leggatt 1992).

There is, though, still a gap our students cannot easily cross. For all of the class familiarity and human condition and experience found in his texts, our students and faculty cannot help but see Shakespeare and his work through the critical lens of race, gender, sexuality, and disability. Shakespeare was still a white, wealthy man—discourse communities that are mostly different from those of our students at Atlanta Tech, where more than 90 percent are BIPOC and a majority identify as low-income.[10] Our technical students (as well as members of our faculty) continue to feel like outsiders when reading, analyzing, and writing about Shakespeare's works. It is hard to pick parts of yourself to "see" in Shakespearean works, which is why many of our Arts and Sciences faculty use "canonical" white authors as an amuse-bouche and not the main course. There is great value in having technical students translate Shakespeare into their own speech and vernacular. Shakespeare's was a project of sketching characters that felt alive, and the diversity found in vocational school settings can revitalize this aspect of the work. Students draw on the "aliveness" of language and recreate scripts, collaborating with Shakespeare rather than working against his remote language. Moreover, embedding speeches and episodes of Shakespeare's works in current, cultural affairs not only bridges the contextual gap somewhat but likewise places the drama in the world of action. In this way, technical students remind us that theater is home to action and activity, a space of doing and creation.

Even so, there is a balancing act with which all educational systems must engage, especially in terms of time, space, and the viability of a program and its curriculum and competencies. Although general education (Gen. Ed.) is widely intertwined with traditional vocational programs, those pathways dictate what type of general education courses are deemed integral to student advancement within the workforce. Industry needs and students' future economic development, via the successful completion of their "technical education" and training, also dictate what general education courses are offered or what courses are financially covered under their chosen programs. General education standards are in the center of an ever-packed boxing ring, always on the ropes fighting against both old requirements and newcomers. When programs introduce additional curriculum considerations, Gen. Ed. is usually the first set of courses reconsidered for relevance in the program—the first set of courses minimized or completely removed (as seen in diploma programs).

Transformation in a technical classroom is a collaborative effort with the goal of developing a holistic student who will challenge and innovate solutions for their educational and workforce journeys. As we mentioned above, "transformation" is derived directly from ATC's mission statement. We ask our students to challenge real-life issues from different perspectives with the hope that bridges will appear between the content and their "home" language, between their chosen career and the culture they are studying, between the socially constructed barriers of gender, race, class, and disability that they might experience in their future careers and communities. Indeed, technical and vocational students actively see themselves as creators and collaborators. The centrality of *doing* and *making* should not be confused, however, with an ever-calculating utilitarianism. Ours is a program of transformation centered on how the individual might make room for themselves within a community. The inclusion of Shakespeare's works recenters that shared sense-making, not because the works themselves are transcendent, but because they tender possibilities ripe for testing, for more *doing* and *making*. The classroom is the place of transformation, and our students, its agents, not the other way around. Teaching Shakespeare's work at a two-year technical college in the heart of a major metro area has reminded us of that important fact.

NOTES

1. Atlanta Tech Strategic Plan 2018–2022. https://atlantatech.edu/wp-content/uploads/strategic-plan-2018-2022_posting-revised-12_2018.pdf.
2. Moreover, it is still assumed that students who matriculate at two-year institutions may plan to eventually attend a four-year university. Transferring from a four-year to a two-year school, however, is considered a "reverse transfer" and assumed to be incredibly rare, despite *The Chronicle*'s dubbing community college as the "preferred institution" of transfer students. J Gonzlez, "A Third of Students Transfer Before Graduating," *The Chronicle of Higher Education* (2012).
3. We have chosen not to include specific anecdotes and lists of our students' traumas in this chapter. We hope readers will understand this decision and trust that ATC's mission "to serve low-income, low-achieving, underserved populations," speaks to a truly heterogeneous student body. "Strengthening Predominantly Black Institutions (Competitive Grants) Program: FY 2011

Project Abstracts," *Predominantly Black Institutions Program* (2011), 2 https://www2.ed.gov/programs/pbi/pbi-abstracts2011.pdf.
4. "About," Technical System of Georgia. Retrieved December 28, 2021, https://www.tcsg.edu/about-tcsg/.
5. "Arts and Sciences," Atlanta Technical College. Retrieved December 28, 2021, https://atlantatech.edu/programs/arts-and-sciences/.
6. Faculty Handbook, Atlanta Technical College (Updated 2019).
7. See the Center for Workforce Innovation website for more information on this initiative: https://atlantatech.edu/community-and-business/center-for-workforce-innovation-cwi/.
8. "swagger, v.". OED online. December 2021. Oxford University Press. http://www.oed.com/viewdictionaryentry/Entry/195354   (accessed March 05, 2022).
9. "green-eyed, adj. 2". OED online. December 2021. Oxford University Press.   http://www.oed.com/viewdictionaryentry/Entry/81188 (accessed March 05, 2022).
10. "Campus Snapshot, TEC0181". Atlanta Technical College. https://atlan-tatech.edu/wp-content/uploads/Campus-Snapshot-by-Year-TEC0181.pdf.

References

Adams, Jeff. 1992. "The Play's the Thing: Integrated Curriculum Makes Even Shakespeare Relevant to Vo-Tech Students." *Vocational Educational Journal* 67.8 (1992): 32–33.

Benedicks, Crystal. 2007. "The Shakespeare Portal Teaching the Canon at the Community College." In *Reclaiming the Public University: Conversations on General & Liberal Education* 18: 177–186.

Boutry, Katherine. 2019. "Creativity Studies and Shakespeare at the Urban College Classroom." In *Shakespeare and the 99%*, ed. Sharon O'Dair and Timothy Francisco. Springer.

Carleton, David. 2002. *Landmark Congressional Laws on Education.* Greenwood Press.

Davidson, Cathy. *The New Education: How to Revolutionize the University to Prepare Students for a World in Flux.* Basic Books, 2017.

Forrester, Ann. 1995a. "Why Teach Shakespeare? (or Any Other Dead White Male?)," (Paper presented at the Community Colleges Humanities Association Conference, November).

Tippens, Dora. "Crossing the Curriculum With Shakespeare," *Shakespeare Quarterly* 35.5 (1984): 653–656.

O'Dair, Sharon. *Class, Critics, and Shakespeare.* Ann Arbor: University of Michigan Press, 2000.

Forrester, Ann. 1995b. "Why Teach Shakespeare? (or Any Other Dead White Male?)," (Paper presented at the Community Colleges Humanities Association Conference, November).

Mareneck, E.C. 2018. "Teaching Introduction to Acting At Bronx Community College: From Shakespeare to Sza." *International Journal of Whole Schooling* 3.

Koon, Mary Downing. 2007. "Technical College System of Georgia," New Georgia Encyclopedia, last modified Oct. 20, 2015. https://www.georgiaencyclopedia.org/articles/education/technical-college-system-of-georgia-tcsg/.

Leggatt, Alexander. 1992. *Jacobean Public Theatre*. Routledge.

CHAPTER 12

"Let the Sky Rain Potatoes": Shakespeare Through Culinary and Popular Culture

Sheila T. Cavanagh

Nobody "needs" Shakespeare, but university students often demonstrate a desire to learn about his work, even if they are not majoring in the Humanities. My students at Emory University are typically academically adept and eager learners, but some pre-medical, pre-professional, first-generation, and international students hesitate at the level of prior expertise they fear will be needed in order to tackle a full semester of early modern drama, with its unfamiliar language and other perceived obstacles. I have always encouraged a broad range of students to incorporate their personal and prior educational knowledge into Shakespearean studies, but COVID-19 led me to develop two courses that offer new avenues of engagement to particularly diverse groups. The few English majors in these cohorts find numerous ways to deepen their literary expertise, but their classmates from other backgrounds also find many entry points into the course material. Everyone expands their understanding of Shakespeare, but they also gain additional theoretical and practical knowledge and find

S. T. Cavanagh (✉)
Emory University, Atlanta, GA, USA
e-mail: engstc@emory.edu

S. Freeman Loftis et al. (eds.), *Inclusive Shakespeares*, Palgrave
Shakespeare Studies,
https://doi.org/10.1007/978-3-031-26522-8_12

numerous ways to succeed. The courses, "Cooking with Shakespeare" and "The Many Faces of Shakespeare: Literature and Popular Culture," link common interests in foodways and television with relevant segments of Shakespeare. The asynchronous sessions, required by pandemic Zoom classes, are designed to be both entertaining and informative. By the end of term, most students have excelled in numerous ways: the courses encourage students to combine their own personal and cultural experiences with the study of Shakespeare, and they soon recognize that Shakespeare is already embedded in their daily lives in ways they had not previously realized.

"Cooking with Shakespeare" offers innumerable opportunities for students to expand their educational and culinary horizons while drawing from their personal and cultural backgrounds in unexpected ways. This greatly reduces the levels of intimidation commonly associated with more traditional Shakespearean syllabi where students fear encountering lengthy examples of the playwright's complex language without overtly welcoming contextualization. Emory lacks appropriate early modern culinary spaces and equipment, but the cooking course can be taught either electronically or in person, using the university's modern kitchen. Alternative class assignments are available for any undergraduate lacking access to necessary environments or utensils, but during this Maymester version, all students had kitchens readily available, often with friends or relatives available for culinary consultation. The students write regularly and each of them cooks, bakes, or concocts beverages, but they are able individually to balance these tasks so long as they submit sufficient prose to fulfill the writing requirement. They also choose which dishes or drinks to prepare, so that they can accommodate their budgets and local access to ingredients.

The course includes pertinent Shakespeare daily, but the students also encounter significant material involving farming, economics, relevant early modern legal circumstances, international trade expansion, calendar customs that involve food, religious influences on dietary habits, and the importance of climate for food production and storage. In ordinary times, Maymester classes meet for 3.5 hours daily over a period of three weeks. This schedule can be arduous, so Zoom brings surprising benefits. We gather on Zoom for 90 minutes daily, then the students engage in another 90 minutes of asynchronous work. In addition, they have daily reading and writing to complete. An abundance of high-quality streaming material, the opportunity to spend part of this time covered with flour or investigating beef recipes, and a wide variety of reading keep the students engaged and reduce the fatigue and anxiety that often accompanies more conventional Maymester classes. Student participation has been consistently high, with few absences. Our recent group included an ardent vegan, an equally committed carnivore, several international students, a couple of playwriting majors, an economist, at least one first-generation student, and a number of undergraduates majoring in the sciences or math. Their contributions to the course were as diverse as their backgrounds. While we were never able to enjoy a communal feast, we marveled at various cooks' ingenuity while acquiring a newfound understanding of the wide disparities between food production in early modern times and our own. Everyone was continually struck by how much labor was involved for those without servants. With a nod to pop-singer Gloria Gainer, a general sentiment among the students was "I would NOT survive" (Gainer 1978). In addition to learning about early modern culture, they gained a new appreciation for how little of their own physical effort went into their daily food consumption and how often they possessed little detailed information about what they were eating and where it had originated.

To offset this initial limited knowledge about food culture, the compressed Maymester schedule includes varied asynchronous assignments, beginning with one season of a popular BBC series focused on life in varying time periods, from conditions in a medieval castle to those on a farm during the First World War. In each season, the "stars" (frequently domestic historian Ruth Goodman with archeologists Peter Ginn and Alex Langland) move into an appropriate historical property and endeavor to recreate the jobs and challenges facing working people during the chosen era over the course of a calendar year. For this class, the students watch *Tales from the Green Valley* (2005), set in 1620, with a few segments from the *Tudor Monastery Farm* of 1520 (2013). Emory students find the historical/archeological trio to be personable and informative. After watching the entire season of *Green Valley*, recent students were delighted to encounter some of the same figures, now seen as old friends, in *Monastery Farm*. Each segment lasts 30 minutes and students view two episodes per weekday, then complete the series over the first Maymester weekend. The program proves remarkably successful, since it demonstrates the real-life obstacles and achievements faced by a talented and knowledgeable group who need to contend with the vagaries of the weather and locate appropriate experts as they engage with diverse aspects of early modern farming, husbandry, dairying, cooking, and household chores. These figures are generally cheerful and ingenious, but make it clear that their tasks require extensive labor. While most of the students have never thought about the topics considered, they invariably find the episodes thought-provoking and engaging.

Classes include Shakespeare daily, ranging from plays encountered in high school to other less common texts. We discuss the culinary and household preparations for the Capulets' feast in *Romeo and Juliet*, for instance:

> A hall in Capulet's house.
> Musicians waiting. Enter Servingmen with napkins
> FIRST SERVANT
> Where's Potpan, that he helps not to take away? He
> Shift a trencher? he scrape a trencher!
> SECOND SERVANT
> When good manners shall lie all in one or two men's
> Hands and they unwashed too, 'tis a foul thing.
> FIRST SERVANT
> Away with the joint-stools, remove the
> Court-cupboard, look to the plate. Good thou, save
> Me a piece of marchpane; and, as thou lovest me, let
> The porter let in Susan Grindstone and Nell.
> Antony, and Potpan.
> SECOND SERVANT
> Ay, boy, ready.
> FIRST SERVANT
> You are looked for and called for, asked for and
> Sought for, in the great chamber. (1.5.1-14)

This scene includes dialogue that students are unlikely to have noticed, even if they have seen or read the play before. Our dual foci on food and on socioeconomic differences in the period make this an illuminating passage, however. It introduces some of the aspects contributing to a festive occasion and begins to denote the ways that status divides characters in the play. We discuss these lines while we are reading about early modern banquets, so the students have seen images of joint-stools, court-cupboards, and trenchers, they have read marchpane recipes, and they have discerned many of the differences existing during this era between wealthy households and homes inhabited by those with more modest means. They will also have witnessed the arduous labor contributing to the concerns expressed about unwashed hands in conjunction with a fancy party. Throughout the class, we consider ways that people from varying social and economic situations interact. In concert with the *Green Valley* episodes and passages such as this description of the Capulet's hosting preparations, class members start to understand some of the central issues surrounding our areas of concern.

Another scene involving dining, from *A Comedy of Errors*, also combines a discussion about food purportedly between people of different stations in the same house, as Dromio berates his supposed employer about his absence at the dining table:

DROMIO OF EPHESUS
Return'd so soon! rather approach'd too late:
The capon burns, the pig falls from the spit,
The clock hath strucken twelve upon the bell;
My mistress made it one upon my cheek:
She is so hot because the meat is cold;
The meat is cold because you come not home;
You come not home because you have no stomach;
You have no stomach having broke your fast;
But we that know what 'tis to fast and pray
Are penitent for your default to-day. (1.246-56)

Here, students encounter capon, which is a castrated rooster fed with a rich diet of dairy or grains, as well as a pig on a spit. Capon was a popular dish for those with means and it often appears within Shakespearean drama. This passage also includes a minor allusion to humoral theory—"She is so hot"—that resonates with students who have been reading and talking about these issues, often comparing them with medical practices such as acupuncture and modern uses for caffeine and alcohol. Once again, many students will not know this play, but they are acquiring knowledge that helps reduce the fear of unfamiliar language while alerting students to the common conversations that often appear in such "high-brow" texts.

We spend significant time investigating the spice trade and encounter numerous allusions to relevant foodstuffs. After watching an episode about sheep-shearing in *Green Valley*, for example, we view and read pertinent scenes from *A Winter's Tale*, such as the Shepherd son's conversation to himself about the items he is instructed to buy:

Shepherd's Son
I cannot do't without counters.   Let me see;
what am I to buy for our sheep-shearing feast? Three pound of sugar,
five pound of currants, rice,--what will
this sister of mine do with rice? But my father
hath made her mistress of the feast, and she lays it
on. She hath made me four and twenty nose-gays for
the shearers, three-man-song-men all, and very good
ones; but they are most of them means and bases; but
one puritan amongst them, and he sings psalms to
horn-pipes. I must have saffron to colour the warden
pies; mace; dates?--none, that's out of my note;
nutmegs, seven; a race or two of ginger, but that I
may beg; four pound of prunes, and as many of
raisins o' the sun. (4.3.37-51)

A further mention of spices also corresponds with social status in *Twelfth Night* when Sir Toby and Feste berate Malvolio:

Sir Toby: Art any more than a steward? Dost thou think, because thou art virtuous, there shall be no more cakes and ale? Feste: Yes, by Saint Anne; and ginger shall be hot i' the mouth too. (2.3.114-117)

Kate Humble hosts a series of documentaries available on YouTube that introduce the spices that emerged in Europe during this period and several of our readings describe the widespread implications of this growing traffic in culinary products produced outside of England (Humble 2011). Spices are commonplace in the students' experience, but facilitating their understanding of the significance of such emerging ingredients increases their understanding of Shakespeare and of the broader historical and cultural implications of food history.

Contextualizing Shakespeare is also facilitated by a number of readings, easily made accessible through Emory's Woodruff Library and our Canvas course management system. We read and discuss essays and book chapters by authors such as Peter Brears (2015), Lena Cowan Orlin (1995), Jillian Azevedo (2017), Joan Fitzpatrick (2007), and John Bohstedt (2010). These texts discuss configurations of households, spaces associated with food preparation and storage, imported goods, societal economic constraints, and other relevant topics. This past May, we also enjoyed

Zoom conversations with a number of visitors, including scholar Sarah Higinbotham, who guided the students through a period recipe for drinking chocolate; Gitanjali Shahani, who discussed several chapters of her book on international food trade (2020); John Tufts (2020), who described how he developed his Shakespearean cookbook *Fat Rascals* through his experiences as an actor with Oregon Shakespeare Festival (he also detailed his family history at Emory, which still boasts "Tufts House" on its campus); and two of the Folger Institute's "Before Farm to Table" post-doctoral scholars Neha Vermani and Elisa Tersigni, who introduced students to their research at the Folger. The combination of reading Shakespeare in conjunction with learning about life in early modern England from visitors, readings, films, and other digital materials enables the students to immerse themselves into the dramatic passages more deeply, but it also provides them with opportunities to demonstrate their own relevant, prior knowledge. The economics major this year, for instance, described some of the theories underlying the various readings we encountered about the range of socioeconomic levels present during this period. Many of the other undergraduates had no academic experience to help them understand the poor laws, the enclosure acts, or the aspects of growing international trade that affected people across England at this time, but their classmate was able to offer helpful contextualization. Similarly, a pre-health student had encountered humoral theory in one of their previous courses and was prepared to explain the gist of these beliefs in ways that supplemented the discussions we read in Shakespeare and scholarly essays. Virtually all of the students were able to contribute to the conversations we had about food and calendar customs, and they each had experience with many of the spices being used in England during Shakespeare's lifetime. One further advantage to meeting over Zoom emerged when we learned that much modern-day "cinnamon" is actually "cassia." When this topic came up in discussion, the students ran to their kitchen cupboards in disbelief, but most soon realized that this ingredient they had never heard of regularly substitutes for the spice they thought they knew.

These few examples illustrate some of the advantages of engaging with Shakespeare through cuisine. As noted, students are often intimidated by Shakespeare, in part, they report, because they believe that their classmates are more knowledgeable than they are. Even though everyone stumbles over Shakespearean language some of the time, they are regularly convinced that they are the only ones who do not understand unfamiliar vocabulary or references. None of the students, however, arrive in this class believing that they should already know the intricacies of Elizabethan husbandry or Jacobean practices relating to cheese-making or fishing. They understand that they are all equally unversed in techniques for cooking lamprey or curing meat, and they do not feel embarrassed when they acknowledge that their first experience of growing vegetables came during the COVID-19 pandemic. Some of the students have extensive experience with cooking, while others have none, but they appear not to believe that they "should" already know such things when they arrive in college. Shakespeare, though often forbidding, is frequently a topic they believe they should have already tackled or that they are incapable of managing. In a course linking certain plays with food, they seem to put these expectations aside. Everyone is a learner together and all students have something valuable to offer. While this is typically true in more conventional Shakespeare courses, "Shakespeare and Cooking" helps students recognize this circumstance.

We also benefit from the students' diverse culinary interests and abilities. Occasionally, they choose similar recipes to try—syllabub is a favorite—but their creations generally range widely. Having an ardent vegan in the course this Spring was a real benefit, since they researched vegan recipes in the period and investigated surprising early modern vegan options, such as almond milk. The international students were unaccustomed to preparing dishes common in early modern England, but they tried adventuresome recipes and shared information about ingredients that were familiar or unknown, respectively, in their own culinary background. Students made tarts, entrees, and marchpane sculptures and explored the circumstances where these items would be located or absent in Shakespeare's time. When they cook, such students benefit from modern food distribution systems and technology, such as electricity, at least in the course's current iteration, but they also gain significant knowledge about the foods available to people of different social standings in the Tudor and Jacobean eras as they prepare dishes as diverse as plain pottage and the much fancier salmon baked in "coffins" made with fat and flour, then topped with pastry crafted to look like the fish it covers. When they present their creations to the class, they talk about where they found the instructions, which historical groups might have had access to the necessary ingredients and other resources, where alterations to the recipe need to be made, and how these items might fit in with some of the Shakespearean meals we encounter in the plays. As they prepare their edible projects, they acquire a variety of related information, including topics such as when potatoes were introduced to England, which spices were limited to the wealthier populace and how they arrived in Europe, how much meat was eaten and what quantities were sold, and the extent of damage done to English teeth by the sugar only a few could afford. Neuroscience demonstrates that people retain knowledge most efficiently when new information is added to related material (Zull, part three) (2002). Since all students have prior experience with food, these culinary lessons support their acquisition of additional information in an accessible fashion.

Not surprisingly, television, games, popular novels, and films also offer enhanced access to Shakespeare for this disparate range of students. Like "Cooking with Shakespeare," "The Many Faces of Shakespeare" facilitates students' ability to access Shakespeare through material they know and enjoy, even though they frequently do not think about possible Shakespearean connections until they encounter them in coursework. Lawrence Levine's *High Brow/Low Brow* is well known to scholars but contains an invaluable contextualizing framework for students who have generally not previously encountered this work (1990). Levine's Shakespeare chapter, combined with a number of Folger Shakespeare Library podcasts[1] and essays from *Borrowers and Lenders[2]: The Journal of Shakespeare and Appropriation* and elsewhere, help students understand possible reasons why Shakespeare appears in so many unexpected popular locations and provides them with tools to investigate the role of Shakespeare in a number of similar sources. Most of the materials we view, read, and discuss are openly available on the Internet, which also supports access. In this class, we begin our discussions with items created from the 1940s onward, although Levine includes earlier sources in his volume. Many of the materials from the mid-twentieth century lack significantly diverse racial, sexual, or socioeconomic representations of society, but this absence fuels searching discussions in today's sociopolitical classroom environment. Similarly challenging, but important, conversations ensue when students contend with the decision of whether or not to view the Shakespearean episodes of *The Cosby Show* (1987) or *House of Cards* (2013–2018), given recent events involving cast members Bill Cosby and Kevin Spacey. Students who opt out receive alternative assignments. While such aspects of these programs are not directly related to Shakespeare, they still help engender consideration of the role of television within our society and the ways that unintended messages can be conveyed through these media in conjunction with the probable cultural and economic goals of the series.

Since Levine speaks at length about the performance of Shakespeare in America's purported "Wild West," we start with a few somewhat oblique, but germane episodes from popular Westerns, including a radio broadcast of *Gunsmoke* (1952), and Shakespeareanized segments from *Maverick* (1960) and *Bonanza* (1965). The Shakespearean allusions are less overt than in some of our other examples, but the *Bonanza* episode in particular illustrates Levine's "high brow/low brow" distinction when female towns-people urge Ben Cartwright (Lorne Greene) to present sophisticated artistic productions in addition to the rodeo events typically associated with a large local festival. He invites an opera singer he has long admired (Viveca Lindfors) to be the chief attraction, but many locals are hoping that Shakespeare will be part of the offerings, including Hoss Cartwright (Dan Blocker), who earnestly endeavors to memorize key passages from the plays. Some students in the class have parents who introduced them to Westerns as children, but these mostly unfamiliar examples of the genre entertain many of these undergraduates, even though the *Gunsmoke* story-line unduly obfuscates its Shakespearean associations. After reading Levine, the students understand the historical antecedents of these interludes, however, and begin to understand that Shakespearean allusions are part of a rich and extensive history.

The texts and programs we investigate include both familiar films and television programming such as *Harry Potter* (Rowling 1997–2007), *Game of Thrones* (2011–2019), and *Star Trek*,[3] as well as examples that are lesser known to today's students, such as *Ozzie and Harriet* (1954) (a class favorite), *My Three Sons* (1967), and *Car Fifty-four Where are You* (1961)? The *Ozzie and Harriet* episode combines a couple of plot charac-teristics that are common in these situation comedies, namely, the intro-duction of a guest star (John Carradine in this case) that some adult audience members will associate with Shakespeare and the conceit that one of the sitcom children is confronted (either happily or in resistance) with Shakespeare in school, then interacts with an adult who encourages them to face the opportunity to excel (or fail) socially through perfor-mance. *Sanford and Son* (1973), *Diff'rent Strokes* (1983), *The Brady Bunch* (1971), *The Cosby Show*, and *Frasier* (2001), among others, incor-porate at least some of these motifs. *The Cosby Show* features famed Shakespearean actor Christopher Plummer, for instance, as a friend of Cliff Huxtable's (Bill Cosby) father Russell (Earl Hyman) who endeavors to introduce Theo Huxtable (Malcolm Jamal Warner) to an appreciation of Shakespeare. The adults recite Shakespeare from memory with evident enjoyment, demonstrating to the children present that they find this drama to be fulfilling and important. *Frasier* turns this trope around, since the guest actor Derek Jacobi (as Jackson Hedley) is the one who introduced Shakespeare to Frasier (Kelsey Grammer) and his brother Niles (David Hyde Pierce) when they were children. Providing a fortuitous link to some of the other course material, Frasier and Niles determine to return Hedley to the classic stage rather than the world of cult science fiction he now inhabits. With a dual nod to baby boomers and current Marvel universe fans, the brothers are able to thwart their own ill-conceived plan (Hedley is a terrible actor) with the introduction of Hedley's father, English actor Patrick Macnee, best known for his role in the 1960s hit *The Avengers* (1961–1969). The famous guest stars, that only audience members of a certain age will recognize, add some of the multi-layered appeal often embedded in popular entertainment. *My Three Sons*, in contrast, rewards viewers with Shakespearean knowledge. In 1967's episode "Both Your Houses," numerous *Romeo and Juliet* references appear. Students paying attention, moreover, are amused when Robbie (Don Grady) and guest star, singer Jackie DeShannon, present some Shakespearean songs to their delighted parents who do not seem to realize that what appears to be a love song actually contains murderous lyrics drawn from *Macbeth*. These sitcoms do not depend on viewers with a Shakespearean background, but they provide bonuses for those who recognize these allusions.

The widely diverse students drawn to "The Many Faces of Shakespeare" appreciate the opportunity to watch television as part of their studies, particularly during the stresses of the pandemic, but they also enjoy playing "watch for the Shakespeare" and engaging their friends and family in conversations about the class assignments. Resembling the students in the cooking course who don't feel uneasy about not knowing how to catch or cook eels, these students do not feel intimidated by watching *Looney Tunes* (2000), *Beverly Hillbillies* (1967), or *Addams Family* (1991). Since most of these episodes highlight familiar Shakespearean plays, such as *Romeo and Juliet*, *Hamlet*, and *A Midsummer Night's Dream*, they also feel equipped to spot many references when they occur, even if they miss numerous nods to Shakespeare early in the term, such as the appearance of Hermione in both *The Winter's Tale* and *Harry Potter*. In fact, they generally express delight at their newfound ability to see Shakespeare in materials they thought they already knew well. One student, for example, had grown up watching lots of *Sanford and Son*, since that was his father's favorite show. He assumed that he was an expert on this program but was nonetheless thrilled at the unremembered sight of Lamont (Demond Wilson) playing Othello in 1973. Many of the students are long-time fans of *Star Trek* and/or *Star Wars*[4] and enjoy learning aspects of these narratives that previously eluded them. Since most of these students are not English majors and are frequently first-generation, science, or international students, they relish the opportunity to speak with others about their academic work through the lens of well-known and extremely popular books, films, and television programs. During the extra stresses introduced by COVID, these students also appreciate the fact that they can offset doing their scientific lab assignments at home and their intensive pre-medical exams with assigned viewings of *Gilligan's Island* (1964–1967), *Breaking Bad* (2008–2013), and *Succession* (2018–2023).

The students' classroom presentations further enabled them to explore their own interests, often leading in fascinating directions. One student focused on the TV show *Barry* (2018–2023), which was new to me. In this program, Bill Hader stars as Barry Berkman, a hit man who unexpectedly becomes drawn to acting. Shakespeare appears frequently. *Barry* will be included in a future iteration of this course, as will some of the materials other students focused upon, from Taylor Swift to Tupaq. We were fortunate enough to have a zoom visit with The Sonnet Man (Devon Glover),[5] which piqued students' interest in intersections between Shakespeare and modern forms such as rap and Hip Hop which they had previously not considered. For their final projects, numerous students created their own Shakespearean adaptations that included choreographed dance, make-up palettes, computer-generated imagery, and musical compositions. In each instance, they detailed their rationale for adapting Shakespeare through their chosen medium and typically demonstrated keen understanding of the drama as well as the environment in which they embedded Shakespeare's work.

Throughout the semester, we read passages from Shakespeare aloud and discuss the plays in historic and performative contexts, but the students do not read plays in their entirety until they are working on their mid-term or final projects. Some of them work with texts that had been unfamiliar to them before such as *Richard III*, since so many of the adaptations we consider include references to this play. It remains rare for the students to delve into less widely known dramas, such as *All's Well That Ends Well* or *Henry VI, part two*, but I discuss characters and situations from a variety of plays as we move through the term, hoping that at least something about the breadth of Shakespeare will resonate despite the comparatively restricted number of texts that recur in much Shakespearean popular culture. The course banner introduces them to the chef-like image of Anthony Hopkins as *Titus Andronicus*[6]; they occasionally encounter the many bawdy puns associated with *Coriolanus*; and there are some surprising Shakespearean moments in advertising, as Douglas Lanier also describes, such as the reference to *Two Gentlemen of Verona* in a plug for Sabena Airlines or the Fairbanks lard ads that refer to a range of plays, such as *Henry IV* (Lanier 2014). These ads can easily be shared either in person or via zoom and they tend to provoke interesting discussions about the ways that marketing incorporates Shakespeare much more often than the students realize. Emory boasted an extensive exhibition on Shakespeare and Popular Culture entitled "A Goodly Commodity" during the Shakespeare anniversary year in 2016 (http://shakespeare.folio.emory.edu/). Most of the artifacts included, from shower curtains and toasting forks to Barbie and Wishbone dolls, now reside in my office, making them readily available to share with students on a regular basis, as needed. Students may not know much about *Richard II, Cymbeline*, or another lesser performed play, but there is typically a tea towel, a playing card, or some other bit of obscure ephemera that includes them. The students will undoubtedly not learn as much from these mementoes as they would from reading and/or seeing these plays, but it still broadens their familiarity with Shakespeare and helps activate the synapses that may fire when related information is encountered in the future (Zull, part two). Some germane popular culture items seem designed to plant these kinds of Shakespearean seeds for young people; others appear to "reward" adults who recognize the allusions. In both instances, these books, songs, games, puzzles, films, and TV programs further embed Shakespeare into many people's shared cultural spaces. Many people are currently questioning Shakespeare's comparative ubiquity in a world where there are many other voices unheard and these queries are appropriate. Shakespearean allusions are not a necessary part of students' education but learning to recognize and analyze them can help provide a prominent literary aspect of the broad knowledge many expect from a university education. This practice can also help readers and viewers understand some of the complexity that contributes to many popular books and movies. As curricula expand to incorporate texts and voices that have often previously been marginalized by conventionally canonical texts, Shakespeare can also participate in these expansions of perspective. People everywhere have many stories to tell, and Shakespeare may well capture more than his "fair share" of adaptations. Nevertheless, the role of Shakespeare in global conversations warrants examination and at least some students will choose to learn from these canonical artifacts.

"Cooking with Shakespeare" and "The Many Faces of Shakespeare" introduce undergraduates to a wide range of perspectives. The culinary class raises questions about food production and allocation that resonate both for the early modern period and for today. It also provides undergraduates with access to the kind of hands-on learning that is beneficial for education but that is often minimized in university curricula. Given that Shakespeare is often perceived as "foreign" from modern times and circumstances, it is striking that the food-related passages in the plays often bring characters and situations more clearly in focus and help them become more clearly relevant for students who may find Shakespeare off-putting or dated. The popular culture course helps undergraduates to recognize the integration that often subtly exists between their academic endeavors and the material they consume for pleasure. The conversations generated in these classes can easily transfer to home or social settings in ways that college curricula often resist. First-generation students, international students, pre-medical students, and pre-professional undergraduates all benefit from classes that make Shakespeare more approachable: students frequently engage in dialogues about the books, movies, music, games, and TV shows they encounter. Food, a subject everyone has experience with in one form or another, garners additional interest, both on television and in "real" life. Recognizing the ways that Shakespeare is communicated through these avenues, therefore, provides students with unusual opportunities to integrate very different aspects of their lives.

NOTES

1. Folger Library Podcasts. https://www.folger.edu/podcasts-and-recordings.
2. *Borrowers and Lenders: The Journal of Shakespeare and Appropriation.* 2005–present. https://openjournals.libs.uga.edu/borrowers/index.
3. *Star Trek.* https://intl.startrek.com/.
4. *Star Wars.* https://www.starwars.com/.
5. The Sonnetman. http://sonnetman.com/.
6. *Titus.* Directed by Julie Taymor. https://www.imdb.com/title/tt0120866/.

REFERENCES

Addams Family. 1991. https://www.imdb.com/title/tt0101272/.

Azevedo, Jillian. 2017. *Tastes of the Empire: Foreign Foods in Seventeenth Century England*. New York: McFarland and Company.

Barry. 2018–. https://www.imdb.com/title/tt5348176/.

Beverly Hillbillies. 1967. *The Clampetts in London*. https://www.imdb.com/title/tt0522601/.

Bohstedt, John. 2010. *The Politics of Provisions: Food Riots, Moral Economy, and Market Transition in England, c. 1550–1850* (History of Retailing and Consumption). London: Routledge.

Bonanza. 1965. *The Spotlight*. https://www.imdb.com/title/tt0529828/.

Breaking Bad. 2008–2013. https://www.imdb.com/title/tt0903747/.

Brears, Peter. 2015. *Cooking and Dining in Tudor England*. London: Prospect Books.

Car Fifty Four Where are You? 1961. *The Taming of Lucille*. https://www.imdb.com/title/tt0536400/.

Diff'rent Strokes. 1983. *Romeo and Juliet*. https://www.imdb.com/title/tt0560016/.

Fitzpatrick, Joan. 2007. *Food in Shakespeare: Early Modern Dietaries and the Plays* (Literary and Scientific Cultures of Early Modernity). London: Routledge.

Frasier. 2001. *The Show Must Go Off*. https://www.imdb.com/title/tt0582551/.

Gainer, Gloria. 1978. "I will Survive." https://www.youtube.com/watch?v=fCR0ep31-6U.

Game of Thrones. 2011–2019. https://www.imdb.com/title/tt0944947/.

Gilligan's Island. 1964–1967. *Hamlet*. https://www.youtube.com/watch?v=MKMOClN9ITg.

Gunsmoke. 1952. https://www.oldtimeradiodownloads.com/western/gunsmoke/shakespeare-1952-08-23.

House of Cards. 2013–2018. https://www.imdb.com/title/tt1856010/.

Humble, Kate, 2011. *The Spice Trail*. https://www.imdb.com/title/tt1855043/?ref_=fn_al_tt_1.

Lanier, Douglas. 2014. *Marketing Shakespeare. The Oxford Handbook of Shakespeare*, edited by Arthur F. Kinney. Oxford: Oxford University Press. 498–514.

Levine, Lawrence. 1990. *HighBrow/LowBrow: The Emergence of Cultural Hierarchy in America*. Cambridge, MA: Harvard University Press.

Looney Tunes. 2000. *Looney Tunes Shakespeare*. Dvd.

Maverick. 1960. *Maverick and Juliet*. https://www.imdb.com/title/tt0644467/.

My Three Sons. 1967. *Both Your Houses*. https://www.imdb.com/title/tt0654985/.

Orlin, Lena Cowan. 1995. *The Elizabethan Household*. Washington, D.C.: Folger Shakespeare Library.

Ozzie and Harriet. 1954. *An Evening with Hamlet*. https://archive.org/details/OZZIE_AND_HARRIET_An_Evening_With_Hamlet.

Rowling, J.K. 1997–2007. *Harry Potter Series*. London: Bloomsbury.

Sanford and Son. 1973. *Lamont as Othello*. https://www.imdb.com/title/tt0694113/.

Shahani, Gitanjali. 2020. *Tasting Difference: Food, Race, and Cultural Encounters in Early Modern Literature*. Ithaca, N.Y.: Cornell University Press.

Shakespeare, William. 2015. *The Norton Shakespeare*, edited by Stephen Greenblatt et al. New York: W.W. Norton.

Shakur, Tupaq. 1983. *Something Wicked*. https://www.youtube.com/watch?v=-ksBTXQdc5Q.

Succession. 2018–. https://www.imdb.com/title/tt7660850/.

Tales from the Green Valley. BBC. 2005. www.imdb.com/title/tt0478958/.

The Avengers. 1961–1969. https://www.imdb.com/title/tt0054518/.

The Brady Bunch. 1971. *Juliet is the Sun*. https://www.imdb.com/title/tt0531103/.

The Cosby Show. 1987. https://www.imdb.com/title/tt0547064/.

Tudor Monastery Farm. BBC. 2013. https://www.imdb.com/title/tt4103600/.

Tufts, John. 2020. *Fat Rascals: Dining at Shakespeare's Table*. http://www.johntufts.com/fatrascalsbook.

Zull, James E. 2002. *The Art of Changing the Brain: Enriching the Practice of Teaching by Exploring the Biology of Learning*. Sterling, VA: Stylus.

CHAPTER 13

"Let Gentleness My Strong Enforcement Be": Accessing San Quentin Prison with Inside-Out Shakespeare

Perry Guevara

When Shakespeare writes of "inaccessibility," he often has in mind physical space, a rugged terrain, or an arboreal wilderness that tests his characters. In *The Tempest*, shipwrecked Adrian worries that the island is "uninhabitable and almost inaccessible," contrary to the local knowledge of those who have lived there for so long: Caliban, Ariel, Sycorax, even Prospero and Miranda as latecomers (Shakespeare n.d., 2.1.38). The Forest of Arden in *As You Like It* is rendered similarly remote. Hungry and desperate, Orlando attempts to rob the exiled lords of Duke Frederick's court of their meal only to discover that such force is unnecessary. "Your gentleness shall force / More than your force move us to gentleness," admonishes Duke Senior (Shakespeare 2002, 1.7.101–2). Baffled by their unwarranted hospitality, Orlando replies:

P. Guevara (✉)
Dominican University of California, San Rafael, CA, USA
e-mail: perry.guevara@dominican.edu

© The Author(s), under exclusive license to Springer Nature Switzerland AG 2023
S. Freeman Loftis et al. (eds.), *Inclusive Shakespeares*, Palgrave Shakespeare Studies,
https://doi.org/10.1007/978-3-031-26522-8_13

207

> But whate'er you are
> That in this desert inaccessible,
> Under the shade of melancholy boughs,
> Lose and neglect the creeping hours of time;
> If ever you have looked on better days,
> If ever been where bells have knolled to church,
> If ever sat at any good man's feast,
> If ever from your eyelids wiped a tear
> And know what 'tis to pity and to be pitied.
> Let gentleness my strong enforcement be. (Shakespeare 2002, 2.7.108–117)

He appeals to a vision of a shared, past life outside of "this desert inaccessible," where mutual pity once gave way to gentleness. Here, even if only momentarily, gentleness is possible where it is least expected.

Orlando's promise to "let gentleness" be his "strong enforcement" retroactively critiques a contested site of enforcement in our present-day society, where, more often than not, gentleness fails to guide politics and where access is barred, quite literally: prison. My upper-level Shakespeare course brings undergraduate students inside the walls of San Quentin State Prison, just north of the Golden Gate Bridge on the shores of San Francisco Bay, so that they may learn, study, and perform Shakespeare alongside incarcerated actors. A mere five miles from campus, the prison bears the name of Quentín, a Miwok warrior who was once imprisoned there. The prison's namesake is a crucial reminder of overlapping histories of land on which the prison is built—of the Coast Miwok peoples, Catholic Spanish mission, trans-Pacific migration, and African-American shipbuilding in the Second World War—what Chickasaw scholar Jodi A. Byrd might recognize as an "incommensurable" place that now manifests the tragedy of mass incarceration (Byrd 2011). I developed the course on the premise that Shakespeare ought to be read in terms of where he lands—however unlikely that place might seem—that the study of Shakespeare can help communities reckon with the incommensurability of the lands they inhabit and that Shakespearean theater has the potential to promote community. Above all, my pedagogy pursues the practice of gentleness through theater in prison, a space profoundly hardened by recalcitrant and racist cultural narratives of criminality and a penal system that privileges retribution over reintegration.

As Ayanna Thompson rightly points out in *Passing Strange: Shakespeare, Race, and Contemporary America*, teaching Shakespeare in prison is fraught: Black and Brown populations are disproportionately and unjustly subjected to the violence of law enforcement as well as to America's capitalist investment in incarceration, and far too often is Shakespeare deployed as an antidote, when, in fact, Shakespeare historically has contributed to the maintenance of the university as a settler colonial institution (Thompson 2011). These issues are not lost on my students, most of whom came of age during the Black Lives Matter movement and with the rise of social media activism. Demographically, 71% are students of color and 23% count as first generation, meaning that they are the first in their families to attend four-year college. Many know firsthand what it means to live in over-policed communities, and some even admit to trauma stemming from the criminal justice system.[1] Prison-Shakespeare pedagogy implicitly registers power differentials between those on the inside and those on the outside, but for these students, visiting San Quentin means coming into contact with a community that is adjacent, if not coextensive, with their own through such social mechanisms as the school-to-prison pipeline.[2] Because of their backgrounds, many arrive with an understanding of this contiguity and their own embeddedness in a community unevenly affected by incarceration. That is to suggest, their very emplacement resists complicity in the myth of Shakespeare as savior, because they become his new interpreters, remaking his texts for unintended publics. To reckon with our proximity to incarceration, this course integrates the study of Shakespearean drama with service learning, in partnership with the Marin Shakespeare Company, to bring theater to the following groups: men imprisoned at San Quentin, returned citizens seeking reintegration to society, and at-risk (or better yet, "at-promise") youth in under-resourced schools. While Orlando's vision of the "good life" on the outside might not apply in all places, including present-day California, much less the United States, his trust encourages a radical, pedagogical, and political gentleness that enables access to an otherwise inaccessible place. Marin Shakespeare makes this access possible.

In a recent essay, Jayme M. Yeo characterizes the pedagogy of putting traditional college students in conversation with incarcerated people as "inside-out." Such pedagogy, Yeo suggests, accomplishes two goals: the first, redressing the "problem of testimonial oppression" and "the stereotypes that contribute to it;" the second, creating "a community of readers that more completely understands issues of incarceration" (Yeo 2019, p. 197). "Inside-out" learning strategies include, for Yeo, letter writing and video conferencing between prisoners and students; however, she laments that "combined face-to-face classes are logistically impossible" (Yeo 2019, p. 202). The problem she identifies, without saying as much, is one of access. How does an instructor get college students inside a prison to study Shakespeare? Moreover, how do we design curricula that ensure access, safety, and educational efficacy for both students and the incarcerated? The question of access in prison is layered, so here, I narrow my focus to two matters: practically speaking, the logistics of going from outside to inside the prison within the structure of a semester-long class and then, more conceptually, dwelling in what it means to access a highly disciplinary, heavily policed, and culturally stigmatized space, only then to transform that space through theater.

The course takes its name from Shakespeare for Social Justice, an arts-in-corrections program, led by the directors, artists, and technicians of Marin Shakespeare. Every year, the company mounts three main-stage productions of Shakespeare's plays in our campus' open-air theater, while also providing free educational programming, informed by drama therapy and with guidance from a certified drama therapist, to underserved communities in Northern California, especially those impacted by the criminal justice system. Shakespeare for Social Justice uses theater to recast the roles of prisoner, juvenile offender, and criminal as actor. When enrolling in the course, students commit to spending a minimum of 20 hours with Marin Shakespeare over the course of the semester, collaborating on their mission to bring the restorative potential of theater out into the community. Each week, students put in a couple of hours not only in the Shakespeare classroom but also directly inside a prison, public school, or theater. While all students have the opportunity to work with incarcerated actors inside San Quentin, they also choose where to spend the remainder of their required hours, either with "at-promise" youth in local schools or with returned citizens, who write, rehearse, and stage original theater about reintegrating into society after prison. These triangulated points of access actualize for students the narrative of incarceration in California—prologue and epilogue, to boot—as well as the societal, political, and economic mechanisms that perpetuate its momentum into an industry. These external spaces are coextensive with the academic classroom.

The course is guided, in part, by Theater of the Oppressed, a system of theater techniques elaborated by the Brazilian director Augusto Boal, who famously deconstructed the binary of the spectator and the actor into the figure of the "spect-actor," one who both acts and witnesses in the name of social change (Boal 1985). What emerges from such practice is the illusoriness of separation between an acquiescent audience and industrious players on stage: the breaking of the fourth wall, so to speak. On the first day of class, I arrive to students sitting politely at their desks, notebooks and laptops arranged tidily at their fingertips, obediently facing the front of the room while awaiting the professor's instructions. They appear as good Foucauldian subjects. Before we proceed even with a glance at the syllabus, I tell them to exit the room, back into the hallway, and re-enter the space in a way that disobeys and disrupts the traditional propriety of the college classroom. How they choose to re-enter is up to them. After a few sideways glances and uneasy laughs, students intuit their own embeddedness in a stratified power structure and embrace its disturbance: skipping backward, thumping their chests, whooping, hopping like frogs, rolling on the floor, standing on chairs, and pounding their feet. Once the saturnalian antics subside, I emphasize the point of the exercise: the classroom, like so many physical spaces we inhabit in society, is structured by hierarchy and repetitions of power that solidify into norms. Theater of the Oppressed instructs awareness of how uncritical passivity and idle receptivity result in complicity with oppression. For Boal, however, witnessing activates performance.

After expeditiously introducing theories of power in those first weeks of class, including Michel Foucault's architectonics of the panopticon and Giorgio Agamben's figuration of bare life, students come to see how prisons, schools, and even theaters are disciplinary spaces where they too are subjected to power (Agamben 1998; Foucault 1995). Understanding their situatedness in relation to institutional power is critical to their interaction in the community beyond our campus gates, so that they might resist seeing themselves as privileged avatars of the university dispatched into the community to fix the problems of the truly and authentically oppressed. Rather, they too are embedded in oppression. While it might be easy to parody the "oppression olympics" and the self-righteous heroics of the "white savior complex," the sign of "oppression," under which under-represented groups and those at the margins of society live, proves undignifying and, ultimately, disempowering when "oppressed" takes on the effect of identity. For those with whom we work, such crude identities include "delinquent," "criminal," and "prisoner," whom the mainstream regards not as victims but as victimizers. In prison, such binaries are not so simple. Yeo argues that "inside-out" pedagogy helps decondition "the epistemic violence that accompanies the sign of 'criminal'" by disrupting racial stereotypes and cultural stigmas, instead "positioning incarcerated people … as readers, writers, actors, and artists" (Yeo 2019, p. 201). To facilitate this deconditioning, in the second week of class, students attend a main-stage production at Marin Shakespeare to watch formerly incarcerated actors take on prominent roles as full-fledged theater professionals. Marin Shakespeare hires artists-in-residence who studied Shakespeare in prison and, upon release, came on board as actors. Their performances begin to rewrite the narrative of life after incarceration, emphasizing not criminality but artistic excellence. Witnessing these actors on stage encourages students to challenge received notions of who ends up in prison and, thereby, reconfigure their own positionality in relation to those they eventually will meet on the inside. It also helps them calibrate their relationship to the university's institutional power, which inevitably follows them into the space of the prison.

Before our first theater workshop inside San Quentin, the class embarks on a pre-prison curriculum that combines Theater of the Oppressed, which inform the drama therapy techniques used at the prison, with readings not only of Shakespeare but also of critical scholarship on Shakespeare-prison programs, including important studies by Thompson and Elizabeth Charlebois (Byrd 2011). When it comes to Theater of the Oppressed, we use simultaneous dramaturgy, image theater, and forum theater, each increasing in complexity to gradually arrive in the role of "spect-actor." Simultaneous dramaturgy refers to a process in which audience members freeze a performance and suggest actions for the actors to carry out on stage in an effort to shift the outcome. To practice this technique in class, actors choose a relevant issue inspired by Shakespeare (e.g., patriarchal authority brandished by such begetters as Brabantio in *Othello* or Egeus in *A Midsummer Night's Dream*) and script a scene up to the point of conflict. The actors then pause the performance and invite spectating students to offer potential outcomes to the problem. The actors improvise these possibilities but with the caveat that audience members may intervene whenever they see fit to modify or challenge their actorly decisions. As a low-stakes theater exercise, simultaneous dramaturgy begins to dismantle the wall between actors and spectators.

With image theater, Boal sought to defamiliarize the everyday mechanics and mundane postures of the body by creating still images with actors' bodies as "statues," taking shape from feelings, ideas, or experiences. A still image is then modulated through a series of dynamic adjustments informed by layered meanings, shifting intentions, and mechanical possibilities (not to mention, limitations) of joint, muscle, and bone. Modeling this technique in class, one actor is assigned the role of "sculptor." As in simultaneous dramaturgy, the sculptor identifies an issue or a problem related to the concerns of the course. The sculptor then guides the other actors into static shapes dramatizing the problem. Once realized, the sculptor then reshapes the bodies of the actors into a second image visualizing a solution, destination, or desired outcome to the conflict. The sculptor finally molds a third image that represents how to move from problem to solution. Image theater emphasizes the embodiedness of not only theater but also social change, illustrating how the body and its kinesthetic capacities can drive community action.

The final process from Theater of the Oppressed is forum theater in which, again, actors script a scene confronting a social issue drawn either from Shakespeare or from their service-learning experience in the local community. However, this time, rather than leaving the ending unscripted for the audience to offer suggestions for improvisation, actors write their own conclusions. After rehearsal, they perform the script from beginning to end without interruption. Then, they stage it a second time, but those in the audience are encouraged to directly enter the scene, replacing the original actors, and improvising different choices to which their counterparts must respond and adapt in kind. This exercise, more than any other, actualizes what Boal means by "spect-actor," for here, spectators physically leave the audience to become actors themselves.

Supplementing theatrical praxis—these layered, iterative processes of writing, visualizing, and bodying forth—is instruction on the fundamentals of drama therapy. Nisha Sajnani, a drama therapist and founder of the Theatre and Health Lab at New York University, argues that Theater of the Oppressed lends itself to the practice of drama therapy because it demonstrates the "inseparability and permeability" among "disciplines of art, politics and psychology in the pursuit of progressive individual and social change" (Sajnani 2009, p. 461). To approach this interconnection, students begin with the concept of "aesthetic space" in theater, which Sajnani tells us "is determined by the physical dimensions of space, or platform, and by the mutual agreement of those who gaze upon it." An understanding of space is critical because students will not find a traditional theater—proscenium, thrust, or otherwise—inside the prison. In fact, at San Quentin, stagecraft takes place in a humble mobile unit, surrounded by a chain-link fence, on the far side of the prison yard. Although lacking the conventional trappings of an architectural theater, that trailer nonetheless transforms into aesthetic space because the incarcerated actors collectively regard it as such. Sajnani reminds us that, technically, "theatre can occur in any place" that "stimulate[s] knowledge and discovery, cognition and recognition, and learning by experience."

Drama therapy in this idiosyncratic space seeks recognition of cultural narratives that unjustly represent the incarcerated as failed or dysfunctional citizens. Dysfunction, Sajnani counters, is itself an effect of the pervasiveness of these narratives in our society: "Dysfunction … occurs with the internalization of any message that limits, circumscribes, or otherwise mutes the totality of what an individual or community is able to be and do … in solidarity with their neighbors" (Sajnani 2009, p. 478). As many of the actors at San Quentin admit, these messages limited their own sense of self and concept of personhood, especially the widespread narrative that men of color, from the neighborhoods where they grew up, would, at one point or another, find themselves in trouble with the law. Drama therapy seeks to expose and disrupt the insidiousness of such stereotypes: "The therapeutic process entails the identification and active negotiation of prohibitive and inhibitive messages … which limit or circumscribe the degree to which one is able to experience freedom in addition to awakening the desire to find plausible alternatives in thought and action" (Sajnani 2009, p. 476). In other words, theater spurs a reckoning with the self and, by extension, the community by imagining new narrative possibilities.

While it is necessary for students to connect theory to practice and Theater of the Oppressed to drama therapy, nothing compares to hearing the voices of those directly on the inside who, as Yeo points out, are all too often "rob[bed] of epistemic agency, subjecting their knowledge and voices to the systemic injustice of testimonial oppression" (Yeo 2019, p. 199). Even when given the opportunity to speak, testimonies of the incarcerated are undermined or "rendered suspicious" under the sign of "criminal." By this vexed logic, incarcerated people are unreliable narrators. But who better to speak about the experience on the inside than insiders? Who else has shouldered the burdens of prison? Who wields the authority to tell these stories? To ponder these questions, I assign students podcasts and audio narratives about incarceration in America. Yeo advocates for the importance of close listening, especially in "inside-out" pedagogy: "Our best response to testimonial oppression may simply be the intellectual habit of listening well" (Yeo 2019, p. 203). The 1619 Project, which couples audio with essays in the *New York Times Magazine*, helps students understand what Bryan Stevenson means when he says, "Slavery gave America a fear of black people and a taste for violent punishment.

Both still define our criminal-justice system" (Stevenson 2019). Mass incarceration's origins in American slavery and plantation culture are necessary historical contexts for apprehending testimonial oppression today. A second podcast called Ear Hustle, broadcast by Radiotopia, lifts the veil, so to speak, by enabling prisoners at San Quentin to become radio hosts and storytellers themselves, purveyors of their own experiences, giving an unvarnished take on "the daily realities of life in prison" (Poor et al. n.d.). Created by Nigel Poor, an artist and professor at California State University, Sacramento, Earlonne Woods, and Antwan Williams, both who were incarcerated when the podcast launched in 2017, Ear Hustle covers such diverse topics as living with cellmates (or "cellies"), solitary confinement (or "shu"), and what it is like to grow old and even die in prison. What is unique about teaching Ear Hustle in Shakespeare for Social Justice is that students have the opportunity first to listen to these stories as audio narratives and then meet the storytellers in person when they visit the prison a couple of weeks later.

Adding to these voices are guest speakers, who know firsthand what it means to cross the boundary from inside to outside and who are invited to raise awareness on campus about incarceration. Poor, for instance, described for students the logistical process of making Ear Hustle with Woods and Williams in San Quentin's media lab. Dameion Brown, formerly incarcerated actor and artist-in-residence at Marin Shakespeare, gave an acting masterclass to students and spoke about coming to Shakespeare after 20 years in Solano State Prison. At a panel on "Policing, Prisons, and Marginalized Communities," students listened to the stories of men and women previously incarcerated in the California criminal justice system and the challenges they faced upon release from prison. Such public events affirm the knowledge and untapped power of community voices historically ignored by settler colonial institutions, like prisons and universities, by making space for critique from within those institutions. They also pragmatically cap Shakespeare for Social Justice's pre-prison unit, designed to prepare students to access the prison.

Behind the scenes is a long logistical process of clearing students for entrance. Eight weeks before the first theater workshop with incarcerated actors, Lesley Currier, Managing Director of Marin Shakespeare, and I gather required documentation from students, confirming their legal names, birth dates, and driver's license numbers to verify with prison staff. We cover the prison's strict dress code: absolutely no blue, because that is the color the men wear. (Black, pink, purple, and red are good alternatives.) Other prohibited fashions include open-toed shoes, shorts, skirts with slits, jewelry, and camouflage. And although it might seem like common sense, students are reminded not to conceal such contraband as cellular phones, alcohol, tobacco, and cash. The only permissible items are clear and previously unopened water bottles, required medications, and prepackaged foods like energy bars. In the week leading up to their first visit, Currier again meets with students to review not only these regulations but also other procedures such as where to park, how to interact with guards, and how, in the case of an emergency, to stand for easy identification while the men in blue drop belly down on the ground. Hearing these, students realize the risk involved when going inside the prison, even if that risk is relatively small. I quickly remind them that I have never witnessed an incident nor felt endangered the many times I have been inside San Quentin, but we, nonetheless, arrive in vulnerable bodies. So do the actors. These policies intend to preserve the safety of all Shakespeareans at San Quentin.

When students finally arrive at the gates of the prison, they show identification to a guard, who escorts them to a second checkpoint, where they are scanned by metal detectors and stamped for entry. Once beyond the barred door, the group walks together past the chapel, the exterior of death row, and out-of-service cells from the old prison built in the mid-nineteenth century. (San Quentin is, after all, California's oldest prison.) As the group proceeds, Currier relays harrowing statistics of mass incarceration in the United States: how, for example, Black and Latino men are significantly more likely to be incarcerated than white men and how the national prison population exploded with the so-called War on Drugs in the 1980s. Then suddenly, around a corner, unfurls the expanse of the prison yard, where students observe incarcerated men engaging in various activities: jogging, calisthenics, socializing, resting. Once spotted, our not-so-conspicuous group is enthusiastically welcomed by several of the actors in the Shakespeare program, who join the excursion to the opposite side of the yard, where another prison guard unlocks the fence, giving the group access to the "aesthetic space," the mobile unit where prison-Shakespeare happens. This moment, perhaps more so than any other, is when students realize that they are, in fact, inside an actual prison. It is no longer an academic object of study but instead a live encounter.

The actors, on the other hand, appear more relaxed and keen to chat with students—this routine is familiar to them—but Currier, always the consummate director, dependably leads the troupe into acting warm ups.

Grounded in improvisation, these exercises intend to introduce the students to the men, while giving both the opportunity to express how they feel in this new encounter. Afterward, Currier divides students into small groups with the actors, guiding them into more elaborate improvisational exercises, including simultaneous dramaturgy and image theater. Groups might be asked, for example, to improvise a scene on the meaning of an abstract concept such as freedom, or they might be instructed to embody a series of statues representing the progression from injustice to justice. Through these practices, students and actors begin to collaborate not as strangers but as theater artists. At this point, the group transitions to working directly with Shakespeare's texts, not only for reading comprehension, but also toward a given theme. Last time, they focused on resilience in *As You Like It*, paying special attention to the plight of Duke Senior and the lords exiled from Duke Frederick's court:

> Now, my co-mates and brothers in exile,
> Hath not old custom made this life more sweet
> Than that of painted pomp? Are not these woods
> More free from peril than the envious courts?
> Here feel we not the penalty of Adam:
> The seasons' difference, as the icy fang
> And churlish chiding of the winter's wind,
> Which, when it bites and blows upon my body
> Even till I shrink with cold, I smile and say
> "This is not flattery"; these are counselors
> That feelingly persuade me what I am.
> Sweet are the uses of adversity,
> Which, like the toad, ugly and venomous,
> Wears yet a precious jewel in his head;
> And this our life, exempt from public haunt,
> Finds tongues in trees, books in the running brooks,
> Sermons in stones, and good in everything. (Shakespeare 2002, 2.1.1–17]

In conversation with students, the men searched the text for resonances with their own circumstances in San Quentin, finding irresistible comparisons to Shakespeare's Forest of Arden. They spoke of enduring the "icy fang" and "churlish chiding" of prison life, how their hardships have proven instructive as "counselors." They spoke of loyalty and the bonds of friendship with their fellow actors in the Shakespeare group, "their co-mates and brothers in exile," who collectively hope for parole and eventual freedom. They saw in this "life, exempt from public haunt," the possibility of sweetness—or, as I argue, gentleness—in a place where hardness is valued above all else. Here, literary interpretation is not a mere academic exercise; it is the work of drama therapy.

Most of the workshop is dedicated to translating script to performance, making those practical, actorly decisions of voicing, gesture, blocking, and how best to embody Shakespeare's language for a live performance that the men will eventually live-stream. As Currier regularly reminds the group, theater skills are life skills—creativity, self-expression, critical thinking, communication, problem solving, and teamwork—which will serve the men not only on stage but also when they are eventually released to the outside. When time has nearly expired and the workshop approaches its end, the group of actors and students form a circle; each participant names one thing from this morning at San Quentin for which they are grateful. For some, this final exercise proves emotional. Students admit to being blindsided by the rawness of prison-theater, the unexpected honesty of the actors, and the serendipitous human-to-human connections forged through craft. Others struggle with what it means that they, as students, can leave San Quentin, while the men in blue must stay behind. These farewells, however, do not signal the end of this work. It lasts through the semester in service-learning partnerships and beyond for those students who wish to continue apart from the requirements of the course. It even exceeds the university as students more fully evolve into citizens and take these experiences with them into the voting booth and into our ever-fragile democracy.

As a conclusion, I offer a final description of a theater technique used in Shakespeare for Social Justice, one that disarms me no matter how many times I witness it. Currier instructs the students and actors to mill about the performance space, somewhat aimlessly. When she calls "stop," students find the nearest actor, and the two stand silently face to face, only a couple of feet apart, and looking into each other's eyes. They are encouraged not to break eye contact. Currier then provides a statement to guide the silent interaction of looking, better yet, of seeing the other: "This person knows what it's like to feel pain." Then there is a pause, followed by "just like you." After a moment to process the gravity of mutuality between people who might perceive themselves as so different, as so far apart—and what amounts to a few seconds that somehow feel so much longer—she then instructs them to walk around again, finding another partner. "This person knows how it feels to love someone just like you."

Mill about again. "This person has experienced loneliness just like you." "This person has hurt someone they care about just like you." "This person, at some point in their life, needed forgiveness, just like you." Prompts like these are not so unlike Orlando's series of "if's"—"if ever you have looked on better days," "if ever from your eyelids wiped a tear." Despite all the challenges to this work, logistical as well as political, I wonder if we might be instructed by Shakespeare at San Quentin toward a radical and transformative gentleness.

NOTES

1. Importantly, students who have been traumatized by law enforcement and/ or the criminal justice system are not required to attend theater workshops in prison. On a case by case basis, I work with these students to identify other opportunities with local non-profit organizations to employ Shakespeare in service of transformative justice. Also, during theater workshops, students and actors may opt out of any activity at any point without explanation.
2. The school-to-prison pipeline is the systematic funneling of children from public schools to juvenile detention and, eventually, the prison system. This pipeline is reinforced not only by educational inequities in the United States but also by disciplinary policies that tend to target students of color, those from financially insecure circumstances, and those with learning disabilities.

REFERENCES

Agamben, Giorgio. *Homo Sacer: Sovereign Power and Bare Life*. Translated by Daniel Heller-Roazen, Stanford University Press, 1998.

Boal, Augusto. *Theater of the Oppressed*. Translated by Charles A. and Maria-Odilia Leal McBride, Theatre Communications Group, 1985.

Byrd, Jodi A. *The Transit of Empire: Indigenous Critiques of Colonialism*. Minnesota University Press, 2011.

Charlebois, Elizabeth. "'Their Minds Transfigured So Together': Imaginative Transformation and Transcendence in *A Midsummer Night's Dream*." *Performing New Lives: Prison Theater*, edited by Jonathan Shailor, Jessica Kingsley Publishers, 2011, pp. 256–269.

Foucault, Michel. *Discipline and Punish: The Birth of the Prison*. Translated by Alan Sheridan, Vintage-Random House, 1995.

Poor, Nigel et al. n.d. *Ear Hustle*, earhustlesq.com. Accessed 1 January 2022.

Sajnani, Nisha. "Theater of the Oppressed: Drama Therapy as Cultural Dialogue." *Current Approaches in Drama Therapy*. Edited by David Read Johnson and Renée Emunah, Charles C. Thomas Publisher, 2009, pp. 461–481.

Shakespeare, William. *As You Like It*. *The Complete Pelican Shakespeare*. Edited by Stephen Orgel and A.R. Braunmuller, Penguin, 2002.

Shakespeare, William. n.d. *The Tempest*.

Stevenson, Bryan. "Mass Incarceration." The 1619 Project. *The New York Times Magazine*. 14 August 2019, nytimes.com/interactive/2019/08/14/magazine/prison-industrial-complex-slavery-racism.html. Accessed 1 January 2022.

Thompson, Ayanna. *Passing Strange: Shakespeare, Race, and Contemporary America*. Oxford University Press, 2011.

Yeo, Jayme M. "Teaching Shakespeare Inside Out: Creating a Dialogue Between Traditional and Incarcerated Students." *Teaching Social Justice Through Shakespeare*. Edited by Hillary Eklund and Wendy Beth Hyman, Edinburgh University Press, 2019, pp. 197–205.

CHAPTER 14

Radical Listening and the Global Politics of Inclusiveness: An Afterword

Alexa Alice Joubin

The Hamletian question "Who's there?" opens the introduction to the present volume. It is now time, in the afterword, to ponder the implications of what comes next: "Answer me: stand, and unfold thyself" (*Hamlet* 1.1.2). Surveys and social rituals of inclusion in our times tacitly assume that it is always reparative and desirable, for the sake of solidarity or visibility, to assert one's self-identity publicly. That fantastical clarity of public self-revelation is neither found in Hamlet's universe nor in our world. For instance, it is now commonplace to have everyone self-identify their personal pronouns. However, if deployed as emptied-out rituals, the well-intended practice can be counterproductive as a form of compulsory public confession, which excludes those who change their pronouns depending on context or over time. The same is true of other identities. The insightful dialogue among Sonya Freeman Loftis, Mardy Philippian,

A. A. Joubin (✉)
George Washington University, Washington, DC, USA
e-mail: ajoubin@gwu.edu

© The Author(s), under exclusive license to Springer Nature
Switzerland AG 2023
S. Freeman Loftis et al. (eds.), *Inclusive Shakespeares*, Palgrave
Shakespeare Studies,
https://doi.org/10.1007/978-3-031-26522-8_14

and Justin P. Shaw in the Introduction reminds me of a focus group meeting that Sonya and I attended, where our collaborative research on the phenomenon of exclusive inclusiveness began.

Aiming to craft strategies for inclusion and diversifying its global author recruitment practices, the Press retained a consulting firm to bring together select authors to brainstorm on the design of a questionnaire. The authors came from many different linguistic and cultural backgrounds all over the world, not just the U.K. Therefore, participants took the firm to task over their configurations of nearly every identity category (gender, race, sexuality, age, neurodiversity, disability, and so on), since, even within the Anglophone world, words and cognates have very different connotations in each country, especially in our post-Brexit world and era of the pandemic of COVID-19. We debated whether the questionnaire needs gender and sex as separate categories and whether information about an author's "sex" is even relevant. The draft questionnaire asks interviewees across the globe to select from a list of identity categories, but the well-intentioned project is mired in ineffective communication due to its U.K.-centric vocabulary.

Naming is a powerful act, and it is preferable to defer to people's own self-identification rather than label them. Jack Halberstam has critiqued our society's penchant for categorizing the human experience, noting how "all of these efforts to classify human behavior" contribute to ongoing, divisive projects. Our current "profusion of classificatory options," such as the 51 gender categories offered by Facebook at one point, "fixes bodies in time and space and in relation to favored social narratives of difference."[1] It is the minorities who have to live and contend with flawed knowledge that is created about them. In public health, the practice of studying minorities as "subjects of academic intrigue rather than real people" has also been critiqued. Research projects should benefit the "study populations who experience discrimination" rather than serve the dominant research establishment.[2]

In terms of official forms and questionnaires, pre-populated categories with unspoken assumptions, no matter how inclusive they may seem or how long the drop-down menu may be, are not as effective in community building as open-ended questions that invite self-identification and self-narrative. Pre-set categories may seem useful when one labels someone else, but they can deprive communities of their right to self-determination. For instance, on a form, it is an act of othering to list male and female in addition to a write-in box of "other," because it presupposes normative categories.

This is where global perspectives—multifocal, multilingual, and multicultural viewpoints—become especially important. This chapter demonstrates the application of strategies for global inclusiveness to Shakespeare studies in the classroom and suggests that through radical listening—a set of communication methods that attend to motivations rather than superficial "plots"—students can acquire new skills to analyze complex cultural texts and thereby gain empathy beyond their academic work. Global perspectives can help us tackle the pervasive Whiteness of Shakespeare studies by deconstructing the binary logic of a Black-White order (which inadvertently naturalizes the two as monolithic concepts).[3]

GLOBAL PERSPECTIVES ON INCLUSIVENESS

Beyond the issue of naming, inclusive practices are affected by each country's distinct vocabulary about social difference. For instance, the terms "migrant" and "refugee" signify differently in the U.K. and in the U.S. Discourses about race operate on diverse bandwidths, rendering such terms as "brown people," First Nations, BAME (Black, Asian, minority ethnic), BIPOC (Black, Indigenous, people of color), and AAPI (Asian American and Pacific Islander) only meaningful in certain contexts or time periods across Canada, the U.K., and the U.S. Not all the terms are in use everywhere.

Not only do word choices matter in creating inclusiveness, but it is also important to use them with care and precision. Sometimes, BAME (in the U.K.) and BIPOC (in the U.S.), instead of "Black," are used to discuss Black issues when the speaker feels uncomfortable naming Blackness. This seemingly casual, euphemistic usage smacks of either anti-Black racism, misappropriation, or both. Instead of naming Blackness, the speaker defaults to a purportedly inclusive acronym about people of color (POC) in general. In social and journalistic contexts, those acronyms are sometimes perceived to lessen the discomfort of the dominant group under the pretense of inclusiveness, similar to how the acronym LGBTQ (Lesbian, Gay, Bisexual, Transgender, and Queer) is tossed around in discussions of cis-homosexuality that exclude the "B" and "T" on the list. When an umbrella term such as LGBTQ conflates gender identity with sexual orientation, speakers who use the acronym often render the "T" (transgender community) silent and invisible.[4] In these cases, the speaker does not mean what they say when they use the acronym. They empty out the words and turn them into a harmful social ritual of "inclusion." Such phenomena beg the question of whether inclusiveness is simply a strategy for providing the greatest comfort to the largest number of people. Is it a numbers game dividing the majority from the minority, creating fissures among minorities, or engaging in tokenism?

There are important political ramifications of such practices. For instance, Asian Americans were left out of the #OscarsSoWhite, a campaign to diversify the voting membership of the Academy awards committee, because the operating definition of "diversity" in the United States rarely includes people of Asian descent. Created by April Reign, the campaign seeks to "make the Academy of Motion Picture Arts and Sciences' membership, its governing bodies, and its voting members significantly more diverse."[5] The political invisibility of Asian Americans is partly caused by widely circulated, unfounded claims of their overrepresentation as well as erroneous assertions that the "model minority" is wealthy, autonomous, and exempted from discrimination. In fact, Asian Americans have the largest income disparity and the highest poverty rate of any racial group.[6] Also contributing to the problem are other factors relating to the multiple and contradictory meanings of race in contemporary American culture.

COUNTERACTING THE COLORBLIND GAZE

A non-binary, more comprehensive perspective should not be misconstrued as "whataboutism." Social justice issues are interconnected, and only by taking a global perspective can we effectively resolve local, and all, issues. While local(ized) social justice issues may seem more urgent to solve in the short term, it is paramount, in the long term, to think and act globally in order to create true inclusivity. We can expand our cognitive resources to think beyond the binary by considering the global ramifications of what may seem to be isolated, local cases of discrimination. While being cognizant of, for example, global Blackness, may not seem to solve local problems immediately, it is a more inclusive act to examine comparatively, within Blackness in the U.S., related issues faced by Black immigrants, refugees, expatriates, and international students who do not speak English as their first language, such as the increasingly visible Somali Muslim community in Minnesota.[7] As Ambereen Dadabhoy observes, our gaze is often "implicated in [our] own racial, gendered, and classed positions."[8] Identifying common patterns of racism in interconnected contexts can strengthen local campaigns. Maintaining global perspectives can break down binarism and enhance our cognitive bandwidth.

Students often look through, rather than at, characters who are minoritized in one way or another, especially characters who are unnamed. Audiences of a majority racial group often approach fiction through a colorblind gaze, one that erases the presence of racialized others who are seen but not truly seen. Kenneth Branagh's Japanesque film *As You Like It* (2006) is one such example. The film dresses Wakehurst Place up with a Zen garden, shrine gate, and trappings of a nineteenth-century Japan torn between samurai and European merchants. The intercultural fusion is reflected by Rosalind's and Celia's Victorian dresses during the sumo match between Orlando and Charles. Sitting behind them, Duke Frederick dons dark samurai armor, which smacks of cultural appropriation. Orlando writes love letters in Japanese kanji script. Both Shakespeare and the dream of Japan are deployed ornamentally in the filmmaker's signature visual romanticism.

Such a work is still valuable pedagogically, because it can be a test case to help us place racial discourses across history in a global context and to rethink race through what is commonly regarded as a "non-race" film. The context of Anglophone Shakespearean film history alone is insufficient if we wish to fully unpack the cultural meanings of Branagh's *As You Like It*. Branagh's film participates in the tradition of using racial otherness for ornamental value, particularly in films that draw on Asian cityscapes and food to express exoticism. For instance, Ridley Scott's *Blade Runner* (1982) is set in a futuristic, Japanesque Los Angeles where Rick Deckard (Harrison Ford) eats ramen between missions. Junks, the iconic Hong Kong ships with fully battened sails, adorn the skyline of future New York in Luc Besson's *The Fifth Element* (1997). In San Fransokyo, the fictional city and backdrop of Don Hall and Chris Williams' *Big Hero 6* (2014), the Kabuki-za, the principal theater in Tokyo for the classical form of dance-drama, sits comfortably among American high-rises, merging the two coasts of the Pacific in the sunny future. James Mangold's *The Wolverine* (2013) engages in habitual deployment of Japanese architecture, such as a shiro (castle) and Tokyo's Zōjō-ji Temple, and uses warrior outfits (Ichirō's electromechanical suit, named the Silver Samurai) to signal evil within.

Similar to Branagh's *As You Like It*, these films feature a great deal of Asian script, amplifying the myth that Asian writing is inscrutable. There is no culturally meaningful engagement with the Asian settings in these films. The characters may live in a futuristic Asian-inspired cityscape, but they move through the social and architectural space without giving meaning to the presence of Asian writing, food, and modes of transportation. Asian cities and people, therefore, become disembodied, exotic "aliens." The geographical distance enforces the temporal distance as contemporary Asian urban scenes are reframed as futuristic cinematic space. Maintaining an inherently global, comparative perspective could turn such works into teachable moments by showing the important distinction between color-conscious and colorblind casting, in that the former involves choices made to counteract the erasure of minorities, bringing actors' identities into intentioned, meaningful interactions with plot elements, whereas the latter perpetuates racism by equating social justice with the absence of stereotyping in selection processes.

The colorblind gaze has led to a twofold problem. Films either lack diverse casts—a phenomenon exacerbated by the practice of "whitewashing" (in which white actors are cast in non-white roles)—or they focus on negative portrayals of racialized others, such as Gong Li's performance of Isabella, lover of and financial adviser to a drug dealer in Michael Mann's film *Miami Vice* (2006). The colorblind gaze subsumes minorities under putatively universal themes that appeal to mainstream audiences and transforms what may not hold mainstream interest (such as uniquely Latinx struggles) into American popular culture (such as American pop feminism) that is more palatable for mass audiences, as is the case in Baz Luhrmann's *William Shakespeare's Romeo + Juliet* (1996).[9]

Shot primarily in Mexico City and Boca del Rio in Veracruz, Lurhmann's film is set in a fictional American city called Verona Beach. It pitches White Protestantism against Latinx Catholicism, which is mapped onto cinematic interpretations of the conflict between the Montagues and the Capulets—each clan marked with their distinct accents and sartorial choices. The action scenes, frequently punctuated by freeze frames or slow-motion shots, are "filtered through John Woo's Hong Kong action movies" and hip-hop rap.[10] Even though ethnic difference, such as Latinx culture, is used allegorically to frame the ancient feud in Shakespeare's play, and despite the film's borrowing from several cultures, the film has not typically been taught from the perspective of global or critical race studies. This is due to Luhrmann's use of Shakespeare's text for indexical value. Characters clad in jeans delivering lines from *Romeo and Juliet* give the false impression that the film is a specimen of "Anglophone Shakespeare" rather than "global Shakespeare." Scholarship on Luhrmann's film focuses more frequently on gender issues rather than cross-cultural and racial (mis)representations.[11]

RADICAL LISTENING

The strategy of radical listening can enhance institutional and curricular inclusiveness. As a set of proactive communication strategies that listen for the roots of stories, radical listening, as Rita Charon, founder of narrative medicine, theorizes, can create "an egality between teller and listener that gives voice to the tale."[12] Instead of looking for the what in the plot of a story, students, using this strategy, can examine the why in characters' motivation and behaviors.

Radical listening draws on the methodology of strategic presentism, a term coined by Lynn Fendler.[13] This method acknowledges the readers' position in the present time. It empowers readers to own the text by bringing history to bear on our contemporary issues. By thinking critically about the past in the present—such as the #BlackLivesMatter movement—students analyze Shakespeare with an eye toward changing the present. In this way, Shakespeare ceases to be a White canon with culturally predetermined meanings. This method foregrounds the connection between historical and contemporary ideologies and "the ways the past is at work in the exigencies of the present."[14] In particular, adaptations turn the past from irrelevant knowledge into one of many complex texts in our exploration of present issues. The past is no longer sealed off in a vacuum. Another benefit of encouraging radical listening, enhanced by strategic presentism, in the classroom is that this strategy decenters the traditional power structures that have excluded minoritized students, such as students with disabilities and students of color. Previously underprivileged students are now empowered to claim ownership of Shakespeare through presentist adaptations.

In pragmatic terms, radical listening creates connections between seemingly isolated instances of artistic expression. The ability to recognize ambiguity in these connections helps students to more productively analyze multiple, potentially conflicting, versions of what seems to be the same story. In fact, literary ambiguity, as I have argued elsewhere, "helps connect minds for global change."[15] Because literary ambiguity can allow people to express themselves under censorship, literary ambiguity has proved an ally to oppressed peoples in the Soviet Union, Tibet, South Africa, and elsewhere. As students take into account the ambiguities of adaptations, the modern edition of Shakespeare's plays is no longer the sole object of study. Instead, it is only one of multiple possibilities.

Another inclusive, and inquiry-driven, exercise is collective translation. Teaching Shakespeare through translated versions draws attention to dramatic ambiguities and aspects of the plays that have been dormant. One of the tools to help us teach Shakespeare through translation is Version Variation Visualisation: Multilingual Crowd-Sourcing of Shakespeare's *Othello* (sites.google.com/site/delightedbeautyws/), a project directed by Tom Cheeseman. Comparative analyses of translations of the same passage can shed new light on words that would have elided attention. In Act 1 Scene 3 of *Othello*, after Othello's eloquent defense of his love of Desdemona, the Duke of Venice tells Brabantio, at the end of the court scene, that "If virtue no delighted beauty lack / Your son-in-law is far more fair than black" (289–290). The Duke's remarks are commonly understood as under-handed and racist "praises" of Othello's virtue and appearance, though they provide ample opportunities for multilingual interpretation. Cheeseman's digital project focuses on these two lines. The website lists 200 collated translations in 30 languages and offers English translations of the foreign-language versions of these two lines. Translations of these lines into different languages deal with the meanings of "fair" and "black" rather differently. M. E'temādzāda introduced gendered concepts into the lines, rendering in Farsi, in 2009, the first line as "if masculinity does not lack fascination and beauty." Mikhail Lozinskij's Russian translation says "Since honor is a source of light of virtue, / Then your son-in-law is light, and by no means black." Christopher Martin Wieland and Ángel Luis Pujante used "white" in German and Spanish (respectively) to translate "fair," while Victor Hugo chose "shining." Liang Shiqiu renders the word "fair" as biaozhi (comely) in Chinese with little moral overtone, while Jae-nam Kim expands the notion of virtue to "personality" in Korean while keeping the Duke's racist language that equates blackness with inelegance: "If we can say excellent personality is a beautiful one, / Your son-in-law must be a beautiful person even if he looks black." The translators' choices of word reflect how social markers—gender, class, immigration status—create and amplify one's desires and needs. Pedagogical exercises could be designed around this type of digital project to encourage students to reexamine what they assume to be familiar concepts. Translational differences draw attention to the instability of Shakespeare's texts as well as their variegated terrains that are open for interpretation.

Radical listening can also make other common classroom practices, such as trigger and content warnings, more inclusive. Commonly practiced in secondary and higher education in the U.S., the U.K., and Canada, a trigger warning is a statement, typically on the syllabus, to offer accommodation for people with post-traumatic stress disorder, neurodiverse people, or anyone who has experienced trauma. When used primarily because of a fear of legal action, a trigger warning becomes a ritual about evolving political correctness and not a genuine act of care. In such cases, it serves the educational institution rather than serving the student community. The strategy of radical listening can turn students from passive receivers of such disclaimers to active participants who work together to build an inclusive community. Some trigger warnings may attend only to certain groups' comfort. Misgendering acts (using the wrong pronouns or deadnaming a person) are not typically listed as triggering. Outside of transgender studies courses, transmisogyny is rarely considered "triggering," not even in institutional DEI (diversity, equity, and inclusion) training.[16] Course content warnings, if used, should critique institutionalized cis-sexism—the belief that cisgender people's lives are more natural and legitimate than those of trans people—which has led to the assignment of cisgender status to all characters. This bias makes it seem natural for cis artists and scholars (including those who are heterosexual and homosexual) to claim and exercise authority, while silencing a range of social practices that go under the label of transgender.[17]

In literary and cultural studies, typical themes listed for trigger warning are self-harm (without contextualization), gender-based violence (without spotlighting the perpetrators), "homophobia" (instead of the more accurate term "anti-gay"),[18] negative portrayals of disability (without critiquing pervasive assumptions about able-bodiedness), and explicit racial slurs (while glossing over microaggressions). More often than not, such warnings are based on characters' explicit actions or language. The themes considered traumatizing often reflect the concerns of "mainstream minorities" if not those of the majority community.[19] With radical listening strategies, however, students can attend to characters' intentions that may or may not have been stated and develop, together, a more inclusive list of potentially triggering themes.

Take *Titus Andronicus*, for example. Dominating a typical list of triggering themes are violence and sexual assault, focusing on the rape of Lavinia. While the centering of Lavinia's plight comes with good reasons and could be used to promote social justice in the context of the #MeToo movement, the absence—in some trigger warnings—of anti-Blackness and infanticide is troubling.[20] When trigger warnings focus on Lavinia and gloss over the white Nurse's deriding comments about the yet unnamed Black baby as she urges Aaron to kill the "joyless, dismal, black, and sorrowful issue … as loathsome as a toad" (4.2.69–70), they send a message that prioritizes white women in the classroom. Further, toward the end of the tragedy, Lucius coerces Aaron to confess to his crimes "of murders, rapes, and massacres" (5.1.64) by threatening to hang him and his baby son ("Hang him on this tree, / And by his side his fruit of bastardy" 5.1.47–48). Trigger warnings that ignore these racist incidents contribute to the myths, identified by Celia R. Daileader, about black male rapacity and the need to shield white women from inter-racial contamination.[21]

Using the strategy of radical listening, we can turn trigger warning into a communal enterprise. I begin with a broadly conceived "content warning" about themes of race, gender, sexuality, and disability in the play. I then ask students to play a proactive role in their education. I encourage my students to debate the connection between trigger warnings and social justice. In one class, my students collectively compiled a list of issues and themes, beyond the usual suspects, that could be potentially triggering in the play. Students canvassed a broad swath of issues, including filicide, self-injury, honor killing, premeditated but unexecuted infanticide (two counts), anti-Blackness, involuntary cannibalism, racist misogyny, ableist portrayal of muteness, ableist portrayal of war veterans' post-traumatic stress disorder, and more. The grass-roots approach fostered more diverse voices in the classroom, promoted close reading skills, and enabled students' ownership of trigger warning as a communal practice and collaboratively created knowledge.

That said, it is ineffectual to pursue endless lists of trigger warnings, either, even with student input. The classroom can only be reparative when it is designed, from the very foundations of its pedagogy, to be truly inclusive through transparency: simply replicating political correctness does not create inclusion. It is futile to pursue inclusiveness by way of exhausting exhaustiveness.

CONCLUSION: SHAKESPEARE AND SOCIAL JUSTICE

Inspired by the social justice turn in the arts, the present volume show-cases socially reparative uses of Shakespeare in the classroom and in academic work. Social movements, such as #BlackLivesMatter, which began in 2013,[22] and #MeToo, which began in 2006 and returned in redoubled force globally in 2017,[23] have rekindled reparative interpretations of Shakespeare. For theater and film practitioners, an inclusive Shakespeare gives relevance and purpose to art as well as drawing a larger, more diverse clientele. Since 2015, the Archbishop Fulton J. Sheen Center for Thought and Culture in New York has offered the Justice Film Festivals in the hopes of "inspir[ing] justice seekers by presenting films of unexpected courage and redemption."[24] Also in 2015, the Transgender Shakespeare Company was founded in London as the first company run entirely by trans-identified artists. As Perry Guevara discusses in this volume, Marin Shakespeare Company in San Rafael, California, offers programs on "Shakespeare for social justice" created for people who are incarcerated and at-risk youths. These actors "practice being human together," because they believe Shakespeare offers "deep thinking about the human condition."[25] In London, Donmar Warehouse, led by Phyllida Lloyd, staged a series of all-female productions of *Julius Caesar* (2012), *Henry IV* (2014), and *The Tempest* (2016) that aimed to "create a more ... functional society [and] inspire empathy." The group "believe that representation matters; diversity of identity, of perspective, of lived experience enriches our work and our lives."[26] Social reparation does not reside, in and by itself, within the canon of Shakespeare. Inclusive pedagogical and artistic practices are built on the premise that literary and cultural meanings are relational. It is this multiplicity that enables audiences, educators, and students to find inclusiveness within Shakespeare's works.

NOTES

1. Jack Halberstam, *Trans*: A Quick and Quirky Account of Gender Variability* (Oakland: University of California Press, 2018), 6 and 8.
2. Brian Minalga, Cecilia Chung, J.D. Davids, Aleks Martin, Nicole Lynn Perry, and Alic Shook, "Research on transgender people must benefit transgender people," *The Lancet* 399.10325 (February 12, 2022): 628. 10.1016/S0140-6736(21)02806-3.

3. For example, *Antiblackness*, ed. Moon-Kie Jung and João H. Costa Vargas (Durham, NC: Duke University Press, 2021), critiques the pervasiveness of anti-Blackness in South Africa, Palestine, Chickasaw, precolonial Korea, postcolonial India, and the categorization of Latinx in the 2020 census. The book reveals anti-Blackness to be a globally interconnected, rather than solely American, issue.

4. Chassitty N. Fiani and Heather J. Han, "Navigating identity: Experiences of binary and non binary transgender and gender nonconforming (TGNC) adults." *International Journal of Transgenderism* 20.2–3 (2019): 181–194.

5. Quoted in "A Conversation with the Creator of #OscarsSoWhite," NPR, January 25, 2016. https://www.npr.org/2016/01/25/464244160/a--conversation-with-the-creator-of-oscarssowhite.

6. David L. Eng and Shinhee Han. *Racial Melancholia, Racial Dissociation: On the Social and Psychic Lives of Asian Americans* (Durham, NC: Duke University Press, 2018), 2.

7. Stefanie Chambers, "The Twin Cities: Somalis in the North Star State," *Somalis in the Twin Cities and Columbus: Immigrant Incorporation in New Destinations* (Philadelphia: Temple University Press, 2017), 56–85.

8. Ambereen Dadabhoy, "The Unbearable Whiteness of Being (in) Shakespeare," *Postmedieval* 11.2–3 (2020): 228–235; 230.

9. Courtney Lehmann, "Strictly Shakespeare? Dead Letters, Ghostly Fathers, and the Cultural Pathology of Authorship in Baz Luhrmann's *William Shakespeare's Romeo + Juliet*," *Shakespeare Quarterly* 52.2 (Summer 2001), 189–221.

10. Kenneth S. Rothwell, *A History of Shakespeare on Screen: A Century of Film and Television*, 2nd edition (Cambridge: Cambridge University Press, 2004), 229.

11. One of the exceptions is Nicholas F. Radel's "The Ethiop's Ear: Race, Sexuality and Baz Luhrmann's *William Shakespeare's Romeo + Juliet*," *The Upstart Crow* 28 (2009): 17–34.

12. Rita Charon, *Narrative Medicine: Honoring the Stories of Illness* (Oxford: Oxford University Press 2006), 66 and 77.

13. Lynn Fendler, "The Upside of Presentism," *Paedagogica Historica: International Journal of the History of Education* 44.6: 677–90; 677.

14. David Sweeney Coombs and Danielle Coriale, 2016. "V21 Forum on Strategic Presentism: Introduction," *Victorian Studies* 59.1: 87–89.

15. Alexa Alice Joubin, TEDx Fulbright talk, October 26, 2019.

16. George Washington University has made it obligatory for faculty and staff to complete online DEI training, but the program does not discuss anti-trans attitudes. Study materials use such problematic language as "homophobia" to describe anti-gay and anti-lesbian biases.

17. M.W. Bychowski, "The Transgender Turn: Eleanor Rykener Speaks Back," *Trans Historical: Gender Plurality before the Modern* (Ithaca: Cornell University Press, 2021), 95–113; 95–96.
18. Using the -phobia suffix—a term implying a pathological fear certified by the *Diagnostic and Statistical Manual of Mental Disorders* (DSM)—outside clinical contexts reflects ableist biases and inaccurately describes anti-gay attitudes. Individuals who discriminate against gay people do so not out of pathological fear but rather hate. Lily Rothman, "There Is No 'Neutral' Word for Anti-Gay Bias," *The Atlantic*, December 7, 2012. https://www.theatlantic.com/sexes/archive/2012/12/there-is-no-neutral-word-for-anti-gay-bias/266037/.
19. Serena Hussain, "Missing from the 'minority mainstream': Pahari-speaking diaspora in Britain." *Journal of Multilingual and Multicultural Development* 36.5 (2015): 483–497.
20. David Sterling Brown, "Remixing the Family: Blackness and Domesticity in Shakespeare's *Titus Andronicus*," *"Titus Andronicus": The State of the Play*, ed. Farah Karim-Cooper (London: Bloomsbury, 2019), 111–133. Brown has been promoting the re-reading, through the lens of critical race studies, of works that do not at first glance seem to deal with race as a theme. Brown, "Power, Privilege, and Shakespeare's 'Other Race Plays'," Blackfriars Conference, American Shakespeare Center, October, 2019; Brown, "'Hood Feminism': Whiteness and Segregated (Premodern) Scholarly Discourse in the Post-Postracial Era," *Literature Compass* 18 (October 2021). 10.1111/lic3.12608.
21. Celia R. Daileader, *Racism, Misogyny, and the "Othello" Myth: Inter-racial Couples from Shakespeare to Spike Lee* (Cambridge: Cambridge University Press, 2005).
22. The movement has international impact, but it began with a strong U.S. focus. Following the acquittal of George Zimmerman in the shooting death of African-American teen Trayvon Martin, the hashtag #BlackLivesMatter was used widely on social media since 2013.
23. Tarana Burke, sexual harassment survivor and Black activist, used the phrase "Me Too" to break silence on social media in 2006. The movement spread across the globe in the wake of sexual-abuse allegations against Hollywood producer Harvey Weinstein in 2017, especially after actress Alyssa Milano used "Me Too" as a hashtag.
24. https://www.sheencenter.org/shows/justice/.
25. Marin Shakespeare Company Shakespeare for Social Justice Program. https://www.marinshakespeare.org/shakespeare-for-social-justice/.
26. Donmar Warehouse official website. https://www.donmarwarehouse.com/about/.

BIBLIOGRAPHY

"About." Merced ShakespeareFest. https://www.mercedshakespearefest.org/about. Accessed 2 August 2021.

———. Technical System of Georgia. Retrieved December 28, 2021b. https://www.tcsg.edu/about-tcsg/.

"A Conversation with the Creator of #OscarsSoWhite." *NPR*. January 25, 2016, https://www.npr.org/2016/01/25/464244160/a-conversation-with-the-creator-of-oscarssowhite.

Acton, Kelsie et al. "Being in Relationship: Reflections on Dis-Performing, Hospitality, and Accessibility." *Canadian Theatre Review* 177 (Winter 2019).

Adams, Jeff. "The Play's the Thing: Integrated Curriculum Makes Even Shakespeare Relevant to Vo-Tech Students." *Vocational Educational Journal* 67.8 (1992): 32–33.

Addams Family. Dir. Barry Sonnenfeld. Paramount Pictures, 1991.

Aebischer, Pascale. *Shakespeare's Violated Bodies: Stage and Screen Performance*. New York: Cambridge University Press, 2009.

Agamben, Giorgio. *Homo Sacer: Sovereign Power and Bare Life*. Trans. Daniel Heller-Roazen. Palo Alto, CA: Stanford University Press, 1998.

Albanese, Denise. "Identification, Alienation, and 'Hating the Renaissance'." *Shakespeare and the 99%: Literary Studies, the Profession, and the Production of Inequity*. Eds. Sharon O'Dair and Timothy Francisco. Palgrave, 2019. 19–36.

"Arts and Sciences." Atlanta Technical College. Retrieved December 28, 2021. https://atlantatech.edu/programs/arts-and-sciences/.

© The Author(s), under exclusive license to Springer Nature Switzerland AG 2023
S. Freeman Loftis et al. (eds.), *Inclusive Shakespeares*, Palgrave Shakespeare Studies,
https://doi.org/10.1007/978-3-031-26522-8

Atlanta Tech Strategic Plan, 2018–2022. https://atlantatech.edu/wp-content/uploads/strategic-plan-2018-2022_posting-revised-12_2018.pdf.

Avengers, The. ABC Television, 1961–1969.

Azevedo, Jillian. *Tastes of the Empire: Foreign Foods in Seventeenth Century England.* New York: McFarland, 2017.

"*Bacchae, The.*" Tower Theatre. Accessed August 25, 2021. https://www.towertheatre.org.uk/event/lands17/.

Bailey, Moya. *Misogynoir Transformed: Black Women's Digital Resistance.* New York: New York University Press, 2021.

Bakare, Lanre. "UK theatres promise to only Cast Trans Actors in Trans Roles." *The Guardian,* 26 May 2021, https://www.theguardian.com/stage/2021/may/26/uk-theatres-promise-to-only-cast-trans-actors-in-trans-roles, accessed 30 July 2021.

Barry. HBO Entertainment, 2018–.

Barzilai, Reut. "'In My Power': *The Tempest* as Shakespeare's Antitheatrical Vision." *Shakespeare* 15.4 (2019): 379–397.

Bassett, Kate. "Antony and Cleopatra at the Swan, Stratford." *The Times.* Nov. 15, 2013, https://www.thetimes.co.uk/article/antony-and-cleopatra-at-the-swan-stratford-673qnvhb6db. Accessed Feb. 15, 2021.

Bayton, Douglas C. *Forbidden Signs: American Culture and the Campaign against Sign Language.* Chicago: University of Chicago Press, 1998.

Benedicks, Crystal. "The Shakespeare Portal." *On Liberal Education: Claiming the Public University in the New Millennium.* Eds. Crystal Benedicks and Judith Summerfield. Peter Lang, 2007.

Bérubé, Michael. *The Secret Life of Stories.* New York: New York University Press, 2018. Print.

Berson, Jessica. "Performing Deaf Identity: Towards a Continuum of Deaf Performance." *Bodies in Commotion: Disability and Performance.* Eds. Carrie Sandahl and Philip Auslander. Ann Arbor: University of Michigan Press, 2005. 42–55.

Billson, Janet Mancini and Margaret Brooks Terry. "In Search of the Silken Purse: Factors in Attrition among First-Generation Students." *College and University* 58 (1982): 57–75.

"Bipolar Disorder." National Health Service (NHS). Accessed August 25, 2021. https://www.nhs.uk/mental-health/conditions/bipolar-disorder/overview/#:~:text=Bipolar%20disorder%20can%20occur%20at,likely%20to%20develop%20bipolar%20disorder.

Bissainthe, Toto. "Dèy." Text and translation appear in Julia Wade, RSC/SM/1/2013/ANT1. and associated SM script, also held at the Shakespeare Birthplace Trust, Library and Archives, Stratford-upon-Avon. 1977.

Boal, Augusto. *Theater of the Oppressed.* Trans. Charles A. and Maria-Odilia Leal McBride. New York: Theatre Communications Group, 1985.

Boehm, Claudia and Alejandro Gutiérrez. Personal interview by William Wolfgang. 24 July 2020.

Boffone, Trevor and Carla Della Gatta. "Introduction: Shakespeare and Latinidad." *Shakespeare in Latinidad*. Ed. Trevor Boffone and Carla Della Gatta. Edinburgh: Edinburgh University Press, 2021. 1–18.

Boose, Lynda E. "Scolding Brides and Bridling Scolds: Taming the Woman's Unruly Member." *The Taming of the Shrew: Critical Essays*. Ed. Dana Aspinall. New York: Routledge, 2002. 130–168.

Bohstedt, John. *The Politics of Provisions: Food Riots, Moral Economy, and Market Transition in England, c. 1550–1850*. London: Routledge, 2010.

"Both Your Houses." *My Three Sons*. Season 7, Episode 16. CBS Productions, 1967.

Boutry, Katherine. "Creativity Studies and Shakespeare at the Urban Community College." *Shakespeare and the 99%: Literary Studies, The Profession, and the Production of Inequity*. Eds. Sharon O'Dair and Timothy Francisco. Palgrave, 2019. 121–141.

Bowie-Sell, Daisy. "What's it like for a man to play Ophelia?" *WhatsOnStage.com*, 16 May 2018, https://www.whatsonstage.com/london-theatre/news/ophelia-as-a-man-hamlet-shakespeare-globe_46579.html, accessed 1 September 2021.

Boyd, Michael. "A New and Trusted Voice." Program for William Shakespeare's *Antony and Cleopatra* at the Swan Theatre, Stratford-upon-Avon. Playbill, 2013.

Bradbury, Jill Marie, John Lee Clark, Rachel Grossman, Jason Herbers, Victoria Magliocchino, Jasper Norman, Yashaira Romilus, Robert T. Sirvage, and Lisa van der Mark. "ProTactile Shakespeare: Inclusive Theater by/for the DeafBlind." *Shakespeare Studies* 47 (2019): 81–115.

Bradford, Shannon. "The National Theatre of the Deaf Identity: Artistic Freedom and Cultural Responsibility in the Use of American Sign Language." *Bodies in Commotion: Disability and Performance*. Eds. Carrie Sandahl and Philip Auslander. Ann Arbor: University of Michigan Press, 2005. 86–94.

Brantley, Ben. "A Big Throne to Fill, and the Man to Fill It." *The New York Times*. October 12, 2004.

———. "Shakespeare Hits the Beach." *New York Times*. March 5, 2014. https://www.nytimes.com/2014/03/06/theater/an-antony-and-cleopatra-set-in-the-caribbean.html. Accessed Feb. 15, 2021.

Brathwaite, Edward. *Contradictory Omens: Cultural Diversity and Integration in the Caribbean*. Jamaica: Savacou Publications, 1974.

Breaking Bad. Sony Pictures Television, 2008–2013.

Brears, Peter. *Cooking and Dining in Tudor England*. London: Prospect Books, 2015.

Brown, David Sterling. "'Hood Feminism': Whiteness and Segregated (Premodern) Scholarly Discourse in the Post-Postracial Era." *Literature Compass* 18 (October 2021). https://doi.org/10.1111/lic3.12608

————. "Power, Privilege, and Shakespeare's 'Other Race Plays'." Blackfriars Conference. American Shakespeare Center. October, 2019a.

————. "Remixing the Family: Blackness and Domesticity in Shakespeare's *Titus Andronicus.*" *Titus Andronicus: The State of the Play.* Ed. Farah Karim-Cooper. London: Bloomsbury, 2019b.

Bruno, Christine. "Disability in American Theater: Where is the Tipping Point?" Howl Round Theatre Commons. 2014. https://howlround.com/disability-american-theater. Accessed 14 March 2022.

Bruns, John. "Laughter in the Aisles: Affect and Power in Contemporary Theoretical and Cultural Discourse." *Studies in American Humor* 3.7 (2000): 5–23.

Bulman, James C., ed. *Shakespeare Re-Dressed: Cross-Gender Casting in Contemporary Performance.* Fairleigh Dickinson UP, 2008.

Byrd, Jodi A. *The Transit of Empire: Indigenous Critiques of Colonialism.* Minneapolis, MN: Minnesota University Press, 2011.

Caines, Michael. *Shakespeare and the Eighteenth Century.* Oxford: Oxford University Press, 2013.

Caldwell, Paulette. "A Hair Piece: Perspectives on the Intersection of Race and Gender." *Duke Law Journal* 40.2 (1991): 365–396.

Carleton, David. *Landmark Congressional Laws on Education.* Westport, CT: Greenwood Press, 2002.

Cataldi, Emily Forrest, Christopher T. Bennett, and Xianglei Chen. "First-Generation Students: College Access, Persistence, and Postbachelor's Outcomes." U.S. Department of Education. 2018.

Charlebois, Elizabeth. "'Their Minds Transfigured So Together': Imaginative Transformation and Transcendence in *A Midsummer Night's Dream.*" *Performing New Lives: Prison Theater.* Ed. Jonathan Shailor. London: Jessica Kingsley Publishers, 2011. 256–269.

Chambers, Stefanie. "The Twin Cities: Somalis in the North Star State." *Somalis in the Twin Cities and Columbus: Immigrant Incorporation in New Destinations.* Philadelphia: Temple University Press, 2017.

Charon, Rita. *Narrative Medicine: Honoring the Stories of Illness.* Oxford: Oxford University Press, 2006.

Chernaik, Warren. "Shakespeare at Work: Four Kings and Two Shrews." *Cahiers élisabéthains* 85 (2014): 21–39.

Chess, Simone. *Male-to-female Crossdressing in Early Modern English Literature: Gender, Performance, and Queer Relations.* Routledge, 2016.

Choy, Susan P. *Students Whose Parents Did Not Go to College: Postsecondary Access, Persistence, and Attainment,* Washington, D.C.: U.S. Department of Education, National Center for Educational Statistics (NCES) (2001).

"Clampetts in London, The" *The Beverly Hillbillies.* Season 6, Episode 2. CBS Television Network, 1967.

Clark, Hilary. "Invisible Disorder: Passing as an Academic." *Illness in the Academy: A Collection of Pathographies by Academics.* Ed. Kimberly Rena Myers. West Lafayette, IN: Purdue University Press, 2007. 123–130.

Clark, John Lee. "My Dream Play: A DeafBlind Man Imagines a Pro-Tactile Theatre." *Scene4 Magazine.* 2015. https://www.scene4.com/archivesqv6/2015/apr-2015/0415/johnleeclark0415.html Accessed 14 March 2022.

Cocke, Dudley, Harry Newman, and Janet Salmons-Rue. *From the Ground Up: Grassroots Theater in Historical and Contemporary Perspective.* Ithaca, NY: Cornell University Press, 1993.

Cohen-Cruz, Jan. *Local Acts: Community-Based Performance in the United States.* New Brunswick, NJ: Rutgers University Press, 2005.

Coombs, David Sweeney and Danielle Coriale. "V21 Forum on Strategic Presentism: Introduction." *Victorian Studies* 59.1 (2016): 87–89.

Corcione, Adryan. "9 Signs You're Being Catfished." *Teen Vogue.* January 21, 2020. https://www.teenvogue.com/story/signs-youre-being-catfished. Accessed January 1, 2022.

Corredera, Vanessa. "Complex Complexions: The Facial Signification of the Black Other in Lust's Dominion." *Shakespeare and the Power of the Face.* Ed. James K. Knapp. Surrey, Burlington: Ashgate, 2015. 93–112.

Cosby Show, The. Carsey-Werner Productions, 1984–1992.

Cote, David. "*Antony and Cleopatra*—Theater Review." *Time Out.* March 5, 2014, https://www.timeout.com/newyork/theater/antony-and-cleopatra-1. Accessed Feb. 15, 2021.

Cottom, Tressie McMillam. *Thick, And other Essays.* New York: The New Press, 2019.

Cox, Murray. *Shakespeare Comes to Broadmoor.* London: Jessica Kingsley, 1992.

Craig, Robin. "Past, Present, Future and the Transgender Shakespeare Company." *TheatreForum* 52 (2017): 6–7.

Daalder, Joost. "Folly and Madness in The Changeling." *Essays in Criticism* 38.1 (1988): 1–22.

Dadabhoy, Ambereen. "The Unbearable Whiteness of Being (in) Shakespeare." *Postmedieval: A Journal of Medieval Cultural Studies* 11.2–3 (2020): 228–235.

Daileader, Celia R. *Racism, Misogyny, and the "Othello" Myth: Inter-racial Couples from Shakespeare to Spike Lee.* Cambridge: Cambridge University Press, 2005.

Davidson, Cathy. *The New Education: How to Revolutionize the University to Prepare Students for a World in Flux.* New York: Basic Books, 2017.

Davis, Angela. "Afro Images: Politics, Fashion, and Nostalgia." *Soul: Black Power, Politics, and Pleasure.* Ed. Monique Guillory and Richard Green. New York: NYU Press, 1998. 23–31.

Derby, John. "Accidents Happen: An Art Autopathography on Mental Disability." *Disability Studies Quarterly* 33.1 (2013).

Dickson, Andrew. "*Antony and Cleopatra*—Review." *The Guardian*. Nov. 15, 2013, https://www.theguardian.com/stage/2013/nov/15/antony-and-cleopatra-tarell-alvin-mccraney-rsc-review. Accessed February 15, 2013

Dolan, Frances E. "Taking the Pencil out of God's Hand: Art, Nature, and the Face-Painting Debate in Early Modern England." *PMLA* 108.2 (1993): 224–239.

Dolmage, Jay T. *Academic Ableism*. Anne Arbor: University of Michigan Press, 2017.

Donaldson, Elizabeth J. "Beyond A Beautiful Mind: Schizophrenia and Bioethics in the Classroom." *Disability Studies Quarterly* 35.2 (2015).

Donmar Warehouse official website. n.d. https://www.donmarwarehouse.com/about/.

Drouet, Pascale. "Madness and Mismanagement in Middleton and Rowley's *The Changeling*." *Theta X* (2013): 139–152.

Dunn, Marvin. *Black Miami in the Twentieth Century*. Gainesville, FL: University Press of Florida, 1997.

Eagleton, Terry. "The Ideology of the Aesthetic." *Poetics Today* 9.2 (1988): 327–338.

Edwards, Terra. "Sign-Creation in the Seattle Deafblind Community: A Triumphant Story about the Regeneration of Obviousness." *Gesture* 16.2 (2016): 307–32.

Eng, David L. and Shinhee Han. *Racial Melancholia, Racial Dissociation: On the Social and Psychic Lives of Asian Americans*. Durham, NC: Duke University Press, 2018.

Escolme, Bridget. *Emotional Excess on the Shakespearean Stage: Passion's Slaves*. London: Bloomsbury, 2014.

Eskew, Doug. "Shakespeare, Alienation, and the Working-Class Student." *Shakespeare and the 99%: Literary Studies, the Profession, and the Production of Inequity*. Eds. Sharon O'Dair and Timothy Francisco. Palgrave, 2019. 37–56.

Espinosa, Ruben. "Chicano Shakespeare: The Bard, the Border, and the Peripheries of Performance." *Teaching Social Justice through Shakespeare*. Eds. Hillary Eklund and Wendy Beth Hyman. Edinburgh University Press, 2019. 76–84.

———. *Shakespeare on the Shades of Racism*. London: Routledge, 2021.

Faculty Handbook. Atlanta Technical College. 2019.

Fendler, Lynn. n.d. "The Upside of Presentism." *Paedagogica Historica: International Journal of the History of Education* 44.6: 677–90.

Ferris, Leslie, ed. *Crossing the Stage: Controversies on Cross-Dressing*. Routledge, 1993.

Fiani, Chassitty N. and Heather J. Han. "Navigating identity: Experiences of binary and non binary transgender and gender nonconforming (TGNC) adults." *International Journal of Transgenderism* 20.2–3 (2019): 181–194.

Fitzpatrick, Joan. *Food in Shakespeare: Early Modern Dietaries and the Plays.* London: Routledge, 2007.

Flores, Cathryn. Personal Interview. 12 August 2021.

———, Maria Nguyen-Cruz, and Ángel Nuñez. Personal Interview. 28 July 2020.

Folger Library Podcasts. n.d. https://www.folger.edu/podcasts-and-recordings.

Folkerth, Wes. "Reading Shakespeare After Neurodiversity." *Performing Disability in Early Modern English Drama.* Ed. Leslie C. Dunn. New York: Palgrave Macmillan, 2020. 141–157.

Forrester, Ann. "Why Teach Shakespeare (or Any Other Dead White Male)?" Unpublished Paper. Community Colleges Humanities Association Conference. November, 1995.

Foucault, Michel. *Discipline and Punish: The Birth of the Prison.* Trans. Alan Sheridan. New York: Vintage-Random House,1995.

———. *The History of Madness.* New York: Routledge, 2006.

Fox, Margalit. "Ophelia DeVore-Mitchell, 91, Dies; Redefined Beauty." *New York Times,* March 13, 2014. https://www.nytimes.com/2014/03/13/nyregion/ophelia-devore-mitchell-91-dies-redefined-beauty.html. Accessed December 15, 2021.

Francis, Donette. "Juxtaposing Creoles: Miami in the Plays of Tarell Alvin McCraney." *Tarell Alvin McCraney: Theater, Performance, and Collaboration.* Eds. Sharrell D. Luckett, David Roman, and Isaiah Matthew Wooden. Evanston, IL: Northwestern University Press, 2020. 19–36.

Friedner, Michelle and Pamela Block. "Deaf Studies Meets Autistic Studies." *The Senses and Society* 12.3 (2017): 282–300.

Gainer, Gloria. "I will Survive." *Love Tracks.* Polydor, 1978.

Gainer, Nichelle. "Ophelia DeVore: Bold Beauty and Brains." *Ebony Magazine,* March 16, 2012. https://www.ebony.com/style/ophelia-devore-bold-beauty-and-brains/. Accessed December 31, 2021.

Game of Thrones. HBO Entertainment, 2011–2019.

Garber, Marjorie. *Vested Interests: Cross-dressing and Cultural Anxiety.* Routledge, 2011.

Gard, Robert E. *Grassroots Theater: A Search for Regional Arts in America.* Madison: University of Wisconsin Press, 1954.

Garland-Thomson, Rosemarie. "Integrating Disability, Transforming Feminist Theory." *Feminist Disability Studies.* Ed. Kim C. Hall. Bloomington: Indiana University Press, 2008. 13–47.

Geller, Conrad. Theatre Review: *Richard III.* NextStop Theatre Company at Industrial Strength Theatre. MD Theatre Guide. 2014. https://mdtheatre-guide.com/2014/02/theatre-review-richard-iii-by-nextstop-theatre-company-at-industrial-strength-theatre/. Accessed 14 March 2022.

"genius, n. and adj". OED Online. September 2021. Oxford University Press. https://www-oed-com.ezproxy.library.unlv.edu/view/Entry/77607?redirect edFrom=genius (accessed November 08, 2021).

Glissant, Édouard. *Poetics of Relation*. Ann Arbor: University of Michigan Press, 1997.

Godwin, Simon. Interview by the author. London, August 9, 2018.

Grady, Kyle. "'The Miseducation of Irie Jones': Representation and Identification in the Shakespeare Classroom." *Early Modern Culture* 14 (2019): 32.

———. "Why Front? Thoughts on the Importance of 'Nonstandard' English in the Shakespeare Classroom." *Pedagogy* 17.3 (October 1, 2017): 533–40.

granda, aj and Jelica Nuccio. "Protactile Principles." Tactile Communications LLC. https://www.tactilecommunications.org/ProTactilePrinciples. Accessed 14 March 2022.

"green-eyed, adj. 2". OED online. Oxford: Oxford University Press, 2021. http://www.oed.com/viewdictionaryentry/Entry/81188. Accessed March 5, 2022.

Groce, Nora. *Everyone Here Spoke Sign Language: Hereditary Deafness on Martha's Vineyard*. Cambridge, MA: Harvard University Press, 1985.

Grey, Patrick. "Shakespeare After the New Materialism," presented as part of the panel entitled, "Shakespeare and Intellectual History," at the Shakespeare Association of America (SAA), 30 March–4 April 2021.

Guevara, Perry. "Toward Speech Therapy: Affect, Pedagogy, and Shakespeare in Prison." *Early Modern Culture* 14 (2019): 59.

Gunsmoke. CBS Productions, 1955–1975.

Halberstam, Jack. "Raging Bull (Dyke): New Masculinities." *Female masculinity*. Duke University Press, 2019. 267–76.

———. *Trans*: A Quick and Quircky Account of Gender Variability*. Oakland: University of California Press, 2018.

Hall, Kim F. "Beauty and the Beast of Whiteness: Teaching Race and Gender." *Shakespeare Quarterly* 47.4 (1996): 461–475.

———. "I Can't Love This the Way You Want Me To: Archival Blackness." *postmedieval: a journal of medieval cultural studies* 11.2–3 (2020): 171–179.

———. "'These bastard signs of fair': Literary whiteness in Shakespeare's sonnets." *Post-Colonial Shakespeares*. Ed. Ania Loomba and Martin Orkin. London: Routledge, 1998. 64–83.

Hall, Stuart. "Cultural Identity and Diaspora." *Colonial Discourse and Post-colonial Theory: A Reader*. Eds. Patrick Williams and Laura Chrisman. New York: Columbia University Press, 1994.

Hambley, Heike. Personal Interview. 11 August 2021.

———, and Greg Ruelas. Personal interview. 25 July 2020.

"Hamlet at GableStage: Shakespeare for the Twitter Generation." *Miami New Times*. Jan. 15, 2013, https://www.miaminewtimes.com/arts/hamlet-at-gablestage-shakespeare-for-the-twitter-generation-6511977. Accessed Feb.16, 2021.

"Headlines." Arcola Theatre. Accessed August 25, 2021, https://www.arcolatheatre.com/whats-on/headlines/.

Heilpern, John. "A Sluggish *Richard III*: Where Is Our Royal Psycho?" *The Observer*. October 25, 2004.

Herford, C.H., Percy Simpson, and Evelyn Simpson, eds. *Ben Jonson*. Oxford: Clarendon, 1950.

Heywood, Thomas. *The Fayre Mayde of the Exchange*. English Verse Drama Full-Text Database. Cambridge: Chadwyck-Healey, 1994.

Hobbs, Allyson. *A Chosen Exile: A History of Racial Passing in American Life*. Cambridge: Harvard University Press, 2014.

Holderness, Graham. "Bardolatry: or, The Cultural Materialist's Guide to Stratford-upon-Avon." *The Shakespeare Myth*. Ed. by Graham Holderness. Manchester: Manchester UP, 1988.

Horn, Laura and Anne-Marie Nunez. "Mapping the Road to College: First-Generation Students' Math Track, Planning Strategies, and Context of Support." *Education Statistics Quarterly* 2.1 (Spring 2000): 81–86.

House of Cards. Netflix, 2013–2018. https://www.imdb.com/title/tt1856010/.

Howard, Jean. "Crossdressing, the theatre, and gender struggle in early modern England." *Shakespeare Quarterly* 39.4 (1988): 418–440.

———. *The Stage and Social Struggle in Early Modern England*. Routledge, 1994.

Hughes, Ian. "Electric new production in charged up and vibrant." *The Observer*. Nov. 15, 2013.

Humble, Kate. *The Spice Trail*. 2011. https://www.imdb.com/title/tt1855043/?ref_=fn_al_tt_1.

Hussain, Serena. "Missing from the 'minority mainstream': Pahari-speaking diaspora in Britain." *Journal of Multilingual and Multicultural Development* 36.5 (2015): 483–497.

Iqbal, Nosheen. "How Tarell Alvin McCraney Took Hamlet Back to School." *The Guardian*, Feb. 5, 2010, https://www.theguardian.com/stage/2010/feb/05/shakespeare-school-theatre-hamlet. Accessed Feb. 12, 2021.

Iyengar, Sujata. *Shades of Difference: Mythologies of Skin Color in Early Modern England*. Philadelphia: University of Pennsylvania Press, 2004.

Jackson, Daniel. *Portraits of Resilience*. Cambridge, MA: The MIT Press, 2017.

Jackson, Kenneth S. *Separate Theatres: Bethlem ("Bedlam") Hospital and the Shakespearean Stage*. Newark: University of Delaware Press, 2005.

Jays, David. "Josette Simon: 'Powerful Women are Reduced to Being Dishonourable.'" *The Guardian*, March 21, 2017, https://www.theguardian.com/stage/2017/mar/21/josette-simon-cleopatra-rsc-shakespeare. Accessed Feb. 15, 2021.

Jeamson, Thomas. *Artificial Embellishments*. Oxford, 1665.

John W. Hartman Center for Sales, Advertising & Marketing History. "Black is Beautiful." Race and Ethnicity in Advertising Exhibition at Duke University Libraries https://exhibits.library.duke.edu/exhibits/show/-black-is-beautiful-/-black-is-beautiful%2D%2Dafrocentr. Accessed December 31, 2021.

Johnson, James Weldon. *The Autobiography of an Ex-Colored Man*. New York: Dover Publications, 1995.

Johnston, Kirsty. *Disability Theatre and Modern Drama: Recasting Modernism*. New York: Bloomsbury Press, 2016.

Jones, Bristin. Personal interview. 16 August 2021.

Jonson, Ben. 1609. *Epicoene, or The Silent Woman*. Ed. Roger Holdsworth. New York: Bloomsbury, 2014.

Joubin, Alexa Alice and Lisa S. Starks. "Teaching Shakespeare in a Time of Hate." *Shakespeare Survey* 74 (2021): 28.

"Juliet is the Sun." *The Brady Bunch*. Season 3, Episode 7. Paramount Television, 1971.

Jung, Moon-Kie and João H. Costa Vargas, eds. *Antiblackness*. Durham, NC: Duke University Press, 2021.

Kafai, Shayda. "The Mad Border Body: A Political In-betweeness." *Disability Studies Quarterly* 33.1 (2013).

Karim-Cooper, Farah. *Cosmetics in Shakespearean and Renaissance Drama*. Edinburgh: Edinburgh University Press, 2019.

Kearse-Lane, Kimberly, interviewee. *The Beauty of Blackness*. Directed by Tiffany Johnson and Kiana Moore. *Vox Media*. 2022. https://www.hbomax.com/feature/urn:hbo:feature:GYhpakgyYVMLCwwEAAAAk, 00:07:03.

Keegan, Cáel M. "Transgender Studies, or How to Do Things with Trans*." *The Cambridge Companion to Queer Studies*. Edited by Siobhan B. Somerville. Cambridge UP, 2020. 66–76.

Kemp, Sawyer. "Shakespeare in Transition: Pedagogies of Transgender Justice and Performance." *Teaching Social Justice Through Shakespeare*. Eds. Hillary Eklund, Wendy Beth Hyman. Edinburgh UP, 2019. 36–45.

———. "Transgender Shakespeare Performance: A Holistic Dramaturgy." *Journal for Early Modern Cultural Studies* 19.4 (2019b): 265–283.

Kingsbury, Melinda Spencer. "Kate's Froward Humor: Historicizing Affect in *The Taming of the Shrew*." *South Atlantic Review* 69.1 (2004): 61–84.

Kirwan, Peter. "*Hamlet* (RSC Young People's Shakespeare) @ the Courtyard Theatre." University of Nottingham Blogs, The Bardathon, Aug. 27, 2010, https://blogs.nottingham.ac.uk/bardathon/2010/08/27/hamlet-rsc-young-peoples-shakespeare-the-courtyard-theatre. Accessed Feb. 12, 2021.

Kochhar-Lindgren, Kanta. *Hearing Difference: The Third Ear in Experimental, Deaf, and Multicultural Theater*. DC: Gallaudet University Press, 2006.

Koon, Mary Downing. "Technical College System of Georgia." New Georgia Encyclopedia, 2007. https://www.georgiaencyclopedia.org/articles/education/technical-college-system-of-georgia-tcsg/. Last modified Oct. 20, 2015.

Korda, Natasha. "Household Kates: Domesticating Commodities in The Taming of the Shrew." *The Taming of the Shrew: Critical Essays*. Ed. Dana Aspinall. New York: Routledge, 2002. 277–307.

Kostihova, Marcela. "Richard Recast: Renaissance Disability in a Postcommunist Culture." *Recovering Disability in Early Modern England*. Eds. Allison P. Hobgood and David Houston Wood. Columbus: Ohio State University Press, 2013. 136–149.

Kuppers, Petra. *Disability and Contemporary Performance: Bodies on Edge*. New York: Routledge, 2003.

"Lamont as Othello." *Sanford and Son*. Season 3, Episode 1. NBC Studios, 1973.

Lanier, Douglas. "Marketing Shakespeare." *The Oxford Handbook of Shakespeare*. Ed. Arthur F. Kinney. Oxford: Oxford University Press, 2014. 498–514.

Leary, M., Patton, K., Orlando, A., & Wagoner Funk, W. "The Impostor Phenomenon: Self- Perceptions, Reflected Appraisals, and Interpersonal Strategies." *Journal of Personality*, 68.4 (2000): 725–756.

Leggatt, Alexander. *Jacobean Public Theatre*. New York: Routledge, 1992.

Lehmann, Courtney. "Strictly Shakespeare? Dead Letters, Ghostly Fathers, and the Cultural Pathology of Authorship in Baz Luhrmann's *William Shakespeare's Romeo + Juliet*." *Shakespeare Quarterly* 52.2 (Summer 2001): 189–221.

Levine, Lawrence. *HighBrow/LowBrow: The Emergence of Cultural Hierarchy in America*. Cambridge, MA: Harvard University Press, 1990.

Loftis, Sonya Freeman. *Shakespeare and Disability Studies*. Oxford: Oxford University Press, 2021.

Looney Tunes. "Looney Tunes Shakespeare." Warner Bros., 2000.

Luckett, Sharrell D. "Backstage Pass: An Artist Roundtable on the Work of Tarell Alvin McCraney." *Tarell Alvin McCraney: Theater, Performance, and Collaboration*. Eds. Sharrell D. Luckett, David Roman, and Isaiah Matthew Wooden. Evanston, IL: Northwestern University Press, 2020a. 183–206.

———, David Roman, and Isaiah Matthew Wooden, eds. *Tarell Alvin McCraney: Theater, Performance, and Collaboration*. Evanston, IL: Northwestern University Press, 2020b.

MacDonald, Joyce Green. *Shakespearean Adaptation, Race and Memory in the New World*. New York and Basingstoke: Palgrave Macmillan, 2020.

Mandell, Jonathan. "*Antony and Cleopatra* Review: Shakespeare's Tragedy in Haiti and Miami." *New York Theater*, March 5, 2014, https://newyorktheater.me/2014/03/05/antony-and-cleopatra-review-shakespeares-tragedy-in-haiti-and-miami. Accessed Feb. 15, 2021.

Mareneck, Ellen C. "Teaching Introduction to Acting at Bronx Community College: From Shakespeare to SZA." *International Journal of Whole Schooling* 14.2 (July 2018): pp. 1+. GaleAcademicOneFile, link.gale.com/apps/doc/A631811234/AONE?u=anon~6dfd5fc6&sid=googleScholar&xid=6a0338c0. Accessed 2 Nov. 2022.

Marin Shakespeare Company Shakespeare for Social Justice Program. n.d. https://www.marinshakespeare.org/shakespeare-for-social-justice/.

Margrit, Shildrik. "Critical Disability Studies: Rethinking the Conventions for the Age of Postmodernism." *Routledge Handbook of Disability Studies*. Eds. Nick Watson, Alan Roulstone, and Carol Thomas. New York: Routledge, 2012. 30–41.

Marks, Peter. "Shakespeare's *Timon* takes a rare Washington bow." *The Washington Post*. May 17, 2017.

Marston, John. 1604. *The Malcontent*. Ed. W. David Kay. New York: Methuen, 1999.

Martin, Randall. "Ricardo II: Episode 6." *Cymbeline in the Anthropocene*. 8 February 2021, https://www.cymbeline-anthropocene.com/article/17595-ricardo-ii-episode-6. Accessed 9 February 2021.

"Maverick and Juliet." *Maverick*. Season 3, Episode 18. Warner Bros. Television, 1960.

Mayberry, Susan Neal. "Cuckoos and Convention: Madness in Middleton and Rowley's *The Changeling*." *Mid-Hudson Language Studies* 8 (1985): 21–32.

McCraney, Tarell Alvin. "Director's Notes." Stage Manager's Script and Prompt Book, *Antony and Cleopatra*, RSC 2013, Shakespeare Birthplace Trust Library and Archives, Stratford-upon-Avon.

"catfish, s. and v." Merriam-WebsterDictionary.com. https://www.merriamwebster.com/dictionary/catfish. Accessed December 15, 2021.

Minalga, Brian, Cecilia Chung, J.D. Davids, Aleks Martin, Nicole Lynn Perry, and Alic Shook. "Research on transgender people must benefit transgender people." *The Lancet* 399.10325 (February 12, 2022): 628. https://doi.org/10.1016/S0140-6736(21)02806-3

Miura, Cassie. "Empowering First-Generation Students: Bardolatry and the Shakespeare Survey." *Early Modern Culture* 14 (2019): 46.

Morris, Harry. "Ophelia's 'Bonny Sweet Robin.'" *PMLA: Publications of the Modern Language Association of America* 73.5 (1958): 601–603.

National Health Service. "City and Hackney Mental Health Strategy," 8. Accessed August 25, 2021.

Neely, Carol Thomas. *Distracted Subjects: Madness and Gender in Shakespeare and Early Modern Culture*. Ithaca: Cornell University Press, 2004.

Newstok, Scott. *How to Think Like Shakespeare: Lesson from a Renaissance Education*. Princeton, NJ: Princeton University Press, 2020.

"No Show." Arcola Theatre. https://www.arcolatheatre.com/whats-on/no-show/. Accessed August 25, 2021

Nuñez, Ángel, Maria Nguyen-Cruz, and William Wolfgang. "Ricardo II – EP. 2: Arpa sin Cordón", Ricardo II." YouTube, Merced Shakespearefest. 11 September 2020. https://www.youtube.com/watch?v=czCQDK0l5FQ. Accessed 11 September 2020.

Nunez, Anne-Marie and Stephanie Cuccaro-Alamin. *First-Generation Students: Undergraduates Whose Parents Never Enrolled in Postsecondary Education*,

Washington, D.C.: U.S. Department of Education, National Center for Educational Statistics (NCES) (1998).

O'Dair, Sharon. *Class, Critics, and Shakespeare.* Ann Arbor: University of Michigan Press, 2000.

Ogle, Connie. "The Miami Writer behind 'Moonlight' is Coming Home for a Reading." *The Miami Herald.* Jan. 9, 2017. https://www.miamiherald.com/miami-com/things-to-do/article225704015.html. Accessed Feb. 15, 2021.

"On Redefining What it Means to be Successful." *The Creative Independent.* Feb. 1, 2021. https://thecreativeindependent.com/people/playwright-tarell-alvin-mccraney-on-redefining-notions-of-being-an-artist. Accessed Feb. 12, 2021.

Ophelia DeVore-Mitchell Papers, 1920–2010. Stuart A. Rose Manuscript. Archives, and Rare Book Library, Emory University. https://findingaids.library.emory.edu/documents/devore1224/?keywords=devore. Accessed December 15, 2021.

O'Reilly, Kaite. "The Necessity of Diverse Voices in Theatre Regarding Disability and Difference." Howl Round Theatre Commons (2017). https://howlround.com/necessity-diverse-voices-theatre-regarding-disability-and-difference. Accessed 14 March 2022.

Orgel, Stephen. *Impersonations: The Performance of Gender in Shakespeare's England.* Cambridge UP, 1996.

Orlin, Lena Cowan. *The Elizabethan Household.* Washington, D.C.: Folger Shakespeare Library, 1995.

———. "The Performance of Things in *The Taming of the Shrew.*" *The Taming of the Shrew: Critical Essays.* Ed. Dana Aspinall. New York: Routledge, 2002. 187–210.

Osborne, Jeffrey. "Rural Shakespeare and the Tragedy of Education," *Teaching Social Justice Through Shakespeare: Why Renaissance Literature Matters Now.* Eds. Hillary Eklund and Wendy Beth Hyman. Edinburgh: Edinburgh University Press, 2019. 106–114.

O'Toole, Corbett. "Disclosing Our Relationships to Disabilities: An Invitation for Disability Studies Scholars." *Disability Studies Quarterly* 33.2 (2013).

"An Evening with Hamlet." *Ozzie and Harriet.* Season 2, Episode 32. ABC Productions, 1954. https://archive.org/details/OZZIE_AND_HARRIET_An_Evening_With_Hamlet.

Pascarella, Ernest T., Christopher T. Pierson, Gregory C. Wolniak and Patrick T. Terenzini. "First-Generation College Students: Additional Evidence on College Experiences and Outcomes." *The Journal of Higher Education* 75.3 (May/June, 2004): 249–284.

Pickens, Therí Alyce. *Black Madness: Mad Blackness.* Durham, NC: Duke University Press, 2019.

"Pleasure of Your Bedlam, The." Arcola Theatre. https://www.arcolatheatre.com/whats-on/the-pleasure-of-your-bedlam/. Accessed August 25, 2021.

BIBLIOGRAPHY

Poitevin, Kimberly. "Inventing Whiteness: Cosmetics, Race, and Women in Early Modern England." *Journal for Early Modern Cultural Studies* 11.1 (2011): 59–89.

Poor, Nigel et al. *Ear Hustle*. earhustlesq.com. Accessed 1 January 2022.

Price, Margaret. *Mad at School: Rhetorics of Mental Disability and Academic Life* (Ann Arbor: University of Michigan Press, 2011), Kindle edition.

———, Mark S. Salzer, Amber O. Shea, and Stephanie L. Kerschbaum. "Disclosure of Mental Disability by College and University Faculty: The Negotiation of Accommodations, Supports, and Barriers." *Disability Studies Quarterly* 37.2 (2017).

Program for William Shakespeare's *Antony and Cleopatra* at the Swan Theatre, Stratford-upon-Avon. Playbill, 2013.

"Producer, The." *Gilligan's Island*. Season 4, Episode 3. United Artists Television, 1964–1967.

Quarshie, Hugh. *Second Thoughts about Othello*. Chipping Camden: International Shakespeare Association, 1999.

"Quick Facts: Merced, California, United States." United States Census Bureau, https://www.census.gov/quickfacts/mercedcitycalifornia. Accessed 2 August 2021.

Radel, Nicholas F. "The Ethiop's Ear: Race, Sexuality and Baz Luhrmann's *William Shakespeare's Romeo + Juliet*." *The Upstart Crow* 28 (2009): 17–34.

Rebhorn, Wayne A. "Petruchio's 'Rope Tricks': *The Taming of the Shrew* and the Renaissance Discourse of Rhetoric." *Modern Philology: A Journal Devoted to Research in Medieval and Modern Literature* 92.3 (1995): 294–327.

Richmond, Robert. "From the Director." *Timon of Athens* program. 2017. Folger Theater.

Ridout, Nicholas. *Stage fright, Animals, and Other Theatrical Problems*. Cambridge UP, 2006.

Roach, Joseph. "Theatre History and the Ideology of the Aesthetic." *Theatre Journal* 41.2 (1989): 155–168.

Robles, Cynthia, and Lupita Yepez. Personal Interview. 25 July 2020.

Rodas, Julie Miele. *Autistic Disturbances: Theorizing Autism Poetics from the DSM to Robinson Crusoe*. Ann Arbor: University of Michigan Press, 2018.

"Romeo and Juliet." *Diff'rent Strokes*. Season 5, Episode 23. Tandem Productions, 1983.

Rothman, Lily. "There Is No 'Neutral' Word for Anti-Gay Bias." *The Atlantic*. December 7, 2012. https://www.theatlantic.com/sexes/archive/2012/12/there-is-no-neutral-word-for-anti-gay-bias/266037/.

Rothwell, Kenneth S. *A History of Shakespeare on Screen: A Century of Film and Television*, 2nd ed.. Cambridge: Cambridge University Press, 2004.

Rowling, J.K. *Harry Potter Series*. London: Bloomsbury, 1997–2007.

Ryan, Frances. "How Austerity is Forcing Disabled Women into Sex Work." *The Guardian*. June 5, 2019. https://www.theguardian.com/society/2019/jun/05/austeristy-forcing-disabled-women-into-sex-work.

Saenz, Victor B., Sylvia Hurtado, Doug Barrera, De'Sha Wolf, and Fanny Yeung. *Fist in My Family: A Profile of First-Generation College Students at Four-Year Institutions since 1971*. Los Angeles: Higher Education Research Institute, 2007: 8–10.

Saito, Yuriko. *Everyday Aesthetics*. New York: Oxford University Press, 2007.

Sajnani, Nisha. "Theater of the Oppressed: Drama Therapy as Cultural Dialogue." *Current Approaches in Drama Therapy*. Ed. David Read Johnson and Renée Emunah. Springfield, IL: Charles C. Thomas Publisher, 2009. 461–481.

Salkeld, Duncan. *Madness and Drama in the Age of Shakespeare*. Manchester: Manchester University Press, 1993.

Samuels, Ellen. "'My Body, My Closet': Invisible Disability and the Limits of Coming Out'." *The Disability Studies Reader*, ed. Lennard J. Davis, 4th edition. New York: Routledge, 2013. Kindle edition, 308–24.

———. "Six Ways of Looking at Crip Time." *Disability Studies Quarterly* 37.3 (2017).

Sandahl, Carrie. "Using Our Words: Exploring Representational Conundrums in Disability Drama and Performance." *Journal of Literary and Cultural Disability Studies* 12.2 (2018): 129–144.

——— and Philip Auslander, eds. *Bodies in Commotion: Disability and Performance*. Ann Arbor: University of Michigan Press, 2005.

"Schizophrenia." National Institute of Mental Health (NIMH). https://www.nimh.nih.gov/health/statistics/schizophrenia#:~:text=page%20on%20Schizophrenia.,Age%2DOf%2DOnset%20for%20Schizophrenia,early%20twenties%20%E2%80%93%20early%20thirties). Accessed August 25, 2021.

Sharpe, Christina. *In the Wake: On Blackness and Being*. Durham, NC: Duke University Press, 2016.

Siebers, Tobin. *Disability Theory*. Ann Arbor: University of Michigan Press, 2008.

———. "Shakespeare Differently Disabled." *The Oxford Handbook of Shakespeare and Embodiment: Gender, Sexuality, and Race*. Ed. Valerie Traub. New York: Oxford University Press, 2016. 435–454.

Shahani, Gitanjali. *Tasting Difference: Food, Race, and Cultural Encounters in Early Modern Literature*. Ithaca, N.Y.: Cornell University Press, 2020.

Shakespeare, William. *Julius Caesar*. Ed. David Daniell. Arden Third Series. New York: Bloomsbury, 1998.

———. *Hamlet: The Texts of 1603 and 1623*. Ed. Ann Thompson and Neil Taylor. New York: Bloomsbury Press, 2007a.

———. *As You Like It. The Complete Pelican Shakespeare*. Eds. Stephen Orgel and A.R. Braunmuller. New York: Penguin, 2002a.

———. *The Tempest. Complete Pelican Shakespeare.* Eds. Stephen Orgel and A.R. Braunmuller. New York: Penguin, 2002b.

———. *The Taming of the Shrew. The RSC Shakespeare: The Complete Works.* Eds. Jonathan Bate and Eric Rasmussen. New York: Palgrave Macmillan, 2007b.

———. *The Norton Shakespeare,* 1st edition. Ed. Stephen Greenblatt. New York: W. W. Norton & Company, 2008.

———. *Richard III.* Ed. James R. Siemon. Arden Third Series. New York: Bloomsbury, 2009.

———. *Shakespeare's Sonnets and Poems.* Eds. Barbara A. Mowat and Paul Werstine. New York: Washington Square Press, 2015.

———. *A Midsummer Night's Dream.* Ed. Sukanta Chaudhuri. New York: Bloomsbury Press, 2017.

———. *As You Like It.* The Folger Shakespeare, https://shakespeare.folger.edu/shakespeares-works/as-you-like-it/entire-play.

———. *Twelfth Night.* The Folger Shakespeare, accessed January 1, 2022, https://shakespeare.folger.edu/shakespeares-works/twelfth-night/entire-play.

Shakur, Tupaq. "Something Wicked." *2Pacalypse Now.* Interscope, 1991.

Shapiro, James. Personal Correspondence conducted via e-mail. James S. Sutton. July 8, 2020.

Shaw, Justin. 2019. "'Rub Him About the Temples': *Othello*, Disability, and the Failures of Care." *Early Theatre* 22.2 (2019): 171–84.

Sheridan, Ed. "Hackney's diagnosed depression rates highest of any London borough." *Hackney Citizen.* May 14, 2019. https://www.hackneycitizen.co.uk/2019/05/14/hackney-depression-rates-highest-any-london-borough/.

"Show Must Go Off, The" *Frasier.* Season 8, Episode 12. Paramount Network Television, 1993–2004.

Shuttleworth, Ian. "*Antony and Cleopatra*, Swan Theatre, Stratford-upon-Avon—Review." *Financial Times,* Nov. 15, 2013, https://app.ft.com/content/1b11740e-4d24-11e3-9f4000144feabdc0. Accessed Feb. 15, 2021.

Smalls, C. Isaiah, II. "This 'Moonlight' Oscar winner returned to his alma mater—and he had a message for the kids." *The Miami Herald.* Dec. 16, 2019, https://www.miamiherald.com/article238421728.html. Accessed Feb. 15, 2021.

Smith, Emma. *This is Shakespeare.* New York: Pantheon, 2019.

Smith, Raven. "The Problem with Blackfishing." *Teen Vogue,* October 13, 2021. https://www.vogue.com/article/the-problem-with-blackfishing-jesy-nelson. Accessed January 1, 2022.

Sonnetman, The. n.d. http://sonnetman.com/.

Speaks, Rykener and M. Bychowski. "4. The Transgender Turn: Eleanor." *Trans Historical: Gender Plurality before the Modern.* Eds. Greta LaFleur, Masha Raskolnikov and Anna Klosowska. Ithaca, NY: Cornell University Press, 2021. 95–113.

Spencer, Charles. "*Antony and Cleopatra*, RSC, Review." *The Daily Telegraph.* Nov. 14, 2013, https://www.telegraph.co.uk/culture/theatre/theatre-reviews/10449633/Antony-and-Cleopatra-RSC-review.html.   Accessed Feb. 15, 2021.

"Spotlight, The" *Bonanza*. Season 6, Episode 33. NBC, 1959–1973.

Star Trek. Paramount Television, 1966–1969. https://intl.startrek.com/.

Star Wars. Dir. George Lucas. 20th Century Fox, 1977. https://www.starwars.com/.

Steele, Claude M. and Joshua Aronson. "Stereotype Threat and the Intellectual Test Performance of African Americans." *Journal of Personality and Social Psychology* 69.5 (1995): 797–811.

Stevenson, Bryan. "Mass Incarceration." The 1619 Project. *The New York Times Magazine*. 14 August 2019. nytimes.com/interactive/2019/08/14/magazine/prison-industrial-complex-slavery-racism.html. Accessed 1 January 2022.

Stott, Andrew. "Tiresias and the Basilisk: Vision and Madness in Middleton and Rowley's *The Changeling*." *Revista Alicantina De Estudios Ingleses* 12 (1999): 165–179.

Strand, Lauren Rose. "Charting Relations between Intersectionality Theory and the Neurodiversity Paradigm." *Disability Studies Quarterly* 37.2 (2017).

Succession. HBO Entertainment, 2018–.

"swagger, v." OED online. Oxford University Press, 2021. http://www.oed.com/viewdictionaryentry/Entry/195354. Accessed March 5, 2022.

Tales from the Green Valley. Lion Television, 2005.

"Taming of Lucille, The" *Car Fifty Four Where are You?* Season 1, Episode 12. Eupolis Productions, 1961.

"Tarell McCraney's Hamlet, Now with Explosions." *Miami New Times*. Jan. 10, 2013, https://www.miaminewtimes.com/arts/tarell-mccraneys-hamlet-now-with-explosions-6391530. Accessed Feb. 16, 2021.

Tate, Shirley Anne. "'I do not see myself as anything else than white': Black resistance to racial cosplay blackfishing." *The Routledge Companion to Beauty Politics*. Ed. Maxine Leeds Craig. New York: Routledge, 2012. 205–214.

Tavener, Ben. "From Stratford to Rio: Using Shakespeare to Treat Mental Illness." *BBC News*, April 12, 2015. https://www.bbc.co.uk/news/health-32241100.

Taylor, Paul C. *Black is Beautiful: A Philosophy of Black Aesthetics*. Hoboken: Wiley, 2016.

Terenzini, Patrick T., Leonard Springer, Patricia M. Yaeger, Ernest T. Pascarella and Amaury Nora. "First-Generation College Students: Characteristics, Experiences, and Cognitive Development." *Research in Higher Education* 37.1 (1996): 1–22.

Thomason, John. "*Antony and Cleopatra* is McCraney's Masterpiece." *Miami New Times*. Jan. 16, 2014, https://www.miaminewtimes.com/arts/antony-and-cleopatra-is-mccraneys-masterpiece-6394553. Accessed Feb. 15, 2021.

Thompson, Ayanna. *Passing Strange: Shakespeare, Race, and Contemporary America*. Oxford: Oxford University Press, 2011.

Thompson, Vilissa. "Understanding the Policing of Black, Disabled Bodies." Center for American Progress. 2021. https://www.americanprogress.org/article/understanding-policing-black-disabled-bodies/. Accessed 14 March 2022.

Tippens, Dora. "Crossing the Curriculum with Shakespeare." *Shakespeare Quarterly* 35.5 (1984): 653–656.

Titus. Dir. Julie Taymor. 20th Century Fox, 2000.

Tolman, Albert H. "Shakespeare's Part in the 'Taming of the Shrew'." *PMLA* 5.4 (1890): 201–278.

Touré. "Teaching America that black was beautiful." *New York Times Magazine*. December 28, 2014. https://www.proquest.com/magazines/ophelia-devore-mitchell/docview/1640813180/se-2?accountid=10747. Accessed December 15, 2021.

Trimbur, Lucia. "Buying and Selling Blackness: White-Collar Boxing and Racialized Consumerism" in *Reconsidering Social Identification: Race, Gender, Class and Caste*. Ed. Abdul R. JanMohamed. Routledge, 2011. 177–206.

Tudor Monastery Farm. Lion Television, 2013.

Tuke, Thomas. *A Discourse Against Painting and Tincturing Women*. London, 1616.

Tufts, John. *Fat Rascals: Dining at Shakespeare's Table*. 2020. http://www.john-tufts.com/fatrascalsbook.

Valencia, Richard R. *The Evolution of Deficit Thinking: Educational Thought & Practice*. London and New York: Routledge, 1997.

Verzuh, Jennifer. "Ash Hunnter—Harlots. An Interview." *Starrymag*. https://starrymag.com/ash-hunter-harlots/. Accessed Dec. 27, 2021.

Victor, Regina. "Developing Trans Roles for the Theatre," *American Theatre*. 23 September 2020, https://www.americantheatre.org/2020/09/23/developing-trans-roles-for-the-theatre, accessed 2 August 2021.

Wade, Julia. n.d. RSC/SM/1/2013/ANT1 and associated SM script, also held at the Shakespeare Birthplace Trust Library and Archives, Stratford-upon-Avon.

Wallace, Michele. "A Black Feminist's Search for Sisterhood." *All the Women Are White, All the Blacks Are Men, But Some of Us Are Brave*. Eds. Gloria T. Hull, Patricia Bell Scott, and Barbara Smith. New York: Feminist Press, 2015. 35–40.

Walker, Susannah. "Black is Profitable: The Commodification of the Afro, 1960–1975." *Enterprise & Society* 1.3 (2000): 536–564.

Warburton, Edward C., Rosio Bugarin, and Anne-Marie Nunez. *Bridging the Gap: Academic Preparation and Postsecondary Success of First-Generation Students*, Washington, D.C.: U.S. Department of Education, National Center for Educational Statistics (NCES) (2001).

Wardi, Anissa Janine. *Water and African American Memory: An Ecocritical Perspective*. Gainesville, Florida: University Press of Florida, 2011.

Whelehan, Jeremey. *NOW: In the Wings on a World Stage*. 2014. Treetop Productions. Film.

Wolfgang, William. "Grassroots Shakespeare: 'I love Shakespeare and I live here.'" Amateur Shakespeare Performance in American Communities.' *Shakespeare Bulletin*, 39.3: 355–373, 2021.

——— and Erin Sullivan. "Ricardo II: una producción bilingüe de Merced Shakespearefest." *Lockdown Shakespeare: New Evolutions in Performance and Adaptation*. Eds. Gemma Kate Allred, Benjamin Broadribb, and Erin Sullivan, Bloomsbury Arden Shakespeare Series, 2022.

Yale, Joel. "Black is Busting Out All Over." *Life Magazine* 67.16. 1969.

Yates, Samuel. "Choreographing Conjoinment: *Side Show*'s Fleshly Fixations and Disability Simulation." *Studies in Musical Theatre* 13.1 (2019): 67–78.

Yepez Reyes, Anthony. Personal Interview. 10 August 2021.

Yeo, Jayme M. "Teaching Shakespeare Inside Out: Creating a Dialogue Between Traditional and Incarcerated Students." *Teaching Social Justice Through Shakespeare*. Eds. Hillary Eklund and Wendy Beth Hyman. Edinburgh: Edinburgh University Press, 2019. 197–205.

Zarrilli, Peter B. *Acting (Re)Considered: A Theoretical and Practical Guide*, 2nd ed. New York: Routledge, 2002.

Zull, James E. *The Art of Changing the Brain: Enriching the Practice of Teaching by Exploring the Biology of Learning*. Sterling, VA: Stylus, 2002.

INDEX

NUMBERS AND SYMBOLS
#MeToo movement, 229–230

A
Aaron, Catrin, 32, 76, 154, 230
Able-bodiedness/ableism/ability, 13,
   14, 16, 27, 34, 36, 88, 89, 123,
   127, 148, 156, 164, 181–183,
   198, 199, 201, 229
Accessible/accessibility, 8, 10, 12,
   16–18, 55, 59, 77, 89, 91, 93,
   146, 180, 196, 199
Acton, Kelsie, 19n11
Addams Family, 201
Aebischer, Pascale, 25
Afro, 139, 140
Agamben, Giorgio, 211
Akinbode, Akintayo, 52
Albanese, Denise, 9, 172n2
Alston, Claire, 32

American Sign Language (ASL), 15,
   30–33, 38, 39n8, 40n11
Anishanaabe people, 118
Anti-Blackness, 139, 142, 230, 232n3
Archbishop Fulton J. Sheen Center for
   Thought and Culture, 231
Arenas, Alana, 46
Ariosto, 102
   Supposes, The, 102
Armenian genocide, 9
Aromachology, 37
Asian American and Pacific Islander
   (AAPI), 161, 223
Atlanta Technical College (ATC), 176,
   178, 181, 182
Auslander, Philip, 28
Autism/autistic/autism spectrum,
   2–4, 19, 28, 34
Avengers, The, 201
Azalea, Iggy, 141
Azevedo, Jillian, 196

B

Bacchae, The, 101
Bailey, Moya, 137
Bakare, Lanre, 77
Barry, 202
Barzilai, Reut, 109n25
Bassett, Kate, 54, 55
Bell, Alexander Graham, 39n8
Benedicks, Crystal, 178
Berson, Jessica, 32
Bérubé, Michael, 19n9
Besson, Luc, 225
    The Fifth Element, 225
Beverly Hillbillies, 201
Bilingual, 16, 79–94
Billson, Janet Mancini, 19n13
Bissainthe, Toto, 52, 53
Black, Asian, minority ethnic
    (BAME), 223
Black/blackness, 10, 11, 13, 20, 34,
    44, 45, 49–52, 55, 58, 70, 106,
    116, 131–134, 136–142, 209,
    214–216, 223, 224, 228,
    230, 233n23
Blackfishing, 131–142
Black, Indigenous, people of color
    (BIPOC), 8, 13, 146, 186, 223
Black is Beautiful Movement, 16, 132,
    133, 138–140
Black Lives Matter, 14, 209
Black Power, 139, 141
Block, Pamela, 34
Boal, Augusto, 210–213
Bodymind, 25
Boehm, Claudia, 84, 86, 89, 90, 94
Boffone, Trevor, 83, 84, 94n2
Bohstedt, John, 196
Bonanza, 200
Boose, Lynda E., 108n14
*Borrowers and Lenders: The Journal of
    Shakespeare and
    Appropriation*, 199

Boutry, Katherine, 178, 179
Bowie-Sell, Daisy, 76n10
Boyd, Michael, 46, 48, 53, 57
Bradbury, Jill, 15, 37
Bradford, Shannon, 29
Brady Bunch, The, 200
Branagh, Kenneth, 225
Brantley, Ben, 38–39n4, 55, 56
Breaking Bad, 202
Brears, Peter, 196
Brinkman, Eric, 15, 77
Brokaw, Katherine Steele, 81
Brooks, Gwendolyn, 184
Brown, Dameion, 215
Brown, David Sterling, 152, 233n20
Bruno, Christine, 27
Bruns, John, 76
Bugarin, Rosio, 19
Bulman, James C., 75n6
Burke, Tarana, 233n23
Byrd, Jodi A., 208, 212
Byrne, Antony, 57

C

Caines, Michael, 20n17
Cake, Jonathan, 51, 55
Calderón, Pedro, 92
    La vida es sueño, 92
Caldwell, Paulette, 139
California State University,
    Sacramento, 215
Car Fifty-four Where are You?, 200
Carleton, Dudley, 134, 180
Carmichael, Stokely, 139
Carroll, Diahann, 138
Cash, Rosanne, 145
Cervantes, Miguel de, 80, 90
    Don Quixote, 80
Charlton, Bobbi, 74
Charon, Rita, 227
Cheeseman, Tom, 228

Chess, Simone, 75n5
Chicago, 44, 123
Chicago Shakespeare Theater, 126
Chickasaw, 208, 232n3
Choy, Susan P., 19
Chris, Oliver, 70
Chuter, Sharon, 132
Cibber, Colley, 12
    Richard III, 12
Civil Rights Movements, 138
Clark, Hilary, 105, 106
Clark, John Lee, 35
Cocke, Dudley, 83
Cohen-Cruz, Jan, 83
Coles, Kimberly Ann, 146
Colling, Samuel, 51
Colony Theater (Miami, FL), 44
Connelly, Brendan, 33
Corcione, Adryan, 141
Cosby Show, The, 199, 200
Cosby, Bill, 199, 200
Cote, David, 44, 55
Cottom, Tressie McMillam, 131, 133
COVID-19, 10, 80, 82, 90, 176, 191,
    198, 222
Crenshaw, Kimberle, 146
Crews, Kimberly, 17
Crip time, 2–18
Critical disability studies, 26, 37
Crossdressing, 64–66, 68
Crouch, Tim, 169
Cuccaro-Alamin, Stephanie, 19
Currier, Lesley, 215–218

D
Daalder, Joost, 108n11
Dadabhoy, Ambereen, 13, 148
Daileader, Celia R., 230
Darío, Rubén, 90
D'Avenant, William, 11
    The Enchanted Island, 11

Davis, Angela, 139, 140, 142
DeafBlind, 15, 26, 28, 35–37,
    38n2, 40n11
Death and the King's Horseman, 123
Dekker, Thomas, 64
    The Roaring Girl, 64
Del Marco, Grade, 138, 139
Deliver Us from Eva, 12
DeNiro, Robert, 77
Desai, Adhaar Noor, 147
DeShannon, Jackie, 201
"Dethroning", 160–162
DeVore, Ophelia, 131, 132, 138–141
Dharker, Ayesha, 13
Diagnostic and Statistical Manual of
    Mental Disorders (DSM), 233n18
Dickson, Andrew, 55, 145
Diff'rent Strokes, 200
Dinklage, Peter, 27, 28, 38n4
Disability rights movement, 2
    "nothing about us without us.," 2
Disabled/disability, 2–5, 8, 11–16, 18,
    19, 25–38, 74, 98, 101, 105,
    106, 146–155, 160, 171, 186,
    187, 219n2, 222, 227, 229, 230
Discrimination/discriminatory, 2, 66,
    142, 222, 224
Dog & pony dc, 35, 36
Dolan, Frances, 134
Dolen, Christine, 56
Don Quixote de la Merced, 80, 81, 83,
    84, 88–90, 92, 93, 94n3, 94n4
Donmar Warehouse, 231
Doran, Gregory, 54, 57
Dornquast, Bob, 116–117
Dove, Rita, 184
Dracula, 101
Drama therapy, 210, 212–214, 218
Dryden, John, 11
    The Enchanted Island, 11
D'Silva, Darrell, 57
Dunn, Marvin, 44

E

Eagleton, Terry, 25, 27
Ear Hustle, 215
Early modern, 11, 15, 64, 65, 69, 73,
    75, 98–101, 107n5, 132–136,
    146, 148, 149, 155, 161–166,
    169–171, 176, 177, 179, 182,
    191–194, 197, 198,
    204, 207–219
Ebony magazine, 138
Edwards, Terra, 40n11
Edward's Boys, 75
Eklund, Hillary, 74, 147, 172n9
Embody/embodiedness, 27, 28, 38,
    44, 141, 142, 154, 160, 213,
    217, 218
Emory University, 191
Emotion/ emotional, 4, 6, 34, 37, 66,
    72, 167, 218
English Renaissance, 9, 118
Eskew, Doug, 8
Espinosa, Ruben, 85, 90, 132
Essiedu, Paapa, 74
E'temādzāda, M., 228
Exclusive/ exclusivity, 8, 11–14, 56,
    92, 132, 133, 136, 222
Ezra, Daniel, 73

F

Facebook, 39n8, 222
Fearon, Ray, 74
Fendler, Lynn, 227
Fernandez, Hayley, 15, 49
Ferris, Leslie, 75
First-generation college student, 6,
    8–10, 19, 118, 164, 172n6
Fitzpatrick, Joan, 196
Fletcher, John, 11
    The Sea Voyage, 11
Flores, Cathryn, 82, 85, 86, 93
Floyd, George, 145

Forrester, Ann, 178, 179
Foucault, Michel, 97, 98, 107n2, 211
    Madness and Civilization, 97
Fox, Phoebe, 71, 76, 138
Francis, Donette, 44, 47, 48, 52
Francisco, Timothy, 172n2, 177–178
Friedman, Becky S., 109n24
Friedner, Michele, 34
Frith, Mary, 64, 75
Front Page, The, 125

G

Gainer, Gloria, 193
Gallathea, 65, 75
Gallaudet University, 31
Game of Thrones, 200
Garber, Marjorie, 75, 121
Gard, Robert, 83, 84
Garland-Thomson, Rosemarie, 26
Garnon, James, 76
Gascoigne, George, 102, 103
Gatta, Carla Della, 83, 84, 94n2
Geller, Conrad, 34
Gender/gendered/genderfluid, 5, 8,
    14, 16, 38, 63–74, 133, 137,
    146, 147, 149–152, 154, 155,
    160, 167, 186, 187, 222–224,
    227, 228, 230
GI Bill, 8
Gillen, Katherine, 146
Gilligan's Island, 202
Ginn, Peter, 193
Glissant, Édouard, 48
Godwin, Simon, 15, 66,
    69–74, 76, 77
Goodman, Ruth, 193
Grace del Marco Modeling and Talent
    Agency, 138
Graduate education, 9, 44
Grady, Kyle, 163, 201
Granda, aj, 40n11

Grassroots Shakespeare, 79–94
Greig, Tamsin, 70, 72, 76
Grey, Patrick, 9
Groce, Nora, 32
Guevara, Perry, 17, 170, 231
Guidry, Parker, 63
Gulledge, John, 17
Gunsmoke, 200
Guthrie, Tyrone, 119
Guthrie Theater, 126
Gutiérrez, Alejandro, 84, 86, 89, 90, 93, 94

H
Hader, Bill, 202
Halberstam, Jack, 77, 222
Hall, Don, 225
Hall, Kim F., 11, 133, 136, 137, 146
Hall, Stuart, 56
Hambley, Heike, 82, 88, 89, 91, 93
Harris, Beth, 33
Harry Potter, 200, 201
Haunting of Hill House, The, 168
Headlines, 99
Heilpern, John, 27, 28
Hernandez, Manny, 30, 31
Heteronormative/heteronormativity, 68, 72, 148
Heywood, Thomas, 135
    Fayre Mayde of the Exchange, The, 135
Higinbotham, Sarah, 197
Hobbes, Allyson, 132
Hobgood, Allison, 148, 150
Holderness, Graham, 172n4
Holmes, Federay, 66–69
Homophobia, 229, 232n16
Horn, Laura, 19
House of Cards, 199
Howard, Jean, 75
Hughes, Ian, 55
Hugo, Victor, 228

Humble, Kate, 196
Hunter, Ash, 51
Hyman, Wendy Beth, 74, 147, 172n9

I
I, Cinna, 169
Ijames, James, 13
    Fat Ham, 13
Inclusion/inclusive, 2–18, 25–38, 43, 44, 46, 50–53, 56–59, 64, 73–75, 80, 81, 83, 84, 90, 98, 118, 132, 133, 145–156, 161, 162, 164, 170, 175, 182, 184, 187, 221–224, 228–231
Intersectional/ intersectionality, 14–17, 33, 34, 68, 85, 140, 145–156, 171
Iqbal, Nosheen, 50
Iwuji, Chukwudi, 51, 55

J
Jacobi, Derek, 201
JanMohamed, Abdul R., 76
Jays, David, 57
Jeamson, Thomas, 135
    Artificial Embellishments, 135
Jennings, Lisa, 146
Jet Magazine, 132, 139
Jim Crow South, 132
Johnson, Eunice, 132
Johnson, James Weldon, 132
Johnston, Kirsty, 27
Jones, Bettrys, 69, 70, 76
Jones, Bristin Scalzo, 81, 88, 91, 92
Jones, Caroline, 132, 140, 142
Jonson, Ben, 64, 134–136
    Epicoene, 135
    Masque of Blackness, The, 134, 135
Joubin, Alexa Alice, 3, 17, 18, 74
Jung, Moon-Kie, 232n3

K

Kafai, Shayda, 109n22
Kalukango, Joaquina, 51, 55, 57
Karim-Cooper, Farah, 134, 233n20
Katz, Richard, 69
Kearse-Lane, Kimberly, 132
Keats, John, 184
Keegan, Cáel M., 75
Kelly, Jude, 13
Kemp, Sawyer, 65, 70, 73, 74, 77
Khan, Iqbal, 13, 57, 74
Kim, Jae-nam, 228
Kirwan, Peter, 50
Kochhar-Lindgren, Kanta, 28, 29
Korda, Natasha, 108n14
Kostihova, Marcela, 39n6
Kuppers, Petra, 28

L

LaMotta, Jake, 77
Landau, Tina, 46
Langland, Alex, 193
Lanier, Douglas, 203
Laskey, Jack, 67–69, 76
Lassiter, Ian, 51
Latinx Shakespeares, 83
Lawrance, Tamara, 70, 74, 76
Lesbian, Gay, Bisexual, Transgender,
     Queer (LGBTQ+), 155, 223
Levine, Lawrence, 199, 200
Lieseman, McKenna, 33
Life magazine, 139
Lion King, The, 12
Little Women, 123
Lloyd, Phyllida, 231
Loftis, Sonya Freeman, 221
Long Day's Journey into Night, 125
Looney Tunes, 201
Lozinskij, Mikhail, 228
Luckett, Sharrell D., 44, 46
Luhrmann, Baz, 226, 227
     *William Shakespeare's Romeo +
     Juliet*, 226

M

MacDonald, Joyce Green, 12
Mandell, Even, 55, 56
Mandell, Jonathan, 47, 55
Mangold, James, 225
     The Wolverine, 225
Mann, Michael, 226
     Miami Vice, 226
Mareneck, Ellen, 179
Marin Shakespeare Company, 17,
     209, 231
Marks, Peter, 34
Marston, John, 135
     Malcontent, The, 135
Martin, Trayvon, 233n22
Massinger, Philip, 11
     The Sea Voyage, 11
Matsuda, Mari, 149
Maverick, 200
Mayberry, Susan, 100, 108n11
McCarter Theater Center
     (Princeton, NJ), 45
McCraney, Tarell Alvin, 15, 43–59
     American Trade, 45
     The Breach, 45, 47
     The Brothers Size, 45
     Choir Boy, 45, 49
     David Makes Man, 45,
          47, 58
     Head of Passes, 45, 47
     In the Red and Brown Water,
          45, 47, 48
     Marcus; Or the Secret of Sweet, 45
     Moonlight, 44, 45, 47, 58
     Wig Out!, 45
McKellen, Ian, 28, 98
McMullan, Tim, 72
Mendes, Sam, 32
Mental illness, 97–100, 105–107,
     107n7, 109n22
Merced Shakespearefest (CA), 16, 79,
     80, 82, 84, 85, 88–90, 92,
     93, 94n1
Michael, Chivas, 51

Middleton, Thomas, 64, 99, 100,
    108n11, 119
  Changeling, The, 99, 100,
    108n11, 119
  Roaring Girl, The, 64, 65, 75
Milano, Alyssa, 233n23
Mills, Perry, 75
Milwaukee Repertory Theater, 126
Misgendering, 229
Mississippi Masala, 12
Mitchell, David T., 38n1
Miura, Cassie, 163
Miwok, 208
Moliere, 119, 123
  The Miser, 123
Morrison, Toni, 12
  Desdemona, 12
Msamati, Lucian, 13
Muñoz, José Esteban, 64
My Three Sons, 200, 201

N
Nadarajah, Nadia, 76
National Endowment for the
    Arts, 36, 45
National Theatre of the Deaf, 29
Neely, Carol Thomas, 107n5
Nelson, Jesy, 141
Neumann, Aubrey Helene, 77
Neurodiverse/neurodiversity, 3, 5, 16,
    18, 28, 39n9, 98, 101, 107,
    107n7, 222
Newstok, Scott, 9, 20
New World School of the Arts
    (NWSA), 44, 48, 49
New York Public Theatre, 57
Nguyen-Cruz, Maria, 16, 82,
    85, 86, 89
Nicu's Spoon Theater, 39n7
Niles, Sarah, 51, 201
Nolan, Yvette, 12

Nonbinary, 64–69, 71, 73–75, 77, 224
Nora, Amaury, 19n13
Normative/normativity, 2, 5, 13,
    25–29, 40n12, 67, 69,
    72, 73, 222
Northern Alaska Tour Company, 118
Northern Michigan University,
    16, 116–127
Nuccio, Jelica, 40n11
Núñez, Ángel, 16, 81, 82, 85,
    86, 88, 93
Nunez, Anne-Marie, 19–20
Nunn, Trevor, 76

O
O'Dair, Sharon, 20, 172n2, 177, 178
Oedipus Rex, 126
Ogle, Connie, 48
Oregon Shakespeare Festival, 64–66,
    74, 91, 197
O'Reilly, Kaite, 29
Orlin, Lena Cowan, 196
Osborne, Jeffrey, 9
O'Toole, Corbett, 18n4
Owusu, Jude, 169
Oxford Playhouse, 77
Oxford University Press (OUP),
    19, 20, 222
Ozzie and Harriet, 200

P
Party On, 26, 29, 34–37
Pascarella, Ernest T., 19, 20
Patel, Dharmesh, 49, 50
Peakes, Ian Merrill, 34, 39n9
Philippian, Mardy, 4, 221
Pickens, Therí Alyce, 20
Pierson, Christopher T., 20
Pleasure Bedlam Ltd., 98–102
Pleasure of Your Bedlam, The, 100

Poitevin, Kimberly, 134, 135
Political correctness, 4, 229, 230
Pope, Jeremy, 49
Prescott, Paul, 81
Price, Margaret, 5, 19, 105
Prison-Shakespeare, 209, 216
Profession, 10, 146, 171, 178
ProTactile, 15, 26–38
Public Theater (New York,
    NY), 45, 57
Pujante, Ángel Luis, 228
Punchdrunk, 36

Q
Quarshie, Hugh, 13, 20
Queer/queerness, 13, 15, 58, 64, 65,
    72, 73, 155, 171

R
Rachel, T. Cole, 46, 49, 58
Radel, Nicholas F., 232n11
Radical listening, 17, 221–231
Radiotopia, 215
Raging Bull, 77n19
Ram-Leela, 12
Rauch, Bill, 65, 66
Rebhorn, Wayne A., 102
Red Theatre Chicago, 32
Regendered, 67, 68, 76
Reign, April, 224
Reyes, Anthony Yepez, 80, 84, 89, 90
Ricardo II, 79–94, 94n1
Rice, Emma, 64
Ridout, Nicolas, 66
Roach, Joseph, 27
Robinson, Richard, 64, 75
Robles, Cynthia, 84–88, 93, 94n2
Rodas, Julia Miele, 28
Roman, David, 57, 152, 165, 167, 168
Roundtree, Richard, 138

Rowley, William, 99, 119
    Changeling, The, 99, 100
Royal Court, 45, 77
Royal Exchange, 77
Royal Shakespeare Company,
    13, 15, 126
R+J: The Vineyard, 32, 33
Ruelas, Greg, 88, 90
Rylance, Mark, 98

S
Saito, Yuriko, 38
Sajnani, Nisha, 213, 214
Samuels, Ellen, 4
Sandahl, Carrie, 28
Sanford and Son, 200, 201
San Quentin Prison, 207–219
Saraf, Shubham, 66–69
Saunders, Simone, 50
Savard, Nicolas Shannon, 76, 77
Sawyer, Aaron, 32, 33
Schlesinger, Helen, 68, 76
Scholarship of Teaching and Learning
    (SoTL), 147, 148
Schulman, Nev, 141
    Catfish, 141
Scorsese, Martin, 77
Scott, Ridley, 225
    Blade Runner, 225
Shahani, Gitanjali, 197
Shakespeare, William, 7–17, 20, 26,
    30–33, 35, 36, 39n6, 43, 48–51,
    53–56, 58, 59, 63–65, 67, 74,
    76, 77, 79–94, 97–107, 116–127,
    131–142, 145–156, 159–171,
    175–187, 191–204, 207–219
    All's Well That Ends Well, 202
    Antony and Cleopatra, 11,
        15, 43–59
    As You Like It, 36, 63–74, 81, 175,
        207, 217

Comedy of Errors, The, 98, 195
Coriolanus, 125, 203
Cymbeline, 203
Hamlet, 13, 31, 50, 66, 98, 166–168, 182, 183, 201
Henry IV, Part I, 203, 231
Henry IV, Part II, 231
Henry V, 150, 154
Henry VI, Part II, 202
Julius Caesar, 12, 54, 150, 152, 154, 167–169, 173n10, 231
King John, 12
King Lear, 145
Macbeth, 36, 201
Merchant of Venice, The, 109n24, 182
Merry Wives of Windsor, The, 120, 125
Midsummer Night's Dream, A, 35, 58, 98, 201, 212
Othello, 13, 82, 212, 228
Richard II, 16, 79, 82, 203
Richard III, 12, 27, 32, 34, 39n7, 92, 123, 150, 159, 160, 162, 165, 166, 171n1, 202
Romeo and Juliet, 12, 15, 35, 36, 194, 201, 226
Sonnets, The, 16, 94, 132, 133, 135–138, 142, 182, 184
Taming of the Shrew, The, 98, 102–106
Tempest, The, 11, 106, 109n25, 207, 231
Timon of Athens, 34, 119
Titus Andronicus, 101, 150–152, 203, 233n20
Twelfth Night, 15, 63–74, 119, 196
Two Gentlemen of Verona, 149, 150, 203
Two Noble Kinsmen, The, 98
Winter's Tale, A, 195, 196, 201

Shakespeare Association of America (SAA), 20n15
Shakespeare in Yosemite, 81, 82, 92
Shakespeare's Globe Theater, 126
Shakespeare studies, 8, 9, 13, 20, 177, 178, 223
Sharpe, Christina, 14
Sharrock, Thea, 68
Shaw, Justin P., 34, 148, 222
Sher, Anthony, 27, 28
Shiqiu, Liang, 228
Shuttleworth, Ian, 55
Siebers, Tobin, 27, 28
Simon, Josette, 57
Sinnott, Ethan, 32, 34
1619 Project, 214
Sleep No More, 36
Smith, Charise Castro, 51
Smith, Emma, 9, 20, 28
  "gappiness," 9
Smith, Raven, 141, 142
Snyder, Lindsey, 32, 34
Snyder, Sharon L., 38n1
Social justice, 3, 17, 65–67, 74, 146, 210, 215, 218, 224, 226, 229–231
Spacey, Kevin, 32, 199
Spencer, Charles, 54, 55
Springer, Leonard, 19n13
Starks, Lisa S., 3
Star Trek, 200, 202
Star Wars, 202
Stephens, Katy, 57
Stereotype Threat and Imposter Syndrome, 164
Stevenson, Bryan, 214, 215
Stewart, Patrick, 13, 57
Stimming, 4, 19
Stram, Henry, 51
Stratford Shakespeare Festival (Stratford, ON), 116
Student Learning Outcome, 182

Succession, 202
Swan Theatre (Stratford, ON), 44
Sweeney Todd, 101
Swift, Taylor, 202

T
Tales from the Green Valley, 193
"Talking back," 160
Tavener, Ben, 107n6
Technical college, 17, 175–187
Teen Vogue, 141
Teo Castellanos' Village Improv, 44
Terenzini, Patrick T., 19, 20
Terry, Margaret Brooks, 19
Terry, Michelle, 66, 76
Tersigni, Elisa, 197
Theater of the Oppressed, 210–214
Theatre and Health Lab at New York
    University, 213
Theology/theological, 5
Thompson, Ayanna, 4, 34, 132, 146,
    161, 162, 208, 209, 212
    *Passing Strange: Shakespeare, Race,
    and Contemporary
    America*, 208
Thompson, J. Walter, 140
Thurber, Michael, 52, 53
Tippens, Dora, 175
Tokenism, 11, 224
Tom Patterson Theater, 116
Transgender, 64–71, 73–77, 223, 229
Transgender Shakespeare
    Company, 74, 231
Transmisogyny, 229
Traore, Rokia, 12
    The Death of a Chief, 12
    Desdemona, 12
Tree, Herbert Beerbohm, 12
Trimbur, Lucia, 77n18
Tudor Monastery Farm, 193

Tufts, John, 197
Tuke, Thomas, 134, 136
    *Discourse Against Painting and
    Tincturing of Women, A*, 134
Tupaq, 202
Turchi, Lauri, 162
Tyson, Cicely, 138

U
United States (US), 8, 76, 81, 83, 90,
    109n19, 117, 118, 139, 145,
    146, 161, 180, 209, 216, 219n2,
    223, 224, 233n22
University of California--Merced (UC
    Merced), 81, 93

V
Valencia, Richard R., 172n3
Vargas, João H. Costa, 232n3
Vega, Lope de, 90, 160, 161
Vermani, Neha, 197
Version Variation Visualisation:
    Multilingual Crowd-Sourcing of
    Shakespeare's *Othello*, 228
Vibe Magazine, 140
Vineyard Theatre (New York, NY), 45
Vogue School of Modeling, 131,
    138, 140

W
Wade, Julia, 54
Wallace, Michele, 140–142
Walter, Harriet, 57
Warburton, Edward C., 19
Wardley, Niky, 72
Wardrobe Warehouse, 119, 123
War on Drugs, 216
Whataboutism, 224

White gaze, 13
Wieland, Christopher Martin, 228
Williams, Antwan, 215
Williams, Caroline Randall, 12
  Lucy Negro Redux, 12
Williams, Chris, 225
  Big Hero 6, 225
Williams, Helen, 138
Williams, Katherine Schaap, 150
Wolniak, Gregory C., 20
Woo, John, 226
Wood, David Houston, 16, 148
Woods, Earlonne, 215

Y
Yaeger, Patricia M., 19
Yates, Samuel, 38n3
Yearwood, Tanika, 68, 76
Yeo, Jayme M., 209–212, 214
Yepez, Lupita, 84–88, 93
Young, Pharus Jonathan, 49
Young Vic (London, UK), 45

Z
Zarrilli, Philip, 27
Zoraida, María, 84